Closing the Gender Gap

This book is dedicated to our mothers

Closing the Gender Gap

Postwar Education and Social Change

Madeleine Arnot
Miriam David
Gaby Weiner

Polity Press

First published in 1999 by Polity Press in association with Blackwell Publishers Ltd.

Reprinted 2001

Editorial office:
Polity Press
65 Bridge Street
Cambridge CB2 1UR, UK

Published in the USA by
Blackwell Publishers Inc.
Commerce Place
350 Main Street
Malden, MA 02148, USA

Marketing and production:
Blackwell Publishers Ltd
108 Cowley Road
Oxford OX4 1JF, UK

ISBN 0-7456-1883-9
ISBN 0-7456-1884-7 (pbk)

A catalogue record for this book is available from the British Library.

Library of Congress Cataloging-in-Publication Data
Arnot, Madeleine.
    Closing the gender gap : post-war education and social change/
Madeleine Arnot, Miriam David, Gaby Weiner.
        p.   cm.
    Includes bibliographical references (p.   ) and index.
    ISBN 0-7456-1883-9. — ISBN 0-7456-1884-7 (pbk.)
    1. Sex differences in education—Great Britain.   2. Women—
Education—Great Britain.   3. Sex discrimination in education—
Great Britain.   4. Feminism and education—Great Britain.
I. David, Miriam E.   II. Weiner, Gaby.   III. Title.
LC212.93.G7876   1999
370'.82'0941—dc21   99-25731
                                                        CIP

Typeset in 10½ on 12 pt Adobe Caslon
by Graphicraft Limited, Hong Kong
Printed in Great Britain by T. J. International, Padstow, Cornwall

This book is printed on acid-free paper.

Contents

Preface

This book is about how the schooling of girls and boys has changed since the Second World War. It accounts for how, and in what ways, the gender gap has closed. The concept of gender gap was first used by us in a project for the Equal Opportunities Commission (EOC) as a means of identifying gender differences in patterns of subject study and examination performance over time. It denotes the measure of difference between the sexes in relation to the proportion of girls and boys entering and/or succeeding in particular school subjects.

In this book we explore how the specific gender patterns in education that we identified in two projects – for the EOC and the Office for Standards in Education (OFSTED) – were changed through the actions of the state and teachers and through various social movements, including that of feminism. We analyse how economic transformations have disrupted gender patterns and the extent to which social changes have altered girls' and boys' identities, aspirations and educational choices. We have drawn upon the insights of research developed within modernist, post-modernist, post-structuralist and feminist traditions.

We concentrate on developments in England and Wales for two reasons. The first is that the two studies that form the basis of much of the work in the book investigated English and Welsh educational development and policy-making. Second, the study of gender policy-making in England and Wales in the post-war period provides a fascinating and illuminating case-study of how complex social change transforms the education system.

The 'closing of the gender gap' is of particular interest to us, not least because we were part of such transformations ourselves. First, we are 'products' of the post-war period, since we were all born at the end, or in the immediate aftermath, of the Second World War. We all went from primary to selective secondary school to higher education and continued on to find work in the educational service, initially either as schoolteachers or as academic researchers and lecturers. Like others of our generation of women in the post-war period, we were provided with the possibility of continuous employment, and, despite the lack of adequate childcare in the UK, we accommodated periods of child-bearing and -rearing into our working lives. The difficult demands of home and work, of domesticity and employment, have been constant tensions in our lives, as have the demands of raising sons and daughters in a climate of social change. We have engaged at numerous points, therefore, with the impact of social, educational and family policies, and with attempts to restructure working lives to meet the specific requirements of women workers.

Our lives have been and continue to be deeply affected by the women's movement in the UK and abroad. Even though we are women who have come from different social backgrounds, the expansion of the educational system and particularly the higher educational system gave each of us the chance to move up and away from the narrow confines of domesticity. We have drawn on the energy and diversity of the women's movement, and the challenges it presents to women, to rethink what femininity means, what it means to be a wife and mother, and what it means to be a female educationist and academic. Like others affected by the new social movements of the post-war period, we engaged with the project of modernizing gender through the reform of the educational system. Our strategies have not been simply within the academy. We engaged with the work of teachers, managers, administrators, policy-makers and other professional groups who also sought social change. We saw, and continue to see, educational change as a mechanism, if not the motor, for gender transformation. To that extent, our values still reflect the legacy of thinking of the post-war period.

At the same time, our lives have been characterized by identification and engagement in other social movements of our generation. We have each been involved in socialist and anti-racist movements, specifically in their concerns for economic and structural change. Such a trajectory leaves a legacy of political consciousness and 'belonging', and has provided possibilities for us as individuals to engage with the social order. Pre-eminently this has meant a continuing commitment to address political reforms from a feminist perspective and to consider, as they arose, the impact of policies and practices on women's lives. Through our disciplines – sociology and/or education – we have been provided with the tools to rethink the development and significance of social democracy (latterly in the context of New Right ideologies), but also to think critically about the ways in which we research, teach and understand social change more broadly.

We ask ourselves: how do we go about understanding changes in gender relations of which we were part and which we have influenced? How can we understand our own actions in the context of such changes? Such reflexivity needs to be alert to critiques, reinterpretations and reappraisals. By examining such shifting contexts and ideologies, we draw upon many of our earlier publications and hope in this book to make sense of our past positions and the ebbs and flows of values with which we engaged, either as advocates or opponents.

The subject of this book is the closing of the gender gap, but it also concerns those women who fought for change over the last fifty years and those who strive to continue that process. We would like to acknowledge all those who have helped us think through such issues and those with whom we have collaborated closely: Sandra Acker, Carol Adams, Len Barton, Leone Burton, Jo-Anne Dillabough, Liz Edwards, Ros Edwards, Dulcie Groves, Hilary Land, Meg Maguire, Joanna McPake, Sue Middleton, Val Millman, Caroline New, Janet Powney, Diane Reay, Jane Ribbens, Liz Speed, Kathleen Weiler, Anne West, Lyn Yates, and many others with whom we worked in universities, schools and LEAs over the last twenty years.

The team of researchers who worked on the report *Educational Reforms and Gender Equality in Schools* for the EOC also played a key role in collecting data and drafting the report. We would like to thank, in particular, Jackie Davies, Sarah Delamont, Laura Hart, Sally Mitchell, Jane Salisbury and Johnathan Tritter. Special thanks are due to Elizabeth Gray and Charles Newbould for their contribution to the statistical evidence on examinations which they provided for the project. Anne Madden, Ed Puttick and Liz Speed at the EOC gave us considerable support and encouragement, for which we are very grateful. We would also like to thank the EOC for granting us permission to draw upon the findings of the project and to pay tribute to the late Lynda Carr, whose work for education reform as an officer in the EOC played a key role in the changes we describe in this book.

We would also like to acknowledge the collective contribution of Gerard Duveen, John Gray, Mary James and Jean Rudduck, with Evelyn Arizpe and Delyse Silverstone, to the report *A Review of Recent Research on Gender and Educational Performance*, which was commissioned by OFSTED. Christine Ajambar, David Read and Oonagh Standard at OFSTED were especially supportive of the project. We appreciate having permission to draw upon the findings in this book.

Special thanks are due to Robin Young and David Hamilton for their forbearance in living with this project, and to Kathryn and Adam Arnot Drummond, Toby and Charlotte Reiner and Daniel and Saira Weiner, who provided us with wonderful examples of how a new generation sees gender issues, rejecting many of the assumptions with which we ourselves grew up.

We would also like to thank Leyla Mardin and Pauline Mason for help with the manuscript and Kate Lander for finding all those references. John Thompson at Polity Press was extraordinarily patient and encouraging for which we thank him. He specifically asked us to write a book that was accessible to those unfamiliar with the issues. That task was more challenging than expected, and any errors and flaws that appear in our argument are our responsibility.

Acknowledgements

The authors would like to thank the following for permission to use copyrighted material.

Figure 2.1 and Tables 2.2 and 2.3 originally appeared as Figure 1.3 and Tables 1.3 and 1.5 in the OFSTED report, *A Review of Recent Research on Gender and Educational Performance*. Reproduced with the permission of the Controller of Her Majesty's Stationery Office.

The facsimile from *Sunday Graphic* appears courtesy of Lady Thatcher and The Margaret Thatcher Archive Trust/Thatcher papers, Churchill College, Cambridge.

Figure 2.2, 2.3(a) and 2.3(b) appeared in the report on *Educational Reforms and Gender Equality in Schools* and are reproduced by permission of the Equal Opportunities Commission.

Figure 8.1 appeared as Figure 2.2 from *Young People and Social Change* by Andy Furlong and Fred Cartmel, Open University Press 1997. Reproduced with the permission of the Open University.

Abbreviations and Acronyms

A-level	GCE Advanced Level
AS-level	Advanced Scholarship Examination
AUT	Association of University Teachers
CDT	Craft, Design and Technology
CRE	Commission for Racial Equality
CSE	Certificate of Secondary Education
CTC	City Technology College
DES	Department of Education and Science
DfEE	Department for Education and Employment
EOC	Equal Opportunities Commission
ERA	Education Reform Act (1988)
FE	further education
GCE	General Certificate of Education
GCSE	General Certificate of Secondary Education
GM(S)	grant-maintained (schools)
GNVQ	General National Vocational Qualification
HE	higher education
HMC	Head Masters' Conference (for heads of independent and public schools)
HMI	Her Majesty's Inspectors of Schools
ILEA	Inner London Education Authority
LEA	Local Education Authority
LMS	Local Management of Schools
NAFTHE	National Association for Teachers in Further and Higher Education
NUT	National Union of Teachers
NVQ	National Vocational Qualification

OFSTED	Office for Standards in Education
O-level	GCE Ordinary Level
OPCS	Office of Population, Censuses and Surveys
PPA	Pre-school Playgroups Association
QCA	Qualifications and Curriculum Authority
SAT	Standard Attainment Target or Task
SDA	Sex Discrimination Act (1975)
TVEI	Technical and Vocational Education Initiative
WLM	Women's Liberation Movement

Part I
Refashioning Gender Relations

1

Revisiting Gender in the 1990s

The gender gap in educational performance is currently a major subject of public policy debate internationally. There is a *fin de siècle* flavour to British arguments which suggests a fear of change, particularly of Britain's displacement in the educational and commercial global market. Feverish and highly charged public discussions about the causes and effects of boys' and girls' changing educational fortunes have taken place only relatively recently, even though over the last three decades or more there has been a range of public policy strategies promoting equality in relation to gender as well as class, 'race', ethnicity, sexuality and disability.

Evaluating the impact of these strategies, particularly as they have affected male and female schooling, has been the central concern of sociologists of education and those involved in women's studies. The nature of the impact of social change in family circles and economic, social and public life on educational inequalities has long been the focus of academic debate. At the same time party political disputes in Britain in the 1980s were expressed in terms of support for or hostility against school and local educational authority (LEA) initiatives to promote greater equality. Recent Conservative administrations arguably were more interested in promoting freedom of choice and social diversity than in encouraging greater social equality – a diversionary and fruitless endeavour that, in their view, could only hold back competitiveness and higher standards. Much of the educational legislation put forward under the leadership of Margaret Thatcher enhanced social differentiation rather than commonality, especially since, in that now renowned phrase, she argued that there was 'no such thing as society'. Economic inequalities were thought to be a necessary condition and outcome of contemporary modern societies. The various Conservative administrations between 1979 and 1997 thus appeared eager to exploit the growing trends in social change (especially those of increasing individualism and materialism) rather than focus on the redistribution of wealth or the elimination of social and sexual inequalities. For some ministers, such as Kenneth Baker, 'the pursuit of egalitarianism is now over' (Hatcher, 1989).

By the mid-1990s the EOC became aware that not only had gender patterns changed substantially since the 1970s, when the EOC had been an active agent in the promotion of gender equality in schools, but that the commission had insufficient information on whether or how educational reforms from the 1980s to 1990s had affected the promotion of gender equality in schools. The EOC, which was established by the Sex Discrimination Act (SDA) 1975, had promoted the idea that the spirit of the legislation should be taken up by schools such that each should design and implement its own specific and relevant equal opportunities policy. The work of the commission involved providing advice when sex discrimination was alleged and conducting formal investigations to ensure compliance with the law. By the 1980s officials believed that the main work of the EOC in education had been completed and that few remained ignorant of the issue of sex discrimination and its application to education. With a Conservative appointee as its chair, and following reorganization, the EOC's education department was wound down, leaving remaining departments to focus on training and the law. However, as the EOC itself pointed out, the aspiration to greater sex equality was not a feature of 1980s education legislation, and in fact the proposed national curriculum and other reforms seemed to militate against rather than support equality aims (EOC, 1989). Not surprisingly, by the early 1990s the new reforms implemented by the Conservative government became an object of criticism by a range of feminist writers and scholars (Skeggs, 1994).

With the closure of its education department, the EOC had lost its in-house educational expertise and also its connections with LEAs and schools. Information to the EOC on the impact of the new 'era' came mainly through individual legal cases on employment issues, the majority brought by teachers. There were also no co-ordinated official databases on which to draw, since the Conservative government had also dispensed with much of the work of the Office of Population, Censuses and Surveys (OPCS). In keeping with the marketization of public services, the examination bodies and vocational training awarding bodies had responsibilities only to their immediate clients and none for maintaining a central databank. The reduction in the role of LEAs and 'efficiency savings' meant that none of these bodies could offer comprehensive or co-ordinated information.

In 1993 the EOC therefore took the initiative and invited a number of researchers to tender to undertake research in this area. The politics of the time, and especially the national movements in Scotland and Wales, encouraged the view that no single report could deal adequately with the impact of educational reforms in the UK (e.g., many provisions of the Education Reform Act 1988 did not apply in Scotland or Northern Ireland, and in Wales the particular constellation of schools was unique to the principality). In the event the EOC commissioned and sponsored three interlinked but separate studies, of England (Arnot, David & Weiner, 1996), Wales (Salisbury, 1996) and Scotland (Turner, Riddell & Brown, 1995). As successful bidders, in 1994 we began the task of trying to capture the impact of the so-called revolution in education produced by the reforms of boys' and girls' schooling in England.

Conservative education reforms

The depth, scale and range of education policies of the administrations of Margaret Thatcher and John Major had reformed not only the curriculum and assessment but also the control and financing of education, the allocation of pupils to schools and the diversity of school types. The legislation represented a sustained attempt at redirecting the nature of English education, especially in relation to two key themes; viz.

Modernizing education and training

The reform of school-leaving certification (collapsing the dual academic/vocational routes) saw the establishment for the first time in England of a common examination for all pupils at the age of sixteen. The General Certificate of Secondary Education was established in the early 1980s, and the first results came through in 1988. These examinations introduced new criteria for school content and new examination and assessment strategies, especially the increased use of coursework.

In 1981 the New Training Initiative was set up, which led to a proliferation of pre-vocational courses, including certificates for pre-vocational education and strategies to place value on and rationalize vocational education provision for fourteen to eighteen-year-olds. The Technical and Vocational Educational Initiative (TVEI), piloted in 1983, was extended during the decade and had a major impact on secondary schools nationally. The goal was to stimulate curriculum development in technical and vocational subjects for the fourteen to eighteen age range. Of particular interest was the requirement that efforts should be made to overcome sex stereotyping.

Academic school curricula were standardized by the introduction (in the Education Reform Act 1988) for the first time of a compulsory school curriculum (the National Curriculum) and national targets based on standardized tests of pupils' abilities in the three core subjects (science, maths and English) at ages seven, eleven, fourteen and sixteen.

A related reform was the creation of the National Council for Vocational Qualifications (1984) in an attempt to standardize and validate the numerous vocational courses. New national qualifications were introduced – General National Vocational Qualifications (GNVQs), taken up to age sixteen, and National Vocational Qualifications (NVQs) – and targets were set to encourage schools to attain higher standards.

School performance and school governance

A range of legislation was introduced during the 1980s and 1990s on school management and parental involvement. The Education Act of 1986, for example, created new governing bodies for schools, while the Education Reform Act (ERA) (1988) encouraged schools to opt out of local authority control and to promote open enrolment on a first choice principle. The incentive for school improvement was competition for funding (based on pupil numbers) and local financial management by schools of their own budgets.

Greater independence of schools coupled with increased pressure to improve performance brought with it a new system of regular statutory inspections by Office for Standards in Education (OFSTED). The 1992 Education Act introduced the public 'naming and shaming' of schools through the publication of national league tables, which showed individual school data on pupils achieving five or more higher grade GCSEs and three or more good A-levels.

Such reforms added to rather than reduced the differences between the English and Scottish education systems, as the former became more highly diversified and with the introduction of new types of school (city technology colleges and grant-maintained schools). There were complaints that the English school system had experienced reform overload. In the face of this we were nervous, at the start of the EOC study in 1994, that schools would consider our project on gender equality marginal and inappropriate to their main concern, which had become one of raising examination performance in order to ensure a secure funding base, and, in some cases, survival.

As researchers, we were excited about our involvement in so important a research study, intrigued about the potential contradictory consequences of Thatcherism/Majorism and the education reforms and also fairly pessimistic about whether any shifts in gender equality in education were likely to have emerged, given the stated anti-egalitarianism of government policy-makers. The centrality of the family and traditional family roles within the neo-conservative ideology of the government had been viewed by some feminists as an attempt to restrict women's roles in the labour market, and to encourage female roles and responsibilities in the home and in the privacy of the family. We were aware, however, that the neo-liberal ideas which underpinned some Conservative policy-making aimed at encouraging the free play of market forces and therefore were not predisposed to confining women to the family and domesticity. Thus women were allegedly being allowed their freedom of choice to participate in the labour market (see Chapter 6); however, the extent to which such tendencies affected the performance in schools of the new generation of boys and girls was unclear.

In the event, the EOC project surveyed the views of educational administrators, policy-makers, head teachers and teachers and groups of young people in the schools we visited. The decision by the EOC to evaluate the educational reforms on the basis of gender performance proved especially interesting since we were able to tap into individuals' and institutions' perceptions of whether the reforms (individually or collectively) had reduced or aggravated gender inequalities. However, the project design begged the question about the extent to which research is able to uncover the ways in which national (centrally initiated) educational reforms can affect pupil performance without reference to the complexity of translating policy into practice.

As we were to find, rather than abandoning equality issues, school and LEA strategies for sustaining equal opportunities had been and were in the process of being redesigned and promoted in what could be seen as the 'third wave' of equal opportunities policy-making – to differentiate it from nineteenth-century political campaigns around 'the woman question' and the feminist movements of the 1960s and 1970s. In the context of the new educational reforms, gender equality had become part of the new performance discourse.

The new gender agenda

Each summer since 1992 the results of GCSE examinations have been published, providing a feast of official statistics on changing patterns of examination performance, and notably in recent years the size of the gender gap at sixteen and eighteen. Every summer journalists reinterpret the gender statistics for public consumption. Initially the public's attention was drawn to girls' increasing success at GCSE, but gradually the closing of the gender gap came to be associated with boys' failure. A moral panic ensued about the threat that this failure might represent, especially if associated with a new disaffected male underclass. It is important not to underemphasize or downplay the role that the media took in creating and sustaining recent interest in gender. During the examination results period of 1994 typical headlines in British newspapers included: 'The trouble with boys' (*Sunday Times*, 19 June 1994); 'Girls trounce the boys in examination league table' (*The Times*, 3 September 1994); 'Can girls do better without the boys?' (*Daily*

Express, 11 November 1994); 'Brainy girls are top of the class' (*Today*, 22 November 1994). A similar moral panic over boys also surfaced in other countries: for example, in Australia, Foster (1995: 54) identified a 'backlash period' against gains made by girls as a result of a decade of equal opportunities policy-making deliberately aimed at girls and young women. Examples such as these suggest that the mass media has now become an important element of educational discourse, and one that cannot be ignored.

A parallel shift has been discernible as academic and policy-makers' interest has switched from a concern about how young women can increase their chances in the educational system, and have done so (a story of success), to a new concern in finding explanations for boys' relative lack of improvement. There is particular interest in finding ways in which schools might raise boys' examination performance. In 1996 OFSTED commissioned the EOC to prepare a booklet on the factors that might affect boys and girls which drew selectively on our research (*The Gender Divide*, HMSO 1996).

The momentum established within government circles concerning gender and performance was given considerable boost by the election victory in May 1997 of a Labour government committed to raising standards for all, providing every child with the opportunity to excel, and removing social exclusion. The philosophy of New Labour was articulated by the then Minister for Schools, Stephen Byers, when he argued that all schools would be expected to acknowledge the gender gap in performance and to demonstrate their action strategies (16 January 1998). For the first time in post-war Britain, the reduction of gender differences in education was represented as a national priority. While not articulating the wish to remove girls' education from the agenda, Byers privileged male underachievement by identifying the 'new laddish anti-school culture' as one of the consequences of economic decline and as one of the main causes of boys' failure.

New information on gender differences in education was also published in 1998 when an OFSTED commissioned report summarized recent research evidence. This review (henceforth known as the OFSTED review), conducted by a team of researchers from Cambridge University and co-ordinated by Madeleine Arnot (Arnot, Gray, James & Rudduck, 1998), focused attention not only on boys' underachievement in literacy skills (reading and English) through primary and secondary schooling, but also on girls' failure to take advantage of their success in science at the age of sixteen by choosing scientific careers. Of significance too was the evidence it presented on how the gender gap in the proportions of boys and girls achieving five higher grade passes at GCSE had appeared in the late 1980s and had been sustained ever since. This suggested key inversions in gender patterns in education that were not reflected in the patterns of performance for social class or ethnicity, where no similar transformations have been found despite the sizeable increase in the proportion of pupils achieving school qualifications.

Statistical evidence and research findings presented in the EOC and OFSTED reports identified a range of variables which might be at work in shaping gender gaps in performance. What they failed to offer was any framework with which to understand changing gender relations. Research evidence pointed to the significance of variables which affected boys and girls in their schooling, but few studies were longitudinal and even fewer attempted to map trends over time. Therefore key inversions were identified in gender patterns in education without much reference to changing social patterns. Of central interest to us were the historical influences which lay behind such major shifts in educational inequality in the post-war period.

The EOC and OFSTED studies were not required to offer explanations of how such changes occurred and what factors might have been influential. They seem to us only to scratch the surface of reasons for the variety of changes – educational, social, cultural, political and policy – that we in the UK, as well as those in other countries, have witnessed over the last three decades or so. Behind the educational statistics, we argue, lies a transformation in gender relations: in the economy, in the family, in the welfare provision associated with it, within the cultural realm and personal lives, and, as we shall see, in education. This transformation cannot be laid merely at the door of political ideologies, or of policy and educational reforms, or of the Conservative administrations of the 1980s and 1990s.

Reflections

The task we set ourselves in this book therefore is to show the complex range of educational and social factors which have affected all pupils, and how these social forces have differently affected girls and boys. We set ourselves a number of questions to address in this volume.

- How can we account for the increase in girls' educational and academic achievements even though women continue to experience disadvantage and discrimination in the workplace and in particular occupations?
- To what extent do the patterns of boys' education represent a continuity with the past? Alternatively, to what is their relative lack of progress in examinations over the last ten years attributable?
- How do debates concerning gender mesh with those concerning other educational and social factors, for example, ethnicity, race, school locality, social class?
- Are changes in gender patterns in schools the consequence of national government policy-making, changing cultural expectations, the women's movement, labour-market requirements, or a complex mix of all of these; and, if so, in what ways?

- To what extent are we witnessing a major inversion in a pattern of educational inequality concerning boys' and girls' aspirations and achievement? Are these patterns only temporary (malleable to specific government reforms) or likely to be more permanent?

In trying to address these questions, we go beyond past, somewhat technicist and reductionist debates about why certain subjects (or careers, forms of examination, styles of teaching, classroom groupings, etc.) are or are not attractive to either of the sexes and recent public debates about boys' underachievement. We also distance ourselves from unidimensional explanations, which identify either Conservative educational reforms or feminism as a single causal factor. These factors certainly need to be addressed, but only, we argue, in the light of understanding British education's relation to the wider post-war society. We aim to offer a fresh analysis of gender performance in education by reassessing gender relations in the post-war period and by enhancing understanding of education, other forms of social policy and the impact of new social movements on the educational system in the second half of the twentieth century.

In Chapter 2 we begin our analysis by considering the evidence on changing patterns of gender performance in schools and colleges and by setting such evidence in the context of other research conducted in Britain and in other countries. In Chapter 3 we describe our thesis, that it is the continuity between what were often described as incompatible political agendas – that of social democracy and that of the New Right – which has modernized gender relations. Such continuities grew out of the transformation of working lives of women (described in Chapter 4) and in the struggle by women for new gender identities. Femininity became the target of reform in schools, with girls encouraged to address gender politics directly (Chapter 5). The break with Victorian gender values which had shaped nineteenth-century educational provision for schoolgirls and schoolboys was instituted not just by the advocates of the welfare reforms in the early post-war period, but also by one of its greatest critics – Margaret Thatcher. The expansion of education and its restructuring by Margaret Thatcher in support of the principles of neo-liberalism created the conditions for the narrowing gender divide in education. The iconic status of Margaret Thatcher allows us to explore how her ideas about gender were produced and the impact they had on wider policy-making. We explore facets of her personal and political biography (see Chapter 3), demonstrating the contradictory influences and impacts on her life and political beliefs and, through her, on a new generation of women. Paradoxically, the era of educational reform, while generating social divisiveness, also allowed schoolgirls to 'seize the moment' and penalized boys for sustaining traditional identities (Chapter 6).

In the third part of the book (Chapters 7 and 8) we consider the range of evidence on how different groups of girls and boys responded to the challenges of the various political and social movements of the 1980s and 1990s. The evidence drawn from studies of groups of youth (white and black, working- and middle-class youth) suggests both continuity and change. The tensions which underlie the statistical graphs on performance come to life in the words and aspirations of schoolboys and schoolgirls today.

Finally, in Chapter 9 we revisit our main argument that a range of economic, social and political changes, as well as feminism as a social movement, have shaped the nature of gender differences in education today. We conclude that educational reforms have contributed to those processes; rather than being the motor of development, they legitimized changes that had already begun to percolate through society and provided a key context in which young people could make sense of such social change. Thus, in our analysis, schools both generate gender differences and are the means by which such differences are experienced or challenged.

2

Changing Gender Patterns in Education

The EOC project, *Educational Reforms and Gender Equality in Schools* (Arnot, David & Weiner, 1996), had the explicit aim of assessing the relationship of the educational reforms of the 1980s and early 1990s to gender relations and in/equality in schools. Although the methods used were not sufficiently fine-tuned to assess the impact of specific reforms on educational performance, they were effective in discovering how gender equality was understood as a policy issue throughout the period of educational reform.

Three different criteria or yardsticks were chosen to consider and evaluate gender equality issues. First, attention was given to *educational performance and achievements in public examinations* and in *school-based assessments*. This allowed for the focus on educational outcomes and the differential attainments on the basis of gender – a *cause célèbre* during the course of the research project generated by a BBC television programme in 1994 which suggested that the future was female! The data we focused on were early Standard Attainment Task (SAT) results in primary schools, the changing pattern of entry and levels of performance of boys and girls in different subject examinations at age sixteen (GCSE and O-level) and at age eighteen (A-level). Data from the EOC project were fed into the OFSTED review, which provided additional information on how both boys and girls progressed through the school system (Arnot, Gray, James & Rudduck, 1998). The evidence collected together in these two reports represents the most comprehensive attempt to map gender change in school performance since Her Majesty's Inspectors' (HMI) Report of 1975 which informed the Sex Discrimination Act.

Second, we focused upon *gender-fair cultures* and the extent to which they could be seen to be in existence in schools. The assumption underpinning this notion was that schooling could provide an equitable and supportive experience for both boys and girls, men and women teachers, if the school was consciously committed to gender equality. The notion of a gender-fair culture drew on other contemporary feminist debates and strategies which called upon schools to deal with issues such as sexual/racial harassment and raising girls' self-esteem in order to make schooling more gender fair. However, given the diversity of school cultures in Britain in the context of class, racial and ethnic diversity and regional differences, this became complex and problematic to assess.

Third, we focused upon the level and nature of *equal opportunities policy-making* in LEAs and schools and on the development of policies and strategies for implementing equal opportunities in the experiences of treatment of pupils and/or teachers. Policy-making had been seen as a positive strategy aimed at improving gender awareness among teachers and in schools as a whole, and was assumed to be indicative of commitment, interest and the application of resources. This assumption drew upon the notion developed in the heyday of the partnership between government policy-makers, social scientists and practitioners, that policy could and would inevitably have a positive effect upon behaviour and/or performance – a notion that we hold up to scrutiny not only in this chapter but throughout the book.

Three forms of data collection were employed in the EOC study: statistical analysis of published examination and performance data for England and Wales for the period 1984–94; questionnaire surveys of national samples of primary and secondary maintained schools in England and Wales and a census of all LEAs in England and Wales carried out in 1994; and case-studies of equal opportunities policy and practice in six selected LEAs in England conducted in 1994. The Welsh study (Salisbury, 1996) used many of these examination data, and in addition was based on more case-studies of, and questionnaires from, Welsh LEAs.

The analysis of examination and performance was based on previously collected British data concerning the end-of-school examination results of pupils/students in four chosen years (1985, 1988, 1991 and 1994), two of which preceded the implementation of the relevant education reforms (1985, 1988), one of which occurred amid the period of reform (1991) and one of which (1994) showed how public examinations had been affected by changes in examinations at age sixteen (GCSE) and with the associated national curriculum developments. The data were divided into patterns of entry and patterns of performance: two different sorts of gender gap could then be mapped over the last ten years. As we saw in the introduction, the concept of a 'gender gap' was used as a measure of difference between the sexes in relation to the proportion of girls and boys on entry and/or in performance in a particular subject. The data presented in the EOC report and reanalysed by the OFSTED review team were broken down by subject and as far as possible by age and stage, and gender.

In the survey of 226 secondary schools (including maintained and grant-maintained schools), 390 primary schools, nine city technology colleges (CTCs) and all 52 LEAs, we were able to explore the views and perceptions of the educational reforms from school and LEA administrators, and also institutional policies and practices. The six case-study English LEAs were selected on the basis of differing socio-economic context, political affiliations, educational agendas, and a range of school types. Several LEAs had long histories of equal opportunities policy-making, while others had less experience in this area. LEAs were asked to identify schools and particular local initiatives and concerns which might be of interest to the project (whether drawing attention to high levels of success in relation to gender or to continuing gender inequalities). The perspectives on key educational reforms of school teachers and pupils, school and LEA managers and administrators were sought. Although it was not possible to establish statistically or numerically the precise impact of the educational reforms on children's educational achievements, especially since the impact is likely to be experienced differently by succeeding generations of children, it was possible to gain a sense of the myriad of changes in gender patterns in education over the decade 1984 to 1994 and to begin to speculate on the reasons for such complex trends in gender equalities.

The use of such examination and school data also raised questions about what might be seen to constitute 'improvement' in educational performance by gender. Was the aim to achieve absolute equality in all assessments and examinations throughout the years of schooling between boys and girls, and, if so, were the gaps that remained significant? Or should 'improvement' be interpreted as increased qualifications of each sex, irrespective of the other's pattern of achievement?

The next three sections report some of the main findings of both the EOC research and the OFSTED review.

Closing the gender gap in academic performance

In assessments and examinations, girls and young women are doing better than in previous decades compared with boys. Although in the 1970s girls acquired more higher grade qualifications at age sixteen than boys (Arnot, 1986b), evidence of girls' failure to achieve three good A-levels, allowing them access to higher education, was considered an important indicator of their lower educational achievement. Historically, fewer girls than boys in the UK went on to university, especially since the possibilities to study for a degree had been so limited. The English educational system (especially its elite institutions) had been slow to allow women access to high-status

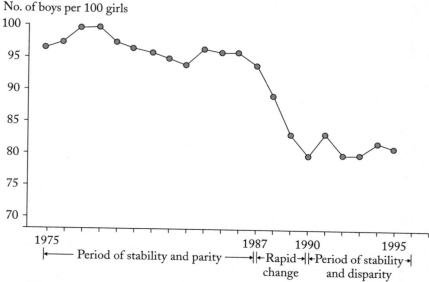

No. of boys per 100 girls

Figure 2.1 *Changing levels of performance at GCE/CSE or GCSE (1975–95): number of boys per 100 girls securing 5+ A*–C grades*
Source: Arnot et al., 1998: 11, fig. 1.3.

education. In the 1980s it was relatively rare for girls to study science and mathematics, to perform well in these subjects, and to study them at university level (Elwood, 1995).

The sizeable increase in girls' educational performance, both in terms of entry into conventionally male subjects (up to age sixteen) and examination success, and in staying on in school after the age of sixteen and entering university, is well documented. It is an extraordinary chronicle of gains since the mid-1980s, especially when girls' progress is contrasted with that of boys. Both sexes are currently far more likely to take GCSE examinations. However, in 1995, for example, 48 per cent of girls compared with 39 per cent of boys achieved five or more A* to C grades at GCSE (Arnot, Gray, James & Rudduck, 1998: 6). Figure 2.1 shows the gap in the proportions of male and female pupils achieving five or more higher grades. Between 1975 and 1987, in a period when a minority of pupils entered examinations, the proportions were roughly comparable. For every 100 girls reaching this level, there were roughly 94 to 100 boys. However, by 1988 the figure for boys had dropped to 89, by 1989 it had dropped again to 83, and by 1990 to 80. Girls' advantage over boys thus appears to have strengthened over the last decade, and there is a clear disparity in performance of these 'high achievers' – a pattern not found in the proportion of girls and boys securing lower levels of performance, which has remained fairly constant over the period (Arnot et al., 1998: 11).

After the age of sixteen, girls continued to match, if not better, boys' performance. Although slightly more boys than girls (taking two or more A/AS-levels) achieved the highest number of point scores in relation to their A-level grades, this gap became minimal in 1995 (boys averaged 14.5 points and girls averaged 14.4) (Arnot et al., 1998: 15).

Girls' raised level of performance at ages sixteen and eighteen has contributed substantially to the rise in the number of students undertaking full-time and part-time courses post-sixteen. The figures have leapt from two-thirds (66 per cent) of the age group to around four-fifths (80 per cent) in the 1990s. In 1995, three-quarters of female students were on full-time post-sixteen courses compared with 69 per cent of boys, with young women increasing their enrolment on A/AS-level courses relative to young men. In the ten years after 1985 young women raised their entry on such courses from one in five (20 per cent) to around two-fifths (39 per cent).

The increase in the proportion of young women staying on after age eighteen (where numbers on full-time and part-time courses have more than doubled), is also already slightly greater than for young men staying on after that age. In 1985 only 26 per cent of young women were in post-eighteen courses compared with 34 per cent of young men; ten years later the figures were roughly equal (47 per cent to 49 per cent respectively). Both young men and young women have more than doubled their numbers in higher education in these ten years; but here again young women have overtaken young men such that in 1995 proportions entering higher education were 20 per cent and 19 per cent respectively.

This extraordinary progress of girls over the last ten years has been associated with two features: namely, girls continuing advantage in English and their improvement in mathematics and science. Their strong performance in English is clearly one of the major factors in their success. The OFSTED review cites the few studies that have tracked boys and girls through primary or through secondary schools, all of which suggest that girls make better progress than boys in reading, mathematics, and verbal and non-verbal reasoning. Data collected from national assessments at the age of seven demonstrate that girls get off to a better start at reading than boys and that the lead they establish in reading and later in English is maintained at Key Stage 2 (age eleven) and Key Stage 3 (age fourteen) (Arnot et al., 1998). Indeed a sizeable gap between boys and girls in reading and English is sustained throughout schooling (see table 2.1).

In 1995, 37.3 per cent of girls achieved A*/A or B grades in GCSE English, compared with only 23.5 per cent of boys; at the other end of the spectrum, 13 per cent of boys scored less than an F grade in comparison with only 5.6 per cent of girls. The fact that boys have not reduced this female

Table 2.1   Performance in English (1995) (percentage of pupils achieving the expected level at each age)

	% Boys	% Girls
Age 7		
Level 2 and above	73	83
Age 11		
Level 4 and above	42	56
Age 16		
GCSE (A*–C)	49	66

Source: adapted from Arnot et al., 1998: 6, table 1.1.

'advantage' in English is one of the key reasons why they have lost overall ground in comparison with girls, especially since by 1995 girls had almost caught up with boys in mathematics and science. Seven-year-old girls had a head start in mathematics (81 per cent of girls reached the expected level compared with 77 per cent of boys), and 86 per cent of girls and 83 per cent of boys reached the expected level in science. By ages eleven and fourteen in 1995, small differences between girls and boys had evened out in mathematics, while boys had a slight advantage in science.

Girls' improvement in science and mathematics at GCSE that year was evident. The proportion of girls who achieved A*/A grades in mathematics was only 2 per cent lower than the proportion of boys, and 45 per cent of boys and 44 per cent of girls reached A*–C grades. Similarly in science, 48 per cent of girls and 47 per cent of boys achieved A*–C grade in combined science.

Figure 2.2 demonstrates girls' two major successes in reducing the gender gap in performance in mathematics and science while holding on to their advantage in English. English is the only subject of the three in which girls have predominated since 1985, and girls sustained their high performance between 1985 and 1994. In comparison, there was a notable shift towards gender equality in science and mathematics. In 1985 there was a clear advantage in favour of boys; by 1994 the size of this advantage had reduced almost to zero in both subjects.

For A/AS-level subjects, girls' reduction (if not elimination) of the gap in overall performance in favour of boys has been a very recent phenomenon which became evident only in the mid- to late 1990s (Arnot et al., 1998). Girls have gradually closed the gaps in performance at A/B grades in the sciences (biology, chemistry and physics) as well as subjects such as English and modern foreign languages). The relative success of boys up to 1988 and

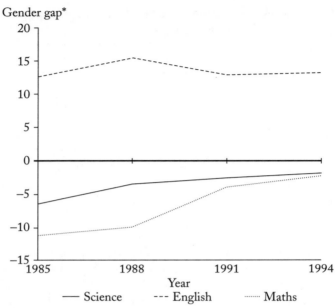

Figure 2.2   *The gender gap in relative performance for core National Curriculum subjects*
Source: Arnot et al., 1996: 30, fig. 3.7.
* For a definition of the gender gap, see page 31.

the tendency after this date for higher proportions of girls to achieve at this high level is clearly visible in figures 2.3(a) and (b) over the page.

Desegregation of subject choices

The second major change identified by the EOC and OFSTED studies was the 'desegregation' of subject choices. The introduction of the National Curriculum as a standardized compulsory set of subjects and the GCSE as a common examination has played a key role in reducing the sex segregation of subjects up to the age of sixteen. Up to the early 1980s boys and girls occupied almost completely different educational tracks. By 1994 most of these differences had reduced, although substantial gender differences still remained in subjects such as physics, craft, design and technology (CDT), economics, home economics and social studies. The male dominance of subjects such as physics, geography, CDT and technology, although sizeable, had decreased, and a more balanced entry pattern was sustained in English, mathematics, history and art and design. The gender gap was found to be on

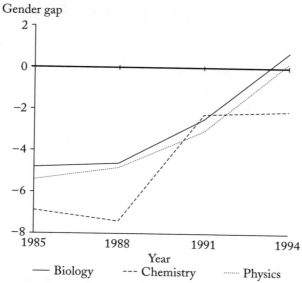

Figure 2.3(a)   *The gender gap in relative performance for the sciences*
Source: Arnot et al., 1996: 53, fig. 4.4.

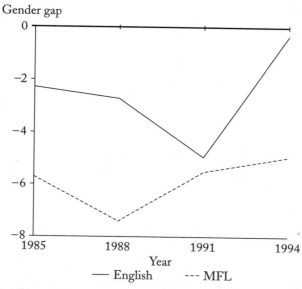

Figure 2.3(b)   *The gender gap in relative performance for English and*
Modern foreign languages
Source: Arnot et al., 1996: 56, fig. 4.8.

Table 2.2   Changes in the gender gap in entry to different subjects at GCSE (1984–94)

Size of gap in 1994	Boys predominate	Balanced entry	Girls predominate	Trend in gap over last decade
Large (30%+)	Physics			Decreasing
	CDT			Decreasing
	Economics			Increasing
			Home economics	Decreasing
			Social studies	Increasing
			Vocational studies	Increasing
Sizeable (15–30%)	Chemistry			Increasing
	Computer studies			Increasing
Small (5–15%)	Technology			Decreasing
	Geography			Decreasing
			Mod. foreign languages	Decreasing
			English lit.	Decreasing
No gap (less than 5% either way)	Science			Decreasing
			Biology	Decreasing
		English		No change
		Maths		No change
		History		No change
		Art & design		No change

Source: Arnot et al., 1998: 13, table 1.2.

the increase in only five of eighteen subjects listed in table 2.2. On the whole the picture was one of reduced sex segregation of subject choice up to the age of sixteen.

Gender legacies

The underachievement of boys, although much debated, is clearly a complex story. At one end of the spectrum, similar proportions of girls and boys seem to be among the underachievers and low performers (Hillman & Pearce, 1998). Proportionally equal numbers of girls and boys get off to a poor start in primary school and similar percentages of young men and women fail to achieve any GCSE qualifications at age sixteen (approximately 9 per cent and 7 per cent respectively in 1995). Evidence from the Youth Cohort Study (Drew & Gray, 1990) in the 1980s and from Furlong and Cartmel (1997), however, indicate that working-class boys have been over-represented in such low achievement categories and have, unlike other social groups, failed to raise their level of achievement during the 1990s. It is important to remember, however, that at the other end of the spectrum professional white men in the last decade have been high achievers, even if not improving their qualifications at the same rate as women in similar class positions (see Chapter 8). Data for 1995 also show that boys remain top achievers in certain subjects: more male (10 per cent) than female students (7 per cent) secured the highest number of points (30 plus) accrued from A-level grades achieved in different subjects (Arnot et al., 1998).

Although, as we have seen, girls have made major inroads into reducing boys' lead in examinations overall, boys have managed to retain and increase their advantage in mathematics and science. After making comparable starts in science, boys pulled ahead of girls by the age of eleven. In 1995, 24 per cent of boys achieved higher than the level expected for their age group in science compared to 20 per cent of girls, and again, at the age of fourteen, more boys (27 per cent) achieved the target level for their age group than did girls (23 per cent). More boys entered single subject science compared with girls. In 1995, for example, 28,000 boys took physics GCSE compared with only 15,000 girls (the comparable figures for chemistry were 28,000 and 16,000 respectively) (Arnot et al., 1998: 10).

The dominance of boys in science, technology and mathematics at A-level has also increased. Between 1984 and 1994 the gaps in entry were sizeable. Over 30 per cent more boys chose physics, mathematics, computer studies, technology, economics and CDT, and in many instances the gender gap had increased. Far larger proportions of girls than boys chose conventional female subjects such as English and modern foreign languages, although here boys had made inroads. More girls chose biology, social studies and art and design (table 2.3).

As we have seen, up to the age of sixteen, sex segregation of subject choices within the compulsory period of school was reduced. However, once subject choice was re-introduced (within, for example, the National Curriculum), young men and women again chose sex-typed subjects and courses. The 'masculinization' of technology and the sciences in post-compulsory education is also a feature of vocational courses. The study by Cheng, Payne & Witherspoon (1995) found that 36 per cent of male students studied one or more mathematics or science-related vocational courses compared with only 16 per cent of female students, and 25 per cent of male students studied at least one subject from engineering, technology, and architecture compared with only 2 per cent of female students. Further, more young women

Table 2.3   Changes in the gender gap in entry to different subjects at A-level (1984–94)

Size of gap in 1994	Boys predominate	Balanced entry	Girls predominate	Trend in gap over last decade
Large (30%+)	Physics			Increasing
	Maths			No change
	Computer studies			No change
	Technology			Increasing
	Economics			Increasing
	CDT			Increasing
			English	Decreasing
			Mod. foreign languages	Decreasing
Sizeable (5–30%)	Chemistry			No change
	Geography			No change
			Biology	Decreasing
			Social studies	Increasing
			Art & design	Decreasing
Small (5–15%)	None		None	
No gap (less than 5% either way)			History	Decreasing

Source: Arnot et al., 1998: 16, table 1.5.

(75 per cent) than young men (56 per cent) chose to take business or social studies. The OFSTED review (Arnot et al., 1998: 18) concluded that 'gender stereotyping in the mid-nineties among the 16–19 age group in terms of the subjects studied for vocational qualifications is just as strong as at A-level.' Young women selected business and commerce, hairdressing and beauty, and caring service courses related to the female-identified sector of the labour market. Again, young men were more likely to choose science and engineering in further and higher education (Felstead, Goodwin & Green, 1995).

The continuing association of masculinity with science and femininity with the arts and social studies/humanities is a historical legacy which still maintains its grip on educational choice and performance, despite the broadening of subject choices at A-level and the introduction of the National Curriculum and the GCSE examination.

To sum up, the evidence collected by the EOC and OFSTED studies at the very least signals the difficulties of generalizing across time, across subjects and across examinations, the content, format and style of which may well be in the process of development and redesign. Nevertheless, the concept of the 'gender gap' allows for the identification of a number of discernible features: overall differences in certification (the numbers of qualifications achieved), and in the proportions continuing into post-compulsory education, entering formal examinations, and achieving higher grades. Despite such difficulties, two clear themes emerge:

1　the extent of girls' success in broadening their subject entry base and increasing their performance, especially in maths and sciences but also in other subjects up to the age of sixteen. This shift in performance is reflected in the higher numbers of girls who proceed to and do well at A-level, and their high entry rates after the age of eighteen into full-time further and higher education.

2　the extent of boys' success in widening their GCSE profiles and by their increased entry into English and modern languages. Boys' performance, however, particularly in terms of these subjects, remains considerably lower than that of girls. Boys appear to have failed to build upon their performance at the same rate as girls in recent decades, especially in relation to the proportions gaining more than five GCSE A*–C grades and the proportions moving through to A-level study. Those boys who do succeed in making the transition to A-level continue to dominate the sciences, and remain successful in gaining top results.

Before the age of sixteen the 'closing of the gender gap' refers predominantly to the reduction in male advantage in science and maths and a reduction in sex-segregated course choices at GCSE. Greater gender equality has also been achieved through a parallel reduction in differences between male and female achievement for most subjects.

After the age of sixteen the 'closing of the gender gap' refers, first, to a decreased 'feminization' of the arts subjects through increased male participation in, for example, English and modern foreign languages, and, second, to the increased success of girls in staying on and achieving A/B grades at A-level.

In the next two sections other findings from the EOC report are presented, helping us to reflect on why educational explanations alone are, perhaps, not sufficient to explain these changes in male and female educational performance.

Gender values, gender cultures

The EOC research study also explored whether there was any evidence that changes made by schools (apart from the creation of equal opportunities policies) had accelerated or influenced the changed patterns that we have outlined above. Had schools indeed become more 'girl-friendly' places? Had pupils and teachers become more aware of gender/equal opportunities issues than in previous decades? Had the feminist movement of the 1970s and 1980s had any impact on the culture of schools in enabling pupils to stand up for their rights and seize opportunities offered by schooling?

The impression we gained from visits to schools around the country in 1995 was that students' perceptions of gender issues across a range of ages and social groups and localities were more open and more sensitive to changed cultural expectations about women's position in society. Girls and young women appeared more confident about their prospects, talking positively about their future lives as involving a combination of work inside and outside the home. As a head-teacher described his pupils, 'girls now have ambition and employers are beginning to see them as reliable and employable. Girls don't see any forbidden areas as in the past' (Arnot et al., 1996: 138).

In interviews and group discussions, boys and young men also seemed more conscious of shifts in gender roles, accepting, in the main, the expansion of women's social and economic influence and its likely impact on their own lives. Yet did this indicate an emerging generation of 'new' boys and girls, conscious and supportive of equality issues? Even though the attitudes of many male (and, to a lesser extent, female) adolescents seem to remain traditionally narrow and stereotyped, the new generation appeared to have a larger proportion of more confident girls and 'softer' boys. An illuminating instance of a new 'caring' male generation was one seventeen-year-old, who, in reflecting on his school's longer day and its business-oriented ethos, argued that the longer day might be dangerous for young students in the darker months of the year. He also expressed concern about the apparent downgrading of the 'softer' humanities in the school's avowedly commercial environment, suggesting that it would be detrimental to the curriculum balance offered by the school (although he himself was specializing in technological subjects) (Arnot et al., 1996: 138).

Career and occupational choices for both sexes, on the other hand, appeared to have remained generally conventional and stereotyped. This apparent contradiction was noted by a teacher interviewed for the EOC project:

> There is great awareness in the classroom of the breaking down of barriers, about what is a traditional girl's job or boy's job. Actually, if you ask the question, they will see no problem with girls wanting to be bricklayers or whatever. Whether that actually affects what happens in reality . . .
>
> *(Arnot et al., 1996: 137)*

Less easy to determine in the research findings was the influence of other factors such as social class, ethnicity and school location on boys' and girls' experiences of schooling. Transformations in student performance may be the consequence principally of change within particular groups; for example, several of the case-studies suggested that some children from upper-working-class or lower-middle-class families seemed most able and willing to exploit the possibilities offered by the New Right policies of deregulation and labour-market flexibility.

Similarly, the OFSTED review suggested that the 'signals' from the labour market, with its entrenched and persistent sex segregation, the collapse of manufacturing industry and the economic restructuring associated with the neo-liberal policies of the Conservative government in the 1980s were experienced differently by different groups of young men and women. While gender might be one of the key factors affecting educational performance, gender functions principally in relation to social class and ethnic origin. The extent to which one ethnic group, one social class or either sex is represented in the highest or lowest achieving educational group depends, to a large extent, on local context and conditions. Thus, national patterns and trends need also to be reinterpreted to accommodate local social and labour-market conditions.

Equal opportunities policy-making

One of the most surprising findings of the EOC research was the level of awareness of gender issues, given the lack of interest of UK governments in the 1980s towards gender equality. Rather than disappearing, as might have been anticipated due to their relative invisibility in the legislation, equal opportunities policies which included gender (81 per cent primary and 93 per cent secondary) were claimed by most schools responding to our survey, many of which were even produced after the 1988 education reforms. Thus a head interviewed for the project was of the view that:

> the reforms have undoubtedly helped to put equality issues higher up the educational agenda, though certainly this has not been prioritised or anticipated by government measures. The inclusion of equal opportunities in OFSTED inspections and in TVEI has been bound to have an effect. Also schools have had more independence to explore chosen priorities and there has been much more media coverage of equal opportunities issues.
>
> *(Arnot et al., 1996: 103–4)*

These reforms appear to have created an atmosphere in some schools where equal entitlement to the curriculum is expected and planned for, particularly the access of girls to the sciences. National publication of GCSE and A-level examination results focused the attention of schools on emergent patterns of achievement. Gender policies had to be reshaped to accommodate the new post-reform language and requirements of schooling. Some schools, for example, integrated gender issues into concerns about performance, standards, school improvement and value-added policies; others incorporated gender into broader-based and more inclusive concepts of entitlement and effective citizenship. Thus, for an infant school involved in the EOC project, gender was viewed as part of the school and community context:

> The gender issue here is seen very much in terms of the particular circumstances of the school and therefore in relation to poverty, lack of rights, sense of worthlessness. The school encourages and rewards assertiveness (rather than aggression) in relation to rights and responsibilities.
>
> *(Arnot et al., 1996: 132)*

School policy-making on gender also appeared more energetic than in previous decades, though there was some discussion of whether this was the consequence of school inspections requiring statements of school policy on gender rather than wider or more deeply held school views on the importance of sex equality. Almost seven out of ten English/Welsh LEAs asserted that OFSTED inspections had encouraged a general interest in, or raised the profile of, equal opportunities, although only 17 per cent reported that inspections had provided a 'strong incentive for equal opportunities'. The EOC project report commented:

> School after school referred to OFSTED reports which they had analysed carefully. They were clearly aware of the need to present their approach to equal opportunities in a positive light and some primary and secondary schools were having to draft their policy statements overnight in preparation for the inspection.
>
> *(Arnot et al., 1996: 118)*

Curriculum and assessment reforms, whether academic (such as the National Curriculum) or vocational (such as the Technical and Vocational Educational Initiative (TVEI)), were also viewed as having had largely positive effects on the promotion of equal opportunities. TVEI, for example, was considered to have had a positive influence by nearly all secondary schools in the survey and the National Curriculum was viewed as helpful in promoting gender equality by 85 per cent of LEAs and 60 per cent of secondary schools (but only 40 per cent of primary schools). Standard assessment of pupils (SATs) were reported as potentially positive for equal opportunities by 84 per cent and 72 per cent of primary and secondary school respondents. The introduction of a common examination (GCSE) at sixteen in 1985 was seen as beneficial by three-quarters of LEAs in England and Wales and 70 per cent of secondary schools in our study.

Both the EOC report and the OFSTED review suggested that the shift in gender performances beginning in the late 1980s might have been the result of the introduction of the GCSE and latterly the National Curriculum, since pupils for the first time were encouraged to take large numbers of subjects and courses, thus extending their subject profile. More pupils were thus entered for subjects which they had not previously taken (e.g., girls taking science, boys taking a modern foreign language) (see above).

Performance at GCSE is associated with particular forms of subject content, skills and focus and with particular styles of teaching and assessment. The move towards project and coursework – girls' preferred assessment style – which had accompanied the GCSE examination raised questions about whether the examination had become more 'girl friendly' in recent years (Whyte, Deem, Kant & Cruickshank, 1985). The OFSTED review found that, while teachers perceived coursework as favouring girls (Arnot et al., 1998: 37–8), the overall effects may well be marginal, and unlikely to have affected boys' relative underachievement over the last twenty years, especially since their performance did not improve when coursework was reduced by John Major's government. The findings were summarized thus:

> There is some evidence that girls do slightly better than boys on the coursework elements of examinations but this may only marginally affect pupils' overall results because other elements in the examination can be more critical in determining final grades. Schools may select syllabuses with different coursework proportions according to their estimation of their teaching strengths or their perception of the relative confidence and ability of their pupils.
>
> *(Arnot et al., 1998: 39)*

The OFSTED review revealed not only the number and range of studies of gender differences in teaching, learning and assessment that have been undertaken in recent years – an indicator at the very least of a shift in consciousness about the importance of gender – but also new levels of awareness about gender differences in learning styles; responses to different teaching and assessment styles, content and feedback; and gender bias in teaching, examining materials and marking. The conclusion reached was that key differences lay in the learning demands made by different subjects to which boys and girls responded differently. At the same time these responses were affected by a range of gender issues. The OFSTED review concluded that boys' failure to gain higher results in English was associated partly with their perception of the subject as feminine, a view encouraged by a complex mixture of feminized literacy in the home and the 'exploration of personal experiences and feelings in stories and poetry' (Arnot et al., 1998: 24). It suggested that perhaps curriculum subjects and modes of teaching and assessment were failing to take account of the fact that:

Boys show greater adaptability to more traditional approaches to learning which require the memorisation of abstract, unambiguous facts and rules that have to be acquired quickly. They also appear to be more willing to sacrifice deep understanding which requires effort, for correct answers achieved at speed.

(Arnot et al., 1998: 28)

In contrast, girls appear to 'do better on sustained tasks that are open-ended, process-based, related to realistic situations and that require pupils to think for themselves' (ibid.).

Which girls and which boys?

Such findings raise important questions about what shapes such gender patterns of learning and preferences for particular knowledge styles and about the gender assumptions which underlie schooling. The OFSTED research review illuminated, for the first time, how the curriculum reforms were not able to be causally linked to the changes in gender patterns. Even the question of school type, for example, whether single-sex and mixed schools favoured one sex or the other, seemed only marginally connected to changing gender patterns of performance. Of greater significance to schools' success in gaining high performances from their pupils, it seems, is the nature of the schools' intake, as indicated also by the analysis of annual published league tables.

The categorization of 'girls and boys' in performance data across schools which we have used so far thus renders explanations of educational change deeply problematic. As Moore (1996) has argued, such categories allow for discussions about 'relative educational' achievements, with one group always being constructed as 'the problem' or, even worse, 'the victim' of the system. But they fail to uncover the differences between those who are successful and those who fail to achieve within the current system of schooling. Girls' achievement is not uniform – as an Australian study by Teese, Davies, Charlton & Polesel (1995) showed and as the EOC project indicated. As in Britain, while it is clear that girls as a category have been largely successful at school, social class remains a key factor in educational success.

Teese and his colleagues' study, entitled *Who Wins at School?*, found not only that working-class girls had higher rates of failure in some subjects than other girls (for example, English) but that working-class boys were more likely to depress the overall scores for boys in literacy and in language more generally. Gender differences appeared narrowest where students have the greatest cultural and material advantages and sharpest where their parents were more socially disadvantaged. Descending the social scale, the gender gap in the Australian context was found to widen. The lower the social status of girls, the less likely they were to take mathematics and the more likely they were to fail when they did. Teese et al. found that Australian working-class girls had higher rates of failure in English than other girls, and also that working-class boys over-enrolled in mathematics and physics. Moreover, working-class boys were more likely to play truant from classes in literature, history or modern languages. 'Thus the real question is not whether girls as a group or boys as a group are more disadvantaged, but *which* girls and *which* boys' (Teese et al., 1995: 109).

Such findings resonate with the view of one head-teacher interviewed for the EOC project, who also noted the impact of social class on educational opportunity and access:

> Society works so much against working class kids in terms of being able to access higher education, being able to afford A-levels, the negative experiences parents had in their own schools. All these sorts of things.
>
> *(Arnot et al., 1996: 106)*

We return to disparities of performance among girls and among boys from different social groups later in the book (chapters 7 and 8).

Ethnicity and racial identity also interact with gender and social class to produce different patterns of participation and performance according to minority group membership. There is frequently a more intense (and longer) investment in education by black students as they struggle to achieve the qualifications needed to gain access to (often racist) segments of the labour market. Thus Modood and Shiner (1994) show that, in respect of the overall population, minority ethnic students might be viewed as 'overrepresented' in higher education, whereas white students may be seen as 'underrepresented'. But as Mirza (1997) also points out, this could be because discrimination in the workplace forces black students back to education. Young men and women from minority ethnic groups are also more likely to invest in vocational qualifications (Felstead et al., 1995). As the recent review of the achievements of ethnic minority pupils by Gillborn and Gipps (1996) found, the effects of class and locality also critically shape the patterns of performance of different groups of ethnic minority pupils.

The reorganization of schooling following the 1988 Education Reform Act was likely to have differential effects on schools in different localities. The EOC study found that the impact of the organizational reforms of schools after 1988 on gender equality was viewed less positively than other elements of the legislation by LEAs compared to schools or individual teachers. Indeed the introduction of local management of schools (LMS), the sharp reduction in the powers and funding of LEAs which had a history of promoting equal opportunities, and the creation of new types of schools (e.g., grant-maintained schools (GMS)) drew the most criticism. While appearing to strengthen local discretion in tackling gender inequalities, such organizational reforms were viewed as a hindrance to gender equality – an issue we return to in Chapter 6.

Reflections

The changing pattern of gender achievement identified in the two research reports is also reflected in gender patterns in other countries, especially the increased educational achievements of girls (e.g., Powney, 1996; Ministry of Health and Social Affairs, 1995; Yates and Leder, 1996). What has been revealed is that, of all the educational inequalities which form the terrain of policy-making since the Second World War, gender has shown the most dramatic shift. Specifically, in England and Wales the closure of the gender gap up to age sixteen and changing patterns of achievement in post-compulsory education and training stands as a testimony to this transformation.

But in other respects the two research studies show that the extent of gender change has been less convincing. Interest in, and take-up of, gender issues has been patchy, and, although many schools in England and Wales reported having equal opportunities policies and initiatives on gender, many teachers viewed gender equality as low in the priorities of their schools; similarly LEAs viewed gender equality as low on their agendas. School and LEA management cultures seemed particularly impervious to change. This meant that there was a frequent dominance by white male cultures of school and LEA hierarchies – and a consequent underrepresentation of women and minority ethnic staff in senior management positions. A description offered by one male head-teacher was of 'grey-suited men running the authority in a paternalistic rather than [a] partnership sort of way' with 'blunt autocratic reputations' and with 'uncomfortable, defensive, dismissive, sceptical, [and] hostile' responses to gender issues (Arnot et al., 1996: 133).

Two distinct but interrelated themes warrant further exploration and discussion. First, what is the connection between educational achievement, government ideology, and education policy? And, second, what explanations can be found for the changes in how young men and women see their future lives and relationships, which were glimpsed in the EOC research and were also reported by researchers in the UK and in other countries and cultures (Gipps & Murphy, 1994; Bron-Wojciechowska, 1995; Foster, 1995; Yates & Leder, 1996; and Valente et al., 1996)?

Rather than relying on past educational discourses on gender, which were derived from ideas about natural or biological difference (see Chapter 3), we now have to search elsewhere for explanations. The forms of data collection and analysis we have described in this chapter cannot 'prove' a relationship between changes in end-of-school examination performances and government policies and reforms, although they may occur during the same historic period.

In fact, it is more likely that changes – whether in performances or policies – derive from the same cultural sources rather than that each influences the other. Moore (1996) has argued that explanations drawn from within education alone cannot account for the changes we have identified; wider social and economic factors, whether experienced locally, nationally or globally, are far more important.

In the next chapter we explore what we consider to be the key influence behind current gender patterns in performance – the culmination of an attempt, after one hundred years of struggle, to break the hold of Victorian values upon the education of schoolboys and schoolgirls. Education in the nineteenth century was to play a key role in supporting a division of labour between the sexes – the male breadwinner and the housewife and mother. This division of labour was supported until the 1980s by the organization of the school system, most noticeably by its culture and forms of curriculum provision. In Chapter 3 we suggest that the challenge to such values was a priority neither of post-war social democratic governments nor of the New Right politicians under Margaret Thatcher. Nevertheless, in both periods changes were set in motion to release women from their domestic vocation and conventional roles, and policies were adopted in the social and economic spheres which reshaped male pupils' aspirations and identities. These developments, although not often deliberate, were embedded within the liberal and neo-liberal projects of the post-war period. The transformation of girls' and boys' education was the result of the seemingly unstoppable challenge to Victorian values represented by the restructuring of the educational system and employment after the Second World War, but also by the extraordinary symbol of the age: Margaret Thatcher, the first British female prime minister.

Definition of the gender gap

* By comparing the gender gap in performance and the gender gap in entry it is possible to identify which sex is achieving particularly well or badly. If size of performance gender gap is greater than the entry gender gap, the sex which is predominant in relation to entry is better than could be normally anticipated. The graphs for each subject show whether the performance gap is in favour of girls (+) or in favour of boys (–). Equality in terms of performance between the sexes would be indicated if the line approaches zero. (Arnot et al., 1996, Appendix p. 27)

3

Challenging Victorian Virtues

In this book we argue that the ways in which the values underpinning British society gradually shifted from Victorian to modern principles played a critical role in reshaping the patterns of male and female education found today. The transformation of relations between men and women was not the intended goal of social democratic and welfare reformers in the aftermath of the war, nor was it the aim of the Conservative governments under Margaret Thatcher and John Major between 1979 and 1997. Nevertheless, as we shall show, the major social and educational reforms of the last fifty years brought with them the possibilities of such a transformation. Behind the changing patterns of educational performance described in the last chapter, we want to argue, are far deeper shifts – from what Himmelfarb (1995) refers to as twentieth-century versions of Victorian virtues.

The explicit framing of policy in the name of gender equality is not the key to the transformation of gender relations. Indeed, in the UK such intentions would have been considered inappropriately centralist and authoritarian in a society characterized by its emphasis on individualism and concepts of democratic freedom. Instead it was the tensions between the legacy of Victorian values and the attempts to modernize and transform society in the latter half of the twentieth century that provided the space for the campaigning of the women's movement and the opportunity for women to 'break out' of the gender mould. At the same time such tensions did little to relieve the pressure upon men to remain committed to conventional values and male bread-winning family roles.

In the first section of this chapter we begin the analysis by outlining what are commonly understood as Victorian values and their significance for education. The second section documents, albeit briefly, how by the nineteenth century women had already challenged the distinctions between male public and female private spheres, while sustaining Victorian values within education. The rest of the chapter explores the challenges to such values from those committed to women's rights, to meritocracy and to individualism.

Victorian values and the cult of female domesticity

What do we mean by 'Victorian values'? As Himmelfarb argues (1995: 3), discussion of 'values' has become so commonplace that it is easy to forget its relatively recent history. Margaret Thatcher, perhaps somewhat inadvertently, first mentioned Victorian values as a desirable attribute in the election campaign of 1983. Her initial articulation was followed by a variety of interpretations and reinterpretations and the eventual incorporation of the American family values debate. Himmelfarb (1995: 8) claims that the term has been altered markedly from that used by the Victorians, and Margaret Thatcher herself (1993) claimed that the Victorians were more concerned with 'virtues' than values.

> I had a great regard for the Victorians for many reasons . . . I never felt uneasy about praising 'Victorian values' or – the phrase I originally used – 'Victorian virtues', not least because they were by no means just Victorian . . . they distinguished between the 'deserving' and the 'undeserving poor'. Both groups should be given help; but it must be help of very different kinds if public spending is not just going to reinforce the dependency culture. . . . The purpose of help must not be to allow people merely to live a half-life; but to restore their self-discipline and through that their self-esteem . . .
>
> *(Thatcher, 1993: 627)*

Himmelfarb provides a more scholarly definition of Victorian 'virtues', as:

> neither the classical nor the Christian virtues; they were more domesticated than the former and more secular than the latter . . . Most Victorians even believed them to be . . . 'perennial' . . . the standards against which behaviour could and should be measured . . . And when conduct fell short of those standards, it was judged in moral terms, as bad, wrong, or evil – not, as is more often the case today, as misguided, undesirable, or . . . 'inappropriate' . . .
>
> It is important to recognise . . . the reality and power of the principles themselves – the belief in family and home, respectability and character. Values remain values . . . even if they are not always carried out in practice. They are what people aspire to, knowing that they will not be fully realised.
>
> *(Himmelfarb, 1995: 12–15)*

These values were essentially those of the middle class, part of the newly burgeoning and aspiring bourgeoisie, which, after the second World War, gained increased power and influence. Victorian values were also attractive, to some extent, to some working-class people because they were seen to advocate a particular form of gender relations which gave value to men and women's different roles in the family. Ideas about the naturalness of the Victorian gender order were thus maintained.

According to Victorian advocates of separate spheres, the public world of work and achievement was to be occupied by the independent and autonomous male, and the private, enclosed domain of the 'home, care, harmony and relationships' by the intuitive and dependent female (Brabeck, 1996). This was linked to biologically derived 'natural' characteristics accorded to human males and females. Nineteenth-century ideological beliefs about different male and female biological characteristics and accompanying differences in intellectual and moral orientation also served as a basis for assigning men and women to the separate spheres, buttressed by liberal political values.

In addition, class affiliation was a central feature of masculinity and femininity. According to Vicinus (1972), for upper- and upper/middle-class women, life was expected to be leisurely, if narrow:

> Once married, the perfect lady did not work; she had servants. She was mother only at set times of the day . . . she left heirs in the hands of nannies and governesses. Her social and intellectual growth was confined to the family and close friends. Her status was totally dependent upon the economic position of her father and then her husband.
>
> *(Vicinus, 1972: ix)*

Branca (1975), however, suggests that, for many middle-class women, their lives were more active, energetic, hard-working, well-organized and forward-looking, if restricted to the private sphere. For working-class women, in contrast, the attraction of a life based exclusively in the home was more complex. The forms of work open to women in the nineteenth century were often low paid and grindingly hard. Thus an early goal of the trade unions was to reproduce the middle-class model of family life and *pater familias* with the aid of a male family wage to support a stay-at-home wife and their children. However, such a model of family was also likely to place greater restrictions on the family relations and aspirations of working-class women. Thus an appropriate ideological form was reproduced for working-class families which modified the concept of the 'perfect lady' into one of the 'good woman'. According to Vicinus, 'The perfect lady under these conditions became the woman who kept to her family, centring all her life on keeping the house clean, the children well-disciplined and her daughters chaste' (1972: xiv).

Victorian values were applied to the creation of a 'modern' education system and thus emphasized specific educational experiences and curricula for boys and girls according to their various family, gender and class positions in order to prepare them appropriately for their expected journeys through life. Particularly influential on state schooling, these ideologies embraced a strong family rhetoric, constructing a particular relationship between female and private (home) and male and public (work-related) spheres. With the growth of democracy in the nineteenth century, however, came tensions between the ideological imperatives in education of gender, class and racial differentiation to maintain the male ruling elite and the commitment to wider access to, and a broader role for, education (Burstyn, 1980; Delamont & Duffin, 1978; Dyhouse, 1981).

This tension was evident in the creation of a national system of education in the second half of the nineteenth century. On the one hand, education provision for all classes was expanded to include the establishment of a national elementary education system in 1870, entrance to which was made compulsory two decades later. On the other, the education proposed was sharply differentiated to represent and sustain existing social divisions. Thus, in Britain, distinct nineteenth-century educational traditions emerged, based on social class and gender. For men, schooling was framed according to the perceived class associations contained in 'public/grammar' (upper/middle-class) and 'elementary' (working-class) schools. The education for boys focused on male public roles, in the labour force and as citizens. The public schools educated boys for leadership of the country, while the elementary schools 'schooled' boys for the manual labour force – in reading to understand simple written instructions and in elementary calculations (Lawton, 1975).

Parallel nineteenth-century female educational traditions also emerged, deriving from the notions of 'perfect lady' and 'good woman'. The female curriculum was framed according to the skills, knowledge and accomplishments thought necessary for women as home-based adults, but in classed forms. Thus, household management, Mrs Beeton-style, was reserved for the future 'lady' of the house and housework and laundry skills for the future working 'woman'. Female education was linked with girls' biology and their eventual domestic destinies within the family, exemplified in the claimed link between female 'over-education' and infertility (Delamont & Duffin, 1978; Burstyn, 1980).

Two contrasting educational perspectives on family and gender thus endured from the nineteenth century. The first and most popular view was that women are different from (and inferior to) men, not only biologically but socially, intellectually and psychologically. Girls and boys, it was argued, needed an education which related specifically to their designated roles in society. Motherhood and empire were frequently linked. Motherhood was seen as the supreme vocation for women in the nineteenth century, and one of two imperial callings:

> Marriage and motherhood on the one hand and the 'liberal' professions on the other . . . The confinement of motherhood, like a posting to the far-flung colonies, was recognised as a call to 'higher things' – the disinterested service of the British Empire.
>
> (Hamilton, 1987: 4)

The second perspective on education was that women are equal to men, and that, if girls and women are provided with the same educational experiences as boys and men, they will be able to assume their rightful place in society alongside their male peers. In fact, the Revised Code (1862) appeared to support this position by placing elementary (working-class) girls on an equal footing with boys in terms of the amount of money the schools could earn by successful examination results in the 3Rs (reading, writing, arithmetic). However, gender differentiation was reinserted when the code was widened to include other subjects: sewing, knitting and cookery were introduced for girls in the 1870s, and laundry work, dressmaking, home nursing, element-ary hygiene and physiology in the 1880s (Purvis, 1991). Elementary-school boys were required merely to do more mathematics and technical drawing. Meanwhile, many middle-class girls spent their time in ladies' academies, learning 'accomplishments' such as piano-playing and etiquette, to prepare them for a good marriage and the social setting of the drawing room and parlour. Exceptions were the few girls who attended the newer girls' grammar schools with the view to breaking into hitherto exclusively male professions (Swindells, 1985).

Scholarly achievement sat somewhat uncomfortably alongside the ideal of the 'lady' and the culture of ladylike behaviour, manners and etiquette. The style seen as appropriate to women of the upper classes was antithetical to the promotion of women's intellect (Purvis, 1989). Indeed, the success of middle-class women in campaigning for female education in the late nine-teenth century constituted a challenge to the distinction that had been made between masculinity and femininity. Educating elite women breached the assumption of femininity as associated only with the home, domesticity, virginity and sexual fidelity and masculinity as associated only with public work, strength and superiority (Delamont, 1989). These tensions around separate (and different?) but equal spheres remained until well into the twen-tieth century.

By the beginning of the twentieth century, shifts in the gendered nature of education were forced by new work opportunities open to women, such as typewriting and clerical and telephone work: nevertheless the main purpose of female education was still thought as for motherhood and domest-icity (Dyhouse, 1981). Significantly, a 1923 government report attempted to reconcile moves towards sex equality (notably, extension of the franchise to women in 1918) with contemporary ideas from psychology about 'natural' sex differences. The different but equal theme was well defended:

> We can afford to recognise that equality does not demand identity but is com-patible with, and even depends upon, a system of differentiation under which either sex seeks to multiply at a rich interest its own peculiar talents. Dissimilars are not necessarily unequals; and it is possible to conceive an equality of the

sexes which is all the truer and richer because it is founded on mutual recognition of differences and equal cultivation of different capacities.

(Board of Education, 1923: xiii)

A recurrent theme, noticeable both in nineteenth- and twentieth-century discourses on women's education, was a fear that a woman's intellect was antagonistic to her biological destiny; and that, somehow, academic work would inevitably intervene and destroy her natural destiny as wife and mother (Delamont & Duffin, 1978). Walkerdine identifies such Victorian notions with concerns about empire:

The possession of a womb was thought to render a woman unfit for deep thought, which might tax her reproductive powers or make her less amenable to rearing children. Given the state of the Empire, the concern with the race as with the species, it was considered potentially injurious to allow bourgeois women to reason.

(Walkerdine, 1990: 22)

In the course of the next century the challenge to the concept of separate spheres and to an inferior domestic education for girls was mounted on three fronts: first, in the name of women's rights; second, on the grounds of meritocracy; and third, by the promotion of new forms of individualism by the New Right.

Women's rights

These tensions and debates derived not only from the Victorians but from earlier feminist debate and activity. Perhaps the lack of education itself drove elite women to adopt different values and to develop the arguments and challenges where they were able to. From the eighteenth century onwards, when Mary Wollstonecraft first wrote her great work *The Vindication of the Rights of Woman* (1792), feminists have viewed education both as one of the main sites of female oppression and social exclusion and as a site of distinct possibility and therefore a principal target for challenge and activity.

Not only the virtue, but the knowledge of the two sexes should be the same in nature, if not degree, and . . . women, considered not only as moral, but rational creatures, ought to endeavour to acquire human virtues (or perfections) by the same means as men, instead of being educated like a fanciful half being – one of Rousseau's wild chimeras.

(Wollstonecraft, reprinted in Rossi, 1973: 54)

What has been called the first wave of feminism in the nineteenth century focused among other things on education for the daughters and sisters of the burgeoning bourgeoisie. In the mid-nineteenth century women such as Miss Buss, Miss Beale, Emily Davies and the Shirreff sisters started educational campaigns that became known as the Women's Educational Movement. They argued for schools for girls on a par with those for boys, and after the 1860 Education Act such 'higher education' for girls, as it was then known, was allowed to develop (David, 1980). An independent and public school mix of grammar schools, public day schools and boarding schools was created chiefly but not only on a single-sex basis (Kamm, 1965). By the end of the nineteenth century there was an array of different types of girls' schools funded privately through the payment of fees or, for a small select group, through scholarships.

Emily Davies also campaigned for the opening up of universities to women through the transformation of the entrance and qualifying examination system, known as the Cambridge Locals and Higher School Certificate. She called for the establishment of colleges for women in Cambridge, Oxford, London and the north of England. Although the examination system was eventually modified to allow girls to take the examinations or their equivalents, the universities did not permit their female students to be awarded official degrees until well into the twentieth century. Cambridge, in fact, was the last university officially to block women being awarded degrees, finally conceding only in 1948.

Campaigns to create female elite education went through several stages. Delamont shows that, by the end of the nineteenth century, the principle of equal opportunities had already affected girls' independent schools. Two roles for elite women were available: that of the well-educated/intelligent wife and that of the celibate career woman (often that of teacher), thus disconnecting female sexuality from academic success (Delamont, 1989). However, a perceived threat from lesbianism made the celibate career woman unfashionable, which meant that new ways had to be found to combine female academic ambition with the middle-class ideal of the 'lady' (see Chapter 7).

One beneficiary of early educational campaigns on behalf of women was Margaret Thatcher, who attended a fee-paying girls' grammar school in the late 1930s and Oxford University in the 1940s. She commenced studies there in the midst of the Second World War and obtained her degree in 1947.

As we shall show in Chapter 5, increased provision of grammar and other secondary schools for girls and greater possibilities for female study offered by adult and further education appeared particularly beneficial to upper- and middle-class girls (Deem, 1981; Dyhouse, 1981; Purvis, 1981; Wolpe, 1976). It was this new generation of female professionals and educators who began to think about what could be done for the broad mass of girls and women and who later attempted to reduce the impact of Victorian domestic ideology on educational policy and practice.

Meritocracy

The second major challenge to the dominance of Victorian gender values (alongside and also integral to the challenges of the women's movement) was the restructuring of the educational system after the Second World War, in terms of individual achievement. The term 'meritocracy' to account for these developments was first coined by Young (1963). Dubbed the Butler Act (after the name of the education minister of the time) and also the 'children's charter', the 1944 Education Act provided free state secondary education for all, and implicitly (but not explicitly) afforded girls equal opportunities alongside boys. State education was consolidated through its administration locally by LEAs, and newly built secondary schools were incorporated into what later became known as the tripartite system. In particular, new girls' grammar schools were built or modernized to replace previous fee-paying schools. As we have seen, further and higher education slowly opened its doors to women, thus offering more educational opportunities to a new generation of women – those such as ourselves, born at the end or just after the Second World War (Heron, 1985; Ingham, 1981; Owen, 1983).

Victorian values, however, continued to carry weight in educational circles during this period, despite the apparent commitment to the new political values of social democracy. Deem (1981) characterizes the educational ideology of the post-Second World War period as sustaining the belief of a woman's primary place as in the home. From the Labour government of 1945–51, which was resistant to extending even such basic rights as equal pay to women, through the high point of social democracy and the extension of the welfare state in the late 1960s, to the breakdown of consensus about education and the decline of social democracy towards the end of the 1970s, there was little visible support for any other than the broadest notions of sex equality (Deem, 1981; Dean, 1991). Similarly, in her investigation of girls' education implicit in the ideologies of the Norwood, Crowther and Newsom reports (1943, 1959 and 1963 respectively), Wolpe concludes that all three reports 'provide an ideological basis for the perpetuation of an education system which does not open up new vistas or possibilities to the majority of girls' (Wolpe, 1976: 157).

Despite the various feminist campaigns of the suffrage movement from the early twentieth century onwards, official rhetoric still adhered to the notion of separate spheres, particularly for women as mothers. In the immediate aftermath of the Second World War there was a reinvigoration of such notions through the application of new psychoanalytic and psychotherapeutic ideas. These were applied in particular to the training of schoolteachers and other childcare professionals (see Chapter 4). Bowlby's theories, held in the highest esteem during the 1950s and early 1960s, asserted the necessity of mothers' presence in the early care of babies and in the care of older children well beyond school age (Riley, 1983; New & David, 1985). Thus stay-at-home motherhood became idealized and commonly expected even of the most well-educated or socially privileged mothers. The evils of 'maternal deprivation', as Bowlby's best-known theory was termed, were much debated in teacher training and came to influence future conceptualizations of equality of educational opportunity. In other words, though there was an expectation that girls should be educated 'equally' to and alongside boys, this was not necessarily aimed at equality in employment opportunities. Women were still expected to care for the home and children on marriage, as motherhood became increasingly extolled and codified.

The 1960s and 1970s saw the opening up of educational opportunities to hitherto excluded social groups, particularly influenced by the Civil Rights and Women's Liberation movements from the USA. These developed a new political and ideological purchase on notions of equal opportunities which led the post-war generation of educated women (as feminists) to create a new politics and new approaches to family life. The explicit 'demands' for equal educational opportunities for both sexes and for childcare for pre-school children became two of their first rallying calls (Coote & Campbell, 1982). Many such women became teachers with ambitions to transform the education system in the interests of girls. The one official policy which attempted to accommodate some of these ideas was the Sex Discrimination Act of 1975.

One of the goals of the legislation was to provide the incentive to create a more gender-neutral educational framework. The legislation rendered illegal the practice of excluding pupils from school subjects or courses on the grounds of sex. Yet while, in theory, it removed some discriminatory practices, the Sex Discrimination Act allowed others to continue. For example, coeducational schools were covered by the legislation, but single-sex schools remained able to offer sex-specific curricula. Thus girls in one school could be (and were) treated less favourably than boys in another. It was also left to non-statutory guidelines to urge secondary schools to avoid less overt biases and forms of sex discrimination. 'Be particularly careful', secondary schools were warned, 'not to organise the earlier stages of the secondary curriculum in such a way that it prevents a choice of the full range of options at a later stage' (EOC, 1975: 13).

Another aim of the legislation was to ensure that both girls and boys had a wider range of subject choice at secondary level, rather than the previous narrow sex-divided curriculum. However, subject take-up remained sex-divided and optional throughout the 1970s and early 1980s, as students at thirteen plus were allowed relatively free choice of between four and six subjects (in addition to the 'core' subjects of English, mathematics and PE) to carry forward to the end of compulsory schooling. While a wide range of subjects was theoretically available, Pratt, Bloomfield & Seale (1984) found that girls tended to choose arts, humanities, commercial and 'caring' subjects and boys, science, mathematics and crafts subjects – despite calls from teachers and academics from the late 1970s onwards for a more sex-equitable secondary school curriculum structure (Byrne, 1978). Thus, while government rhetoric promoted sex equality in legislation such as the Sex Discrimination Act and the Equal Pay Act (1970), and through support for the extension of coeducational comprehensive schooling, the outcome in terms of student choice and performance continued to reflect Victorian assumptions concerning private/female and public/male dualisms.

Progressivism, which suffused especially primary education throughout the 1960s and 1970s, also proved unsupportive to the promotion of non-sex-differentiated schooling. Progressivism was premised on a notion of liberatory pedagogy where childhood and learning are best served by leaving children free to develop at their own 'natural' rate. According to this discourse of 'natural' and individual development, girls' early success in reading and language skills was viewed as transgressive, abnormal and 'not real learning'. According to Walkerdine (1983):

> The real discovery and conceptualisation which form the cornerstones of modern pedagogy [progressivism] are contrasted with rule-following and rote-memorising . . . From this point of view, success in terms of attainment or correct work can be achieved in the wrong way. One aspect of the 'problem of female success' is that it turns out to be no success at all! Instead of thinking properly, girls simply work hard – if femininity is defined by passivity, good behaviour, rule-following and the other characteristics of the old methods, then the outcomes cannot be 'real learning'.
>
> *(Walkerdine, 1983: 83–4)*

Thus, it seems that girls' performance *vis-à-vis* progressivism could never be good enough despite their obvious successes, and the notion that girls were different from, and inferior to, boys remained. This view continued to reflect Victorian values, although in a modified form from that of the nineteenth century. Thus motherhood was perceived as more important than women's role in the family *per se*. Family roles were seen as private choices and, despite much feminist campaigning, there remained no official support for the public provision of childcare (New & David, 1985). This rendered it impossible for the majority of women, especially poorer paid or working-class women, to make 'real' choices about how to balance childcare and paid employment. Secondary schools, moreover, continued to provide childcare courses for their female students, often by involving the local infants or junior school, which continued well into the 1990s.

Margaret Thatcher and the cult of individualism

Margaret Thatcher's administrations of the 1980s initiated a once-and-for-all break with Victorianism in terms both of greater gender equality in education and of the modernization of family life and associated work practices. Thatcher's life and work embodies a tension between Victorian family rhetoric and the reality of modern family life. Paradoxically, despite her espousal of Victorian political and family values, she has become an icon of female educational and public achievement for the late twentieth century.

Of interest to us at this point are the contradictions (revealed in her own and her husband's biographies, the latter by her daughter) between public espousal of traditional or 'Victorian' political and family values and the ways in which Margaret Thatcher lived her own family life – contradictions that were to inform her political practice in complex ways. This tension is no more clearly illustrated than in her career, leading to her becoming Britain's first woman prime minister. It could be argued that her particular conservative views enabled her to uphold apparently contradictory values. Her belief in liberal or *laissez-faire* conservatism (and the importance of limited government in the context of the free market) is one which could offer her a number of scripts for her own personal life and direction. Her politics, of individualism and liberalism, in the economic sphere in fact also directed her to a kind of 'liberal, individualistic feminism' which she applied to her politics of family life.

Having benefited from the opening up of educational opportunities for middle-class girls in the 1930s and 1940s, Thatcher embarked upon a career outside the home. On the accession to the throne of the new Queen Elizabeth, in February 1952, she wrote an article in the *Sunday Graphic* entitled 'Wake up, Women'. She argued for 'more and more women combining marriage AND a career', taking only 'a short leave of absence when families arrive'. She even asserted that 'THE IDEA THAT THE FAMILY SUFFERS IS, I BELIEVE, QUITE MISTAKEN.' She went on to argue for equality for women, especially in politics, and concluded that:

> *I should like to see* EVERY woman trying to overcome ignorance of day-to-day affairs; and EVERY woman taking an active part in local life. And, above all, *I should like to see* more and more women at Westminster, and in the highest places, too.

On marrying in 1950, despite the strong Bowlbyism of that period, she switched from her work as an industrial chemist to law, beginning her training as a barrister at the same time as becoming a mother. Her daughter Carol describes this particular combination of career and motherhood in her biography of her father, Denis Thatcher, in the following terms:

A woman of the Queen's age criticises her own sex and calls for a new spirit to meet the challenge at the dawn of the new Elizabethan era.

WAKE UP, WOMEN

A YOUNG Queen, the loveliest ever to reign over us, now occupies the highest position in the land.

If, as many earnestly pray, the accession of Elizabeth II can help to remove the last shreds of prejudice against women aspiring to the highest places, then a new era for women will indeed be at hand.

We owe it to the Queen—and to the memory of a father who set her such a wonderful example throughout his life—to play our part with increasing enterprise in the years ahead.

I hope we shall see more and more women combining marriage AND a career. Prejudice against this dual rôle is not confined to men. Far too often, I regret to say it comes from our own sex.

BETRAYAL, UNLESS—

But the happy management of home and career can and IS being achieved. The name of Mrs. Norman Harper, wife of a Liverpool surgeon and mother of a three-year-old daughter, may mean little to many of you.

But the name of Miss ROSE HEILBRON, Q.C., whose moving advocacy in recent trials has been so widely praised, is known throughout the land.

Unless Britain, in the new age to come, can produce more Rose Heilbrons—not only in the field of law, of course—we shall have betrayed the tremendous work of those who fought for equal rights against such misguided opposition.

The term "career woman" has unfortunately come to imply in many minds a "hard" woman, devoid of all feminine characteristics.

WASTED TALENTS

But Rose Heilbron and many more have shown only too well that capability and charm can go together.

Why have so few women in recent years risen to the top of the professions? One reason may be that so many have cut short their careers when they marry. IN MY VIEW THIS IS A GREAT PITY.

For it IS possible to carry on working, taking a short leave of absence when families arrive, and returning later.

In this way gifts and talents that would otherwise be wasted are developed to the benefit of the community.

THE IDEA THAT THE FAMILY SUFFERS IS, I BELIEVE, QUITE MISTAKEN. To carry on with a career stimulates the mind, provides a refreshing contact with the world outside—and so means that a wife can be a much better companion at home.

Moreover, when her children themselves marry, she is not left with a gap in

by MARGARET THATCHER

who, as Margaret Roberts, was the youngest woman candidate in the last two General Elections. Only a few months older than the Queen, she married three months ago. She has a degree in Natural Science and Chemistry, and is studying for the Bar.

her life which so often seems impossible to fill.

Women can—AND MUST—play a leading part in the creation of a glorious Elizabethan era.

The opportunities are there in abundance—in almost every sphere of British endeavour.

We must emulate the example of such women as Barbara Ward, at 37 one of our leading economists and an expert on foreign affairs; Dr. Janet Vaughan, mother of two children and principal of Somerville College; Mary Field who, as president of

the 90,000-strong British Federation of Business and Professional Women, is one of our most successful "career women"; and Dame Caroline Haslett, Britain's No. 1 woman engineer and founder more than a quarter of a century ago of the Electrical Association for Women.

That there IS a place for women at the top of the tree has been proved beyond question by these, and very many others.

And if there are those who would say: "It couldn't happen to me," they would do well to remember that DAME Caroline Haslett herself started as a 10s.-a-week apprentice in a London boiler works more than 30 years ago.

I have heard it said that American women have far more influence over the nation's affairs than do the women of Britain.

Yet American women have only six out of 435 members in the House of Representatives. We have 17 out of 625 in the House of Commons.

But it is still not good enough. If we are to have better representation in Parliament, the women of England must fight harder for it.

Should a woman arise equal to the task, I say let her have an equal chance with the men for the leading Cabinet posts. Why not a woman Chancellor—or Foreign Secretary?

Why not? And if they made mistakes, they would not be the first to do so in those jobs!

IN HIGH PLACES

To sum up, *I should like to see* the woman with a career holding down her responsibility with easy assurance during the Elizabethan age.

I should like to see married women carrying on with their jobs, if so inclined, after their children are born.

I should like to see EVERY woman trying to overcome ignorance of day-to-day affairs; and EVERY woman taking an active part in local life.

And, above all, *I should like to see* more and more women at Westminster, and in the highest places, too.

It would certainly be a good thing for the women of Britain. And I'm sure it would be a good thing for the men, too!

Meanwhile, Margaret had become a young married woman of comfortable means. Any thoughts of a political career were put on hold, although she still accepted occasional invitations to speak at Conservative party functions. Instead she decided to read for the Bar. Denis supported her decision: 'Do what you like, love,' he told her, and it became his standard response. Fortunately, a barrister's life is also highly compatible with motherhood, an event pencilled in to begin on 29 Sept 1953.

(Thatcher, 1996: 68)

Margaret Thatcher's own account emphasizes the 'jolly' times she was having reading law and pursuing a political career. The following shows how she was able to combine personal family and political involvement and values:

The question . . . [of] how I would combine my home life with politics was soon to become even more sensitive. For in August 1953 the twins, Mark and Carol, put in an appearance . . . Oddly enough, the very depth of the relief and happiness at having brought Mark and Carol into the world made me uneasy. The pull of a mother towards her children is perhaps the strongest and most instinctive emotion we have. I was never one of those people who regarded being 'just' a mother or indeed 'just' a housewife as second best. Indeed, whenever I heard such implicit assumptions made both before and after I became PM it would make me very angry indeed. Of course, to be a mother and housewife is a vocation of a very high kind. But I simply felt that it was not the whole of my vocation. I knew that I also wanted a career. A phrase that Irene Ward, MP for Tynemouth, and I often used was that 'while the home must always be the centre of one's life, it should not be the boundary of one's ambitions'. Indeed, I needed a career because, quite simply, that was the sort of person I was. And not just any career. I wanted one which would keep me mentally active and prepare me for the political future for which I believed I was well suited.

So it was that at the end of my first week in hospital I came to a decision. I had the application form for my Bar finals in December sent to me. I filled it in and sent off the money for the exam, knowing that this little psychological trick I was playing on myself would ensure that I was plunged into legal studies on my return to Swan Court with the twins, and that I would have to organise our lives so as to allow me to be both a mother and a professional woman . . . Usually, however, it was the nanny, Barbara, who took Mark and Carol to the park, except at weekends when I took over.

(Thatcher, 1995: 80)

With the benefit of hindsight, reflection and clarity about these social changes, Thatcher has described how her own unique blend of fortunate circumstances led her to hold relatively unusual ideas for a woman in the early 1950s. Indeed, as we have seen, social commentary during this period shows it as the heyday of Bowlbyism (Wilson, 1980; Riley, 1983; New & David, 1985), when even professionally trained mothers were inculcated with the idea that they should 'return' home and assume sole care of their children. But Thatcher appeared to entertain no such agonizing or maternal 'guilt': she trod her own path coolly, without regard either to her own party's views on motherhood or those of the growing 'psychological and psychotherapeutic' lobbies.

Thatcher's views on women's equality and personal ability to ignore the official rhetoric on motherhood and domesticity suggests an unorthodox perspective at the very least, as she seemed able to hold a personal and political value system which was hugely contradictory, especially given her emphasis on Victorian values in public life. Her public views on values remained unchanged for the next twenty or thirty years and were particularly noticeable when she gained the opportunity, as prime minister, to inject them into the educational system and society. She was elected leader of the Conservative opposition in 1975, which was heralded as a daring step by her somewhat cautious party – significantly in the same year that the Sex Discrimination Act was passed.

Throughout her period in office, both as leader of the Conservative party in opposition and then as prime minister, Thatcher paid attention to issues relating to women's roles in the family and in public life. She tried to deal with the tensions both personally and politically, although they were always contradictory, as we have seen. In her two-volume autobiography she reflected on some of these tensions, on her own particular personal development and on the choices she was able to make as a result of her relatively privileged education. For instance, she mentioned that she saw herself as relatively unusual and privileged in being able to pursue a political career in what she called 'a man's world' (1995: 64, 79). She also espoused the notion that only a select few women were likely to be able to break out of the mould of separate spheres, which remained applicable and attractive to the majority of women, particularly working-class women.

Margaret Thatcher's views of Victorian values, thus, were directed mainly towards the 'ordinary' man and woman. She cites her commitment to Victorian virtues in the context of individualism, and, for example, in defence of her much quoted comment that there is 'no such thing as society', argued that:

> There are individual men and women, and there are families. And no government can do anything except through people, and people must look to themselves first. It's our duty to look after ourselves and then to look after our neighbour.
>
> My meaning, clear at the time but subsequently distorted beyond recognition, was that society was not an abstraction, separate from the men and women who composed it but a living structure of individuals, families, neighbours and voluntary associations. I expected great things from society in this sense . . . The error to which I was objecting was the confusion of society with the state as helper of first resort . . . Society for me was not an excuse, it was a source of obligation. I was an individualist in the sense that I believed that individuals are ultimately accountable for their actions and must behave like it. But I always refused to accept that there was some kind of conflict between this kind of individualism and social responsibility. I was reinforced . . . by the writings . . . on the growth of an 'underclass' and the development of a dependency culture . . .
>
> (Thatcher, 1993: 626–7)

However, while in office as prime minister it was not easy, she found, to develop policies which reflected Victorian values, women's issues and her own life's experience:

The question of how best . . . to support families with children was a vexed one . . . I believed that it was possible – as I had – to bring up a family while working, as long as one was willing to make a great effort to organize one's time properly and with some extra help. But I did not believe that it was fair to those mothers who chose to stay at home and bring up their families on one income to give tax reliefs to those who went out to work and had two incomes.* It always seemed odd to me that the feminists – so keenly sensitive to being patronized by men but without any such sensitivity to the patronage of the state – could not grasp that . . .

The wider influences of the media, schools and above all the churches are more powerful than anything government can do. But so much hung on what happened to the structure of the nation's families that only the most myopic libertarian would regard it as outside the purview of the state.

*I was, though, content to make one minor adjustment. This was to provide tax relief for workplace nurseries. [author's footnote]

(Thatcher, 1993: 630–1)

Margaret Thatcher's educational policies reflected a less libertarian and more contradictory approach to Victorian values. Throughout her period in office, reforms to standardize the school curriculum, particularly for secondary-school pupils, appeared to challenge the concept of separate educational spheres and to delegitimate gender inequality. For instance, the reform of the examination system in the mid-1980s, combining GCE O-levels with CSE examinations for secondary-school pupils, marked the first steps towards a gender-neutral curriculum. The introduction of the GCSE, as the new examination was called, in 1985 seemed to be more effective in encouraging students to be entered for a balanced cluster of subjects and thus offered the beginnings of official change for girls. As a consequence, more girls were entered for science and mathematics than in previous decades, prompting the gradual shift in traditional gender patterns of subject entry and performance that we described in the last chapter.

The final nail in the coffin of the Victorian gendered curriculum, we suggest, was the creation of a national curriculum in 1988 which reduced, but did not eliminate altogether, the possibility of sex-stereotyping in subject choice. Significantly, in the same year some 42 per cent of girls who were entered for GCSE took home economics as one of their subjects; five years later, in 1993, this proportion had dropped to 15 per cent (personal communication with DfEE). There are a variety of explanations available for why such changes occurred. Nevertheless, on the day that the National Curriculum was announced, the then secretary of state for education, Kenneth Baker, told the BBC radio programme *Today* that one reason that all pupils were to be compelled to take the same set of subjects was so that more girls would take up science.

Whatever her intentions, Margaret Thatcher's administrations of the 1980s were associated with a once-and-for-all break with Victorianism in terms of greater gender equality in education and the modernization of family life and associated work practices.

Reflections

In this chapter we have argued that at least one reason for the different patterns of gender performance in schools has been changes in values about women's roles in family life. Key to this process was, firstly, women's struggle for greater access to education and, second, the strategic approach to meritocracy by social democratic reformers, which led to the expansion of educational opportunities for girls and women. Both of these, as we shall show in chapters 4 and 5, were to lay the foundations for a new form of society which included and used women to support its welfare programmes and, at the same time, extended the struggle for women's rights into the mid-twentieth century.

However, until Margaret Thatcher was personally able to demonstrate the link between educational achievement and public success, there had been little public recognition of female educational achievement, or indeed of the possibilities of associating women with power in British society. It is indeed ironic that it was Thatcher herself who argued for women's rights in public life as early as 1952 and who, when she achieved this right for herself, tried to put the genie back into the bottle. Forty years later she tried to reimpose traditional Victorian family values on society – but she singularly failed. Indeed, as we shall argue in Chapter 6, she appeared to accomplish the very opposite and to enhance the advancement of women's educational and public achievements such that even 'ordinary' girls began to desert the traditionally female educational avenues directed towards family life.

Part II
Social Policy and Education Reform

4

Motherhood and Women's Work in the Welfare State

In this chapter we show how greater equality between the sexes developed at the same time as the state began to play a part in promoting economic growth and the collective well-being. Key to these events was the emergence of 'second-wave' feminism in the form of the Women's Liberation Movement (WLM). The social disruption of the Second World War led to the creation of the welfare state and a subsequent boom period which influenced the emergence of the WLM. The WLM challenged the state by constructing a new political agenda on behalf of women. As Connell (1990: 519) reminds us, although government policy actively creates and encourages particular relations between men and women (through, for example, family and education policy), the dynamics between men and women also affect the state, creating new problems to solve and new solutions to those problems. Gender politics, therefore, are both a form of political resistance and a product of government action.

On the face of it, the architects of the welfare state in the 1940s explicitly aimed to maintain the family and its relation to the economy/labour market in the traditional Victorian form (as discussed in Chapter 3). Any changes in gender relations or values were thus *unintended* consequences of government policy and cultural change. They were to some extent an unplanned result of the 'dual repertoire' (CCCS, 1981) of social democracy – supporting economic regeneration and social redistribution. Yet such were these shifts in social practices and the rate and pace of change in relation to gender that, despite intentions and explicit anti-egalitarianism, later attempts by the New Right government in the 1980s and 1990s failed to re-establish Victorian values in relation to the family.

Accounts of the creation of the welfare state during, and in the immediate aftermath of, the Second World War in Britain have been written by feminist policy analysts with increasing degrees of sophistication. Dale and Foster (1986) and Pascall (1986) provide encyclopaedic views of these developments. However, the story has become ever more complicated as newer interpretations challenge the presumption that it is possible to develop one coherent narrative about the relationship between, for example, the 'family' and the 'state'. Although much has been written on the patriarchal nature of the state, this has been counterbalanced by the recognition of the ambivalence of such male-dominated state machinery to gender politics. While some welfare policies explicitly supported traditional family values, these were undermined in practice; others explicitly supported change while implicitly basing practice on conventional assumptions about male and female roles in family life.

From our current vantage point, two phases are particularly noteworthy at the level of ideology and practice. The first phase – the *meritocratic era* – saw a strong commitment to equality of opportunity and individual advancement and, at the same time, sought to maintain the structure of 'normal' family life. Thus women were encouraged to participate in the new meritocratic order. Yet, in providing employment for women in the welfare 'caring' services, Victorian family values (albeit dressed up in new form) regarding women's traditional roles were reinvigorated and supported.

The second phase within social democracy – the era of *feminist politics* – exposed the contradictions between the nuclear family ideal and the realities of women's economic and sexual emancipation. Victorian domestic ideology was put to the test and found wanting. Here, what was scrutinized was not just the family division of labour but also its institutional basis – the marriage contract. As we show in Chapter 5, rethinking the family and women's role meant, in the long run, reconsidering the purposes of female education.

The meritocratic era

Immediately after the Second World War the creators of the welfare state had as their main aims rebuilding Britain and creating a new context for economic growth. There was a large measure of party political agreement that the state should be more interventionist (Mishra, 1984), although there was less consensus on the measures to be taken. In her autobiography Margaret Thatcher implicitly blamed both old Labour and Conservative administrations from the 1940s onwards for an overly 'collectivist' approach to social welfare and the economy, thus inhibiting the growth of market forces for the free play of capitalism (Thatcher, 1995).

In the immediate post-war period there was a commitment to 'slay' what Beveridge in his official report *Social Insurance and Allied Services* (1942) called the five 'giant evils', namely want, squalor, disease, idleness and ignorance.

A range of solutions was developed to address each of these five 'evils' – income maintenance and social security, housing, health, employment, and unemployment and education policies. Over the following five to six years these policy proposals were implemented through a series of legislative measures, first by the Conservatives heading a coalition government towards the end of the war, and later by the post-war Labour administration, fully committed to creating a welfare state. Beveridge's aim, which was accepted by both political parties, was to reinvigorate and support the family in its traditional Victorian form (male breadwinner and head of household and full-time housewife and mother). He did not foresee any changes in the relationships between men and women either at home or at work (Wilson, 1977). In particular, he argued that wives would and should stay at home to take responsibility for their 'other duties', such as caring for husband and family (Land, 1976).

Paradoxically such Victorian family values did not translate into official policies other than those concerned with income maintenance and social security (including the introduction of family allowances); neither were they picked up by developments in the labour market. Land (1976) highlighted the ways in which the policy aims for family allowances and other aspects of income maintenance failed to square with economic developments and their impact upon the labour market. The patterns of paid employment for women, particularly for those who were married and those with caring responsibilities, continued to change, despite the attempts to keep such women at home. The explicit intention, for example, for the National Health Service was to ensure that all citizens would be catered for. Nevertheless, we now recognize that in terms of social services, such as childcare, welfare for the elderly and disabled, and housing policies, the aims of policy-makers were not to provide a universal service, as in health, but rather to create a safety net for those 'families' who fell outside of the mainstream. No gender-explicit language was used to frame the policies, but the presumption remained that women would continue their caring role in the family and community to support 'normal' family life.

The tensions between conventional gender relations in the family and the principle of equality of opportunity were also clearly demonstrated in the field of educational policy – one of the first areas of development of the burgeoning welfare state. Conventional gender relations remained a hidden, somewhat taken-for-granted concept within the 1944 Education Act. As we argued in Chapter 3, no attention was paid in any of the policy documents preceding legislation, or in the Act or its subsequent enabling administrative memoranda, to change gender relations in school or in the family. Instead attention focused on using the family as a support for the school. The assumptions of the legislators and policy-makers was that there should be a close affinity between schools and families. A safety net element was also to be provided within education, with the provision of free school meals and milk, and a school medical and dental service.

Throughout the thirty-year period from the 1944 Education Act to the mid-1970s, policies were developed around the principle of equality of opportunity on the basis that each child was to have educational opportunities regardless of family or parental background or social class. Thus structural changes to the education system were put in place to ensure the enactment of this principle – for example, raising the school leaving age, the transformation of early childhood and primary education in line with the child-centredness of the Plowden Report (1967), and comprehensive education and the reorganization of the secondary curriculum after the Newsom Report (1963). The Conservative administrations of 1970–74, with Margaret Thatcher as secretary of state for education, continued to endorse this policy, which included the expansion of nursery education (circular 2/73), and of higher education, signalled by the government white paper *Education: a Framework for Expansion*.

By the 1970s such educational expansion had also generated moves towards greater family involvement in children's schooling, and by the 1980s it had become accepted that schools could expect parental involvement. The relationship between the family and the state was reinforced in this and other areas of social welfare and social policy. Thus out of the welfare state, with its commitment to individual advancement, came the expectation that women, particularly mothers, would commit themselves to the education of their children, not just at home but also at school. Mothers, as parents, were drawn into the ambit of the state as key players in the promotion of educational opportunities. It was to mothers (rather than fathers) that welfare reformers increasingly looked to promote children's well-being. In much the same way as mass schooling had been built upon the exploitation of women's 'mothering' potential as teachers (Widdowson, 1980), so too in the post-war period were mothers promoted as the key link to children's educational advancement – and fathers were left out.

Ideologies about maternity and motherhood

One of the reasons why a 'motherhood mandate' could be developed was because of the influence of psychological theories of child development in the Britain of the 1950s. In the immediate aftermath of the war there was much concern about how to reduce the destructive social effects of the war and restore social stability through the family. Family life had indeed been disrupted by the absence of many men, especially fathers, who had been away fighting in many parts of the world; and mothers, too, had been involved with the war effort. Children's lives, during the war, were thus regarded as impoverished economically, socially, emotionally and psychologically, as town and country were brought together in war-time evacuation policies. The experience of war-time evacuation thus threw into disarray assumptions about children, their development and the appropriate forms of teaching (Thom, 1992). On the one hand this led to attempts to systematize schooling (for example, in the construction of tiers of primary and secondary schools), and on the other to restore traditional family life. Key to the latter goal was the importance of women remaining in the home as carers of children and husbands.

The Beveridge Report, as Land (1976) has shown, celebrated both the differences between women and men and the need for women to address their 'other duties'. Such other duties were entailed in marriage: women were expected to be full-time home-makers, wives and mothers and to care for their husband and subsequently their children. Where paid employment was taken up, it was clearly to be subordinated to domestic responsibilities.

However, it was not only at this political level that such views were espoused. Predominant psychological and social theories about human growth and development in the 1950s were also committed to sustaining the traditional family (as we saw in the previous chapters) (Wilson, 1980). In particular, official sanction was given to develop notions about 'normal' childcare. Bowlby was invited to write an official report for the World Health Organization entitled *Maternal Care and Mental Health* (published in 1951), which used conventional psychoanalytic notions about mothers and their very young children to confirm traditional family forms. Bowlby aimed to reinvigorate the traditional family, first, by his commitment to ideas about the dangers of 'maternal deprivation' for normal child development, and, second, by his more extensive and carefully developed work on 'attachment' theories. His first study focused on the effects on children of mothers' absence, even though his study was of children in children's homes (rather than in conventional households). The children in Bowlby's study were deprived of parenting at a more fundamental level than merely having their mothers involved in forms of routine employment outside the home. However, his work was taken to mean that mothers' involvement even in part-time employment would have a deleterious effect on children's so-called normal and healthy development.

Despite the limitations of his studies, Bowlby's theories about the dangers of maternal absence on babies were used to underpin official ideologies in the UK about childcare for young children. Significantly they were used to develop an argument for excluding women from paid employment when they had young children, and for restricting the development of day care for young children, except for those not in 'normal' home circumstances. Bowlby's views were taken up particularly in the political realm and also in the growing welfare and (especially) social services, including education. The emphasis in health and social services was that normal child development for babies and under fives needed to take place at home with mother ever present.

Bowlby's study was later popularized as *Child Care and the Growth of Love* (1953). In that same year (August 1953) Margaret Thatcher gave birth to her twins, a matter of delight according to her autobiography, as we have seen in the previous chapter, but also of considerable concern, in particular on account of her ambitions for a political role. For women like Margaret Thatcher who were seeking careers, the mother-at-home nature of prescriptions of 'normal' childhood development provided a critical obstacle. Interestingly, with the benefit of hindsight she refused to conform to these views which were being reinscribed.

The maternal guilt generated by Bowlby's research was an ideological force in its own right, pressurizing mothers to sustain the traditional family form (Rutter, 1972). Indeed, there are accounts of 'girls growing up in the fifties' which illustrate how they felt about the push to 'maternalism' and their mothers' roles within it (Heron, 1985). Those women who were to break out of this individualized and personalized means of regulating mothers needed to be strong indeed. Bowlby's theories, which had initially been welcomed by conservative thinkers and had become pervasive in the 1950s, acted as an obstacle to the development of non-maternal and/or out-of-home childcare.

The Bowlby heritage, so influential in the 1950s and 1960s, lingers on relatively unaffected by later theories and developments and transformations in the social and economic context. In some respects, as we have argued elsewhere, Bowlby was a benign influence on developments in hospital and other forms of health care for young children, enabling parents to stay with children rather than being excluded. On the other hand, his theories were taken up with alacrity by educators involved in training future generations of doctors, nurses, social workers and health visitors, and it became axiomatic in educational and social services that so-called normal child development was dependent upon the presence of mothers (rather than that of fathers). Moreover, the absence of mothers through forms of paid employment was deemed to be detrimental to children's development, long into adulthood. Thus many women recruited to the social services were trained, and indeed may have provided the very training, which aimed to exclude them from forms of employment when they became mothers of young children.

It is important to note that pre-school state provision in the UK was almost non-existent before the Second World War and was provided through the Nurseries and Childminders Act of 1948 only for children 'deprived of normal home circumstances'. In other words, these children were to be supplied with substitute forms of maternal care initially through either residential or possibly day nurseries, which drew on contemporary psychoanalytic principles. This form of provision was viewed as but a second-best solution to the needs of children, focusing as it did on care rather than education. The distinctions between care and education for pre-school children attracted substantial debate throughout the post-war period up to 1950 and, to some extent, blocked expansion. This offers a contrast to experiences and provision in Europe, especially in Italy, Spain and the Scandinavian countries, where major developments in innovative pre-school provision and practice were put into place in the post-war period (Moss & Penn, 1996).

Mothers on the move

By the late 1950s, however, women in Britain began to challenge the construction of motherhood entailed in such doctrinaire approaches to family life. The refusal to extend nursery care or education for ordinary children led middle-class mothers to organize informally to provide some forms of out-of-home collaborative care for their pre-school children (a letter to *The Guardian* was the original spur to this development (Finch, 1984: 3). This developed into the Pre-School Playgroups Association (PPA), where some mothers voluntarily spent time caring for groups of children for a few hours each week, releasing others to pursue individual agendas. The PPA swiftly developed into a national organization, based around mothers' collaborative efforts to provide innovative experiences for their pre-school children on a group basis. At the same time there was some limited expansion of LEA nursery provision for children from disadvantaged home backgrounds or deprived of normal home circumstances, and also for the children of 'married women returners' who were needed to train as teachers at a time of teacher shortage. Thus the official ideology of home-based maternal care began to some extent to give way, even though psychological theories continued to influence education.

During the 1960s, in the UK and elsewhere, women began to question the efficacy of 'maternalist' ideas and theories and also to develop collaborative ways of caring for young children. Simultaneously, some, particularly those involved in the growing women's movement, began to modify psychological theories and develop alternative ideas about forms of normal child development. By the 1970s a substantial body of feminist literature was in existence which provided critiques of, and alternative theories to, conventional social, psychological and psychoanalytic theories about women, motherhood and childcare. In Britain, for instance, Juliet Mitchell (1974) offered a trenchant critique and feminist reinterpretation of psychoanalysis. Revisions and reinterpretations of Freudian theories from a feminist perspective were developed in France (see particularly Kristeva, 1974; Sayers, 1986) and in the USA, for example, Dinnerstein (1976), Baker Miller (1978), Chodorow (1978) and Gilligan (1982). Alternative feminist therapies, initially developed out of

Susie Orbach's work *Fat is a Feminist Issue*, led to the founding of the Women's Therapy Centre in London in 1976.

Some feminist theories about women, motherhood and children were more sympathetic to psychoanalytic theories than others, preferring, for example, psychological or sociological explanations and perspectives. Official ideologies about women's proper family role and about motherhood and childcare were vigorously questioned and criticized, particularly by women. At the same time assumptions about women's economic dependence upon men as husbands and/or partners were also criticized. The challenge to Victorian values in its modernized (or Bowlby-ized form) was not merely ideological: it was also economic. Women, including married women and mothers of dependent children, were increasingly drawn into the labour market on a regular basis, and thus, in the absence of public provision, were often forced to find private solutions for childcare. Many, including those at the lower end of the income range, ultimately ended up with solutions which were largely similar to those of Margaret Thatcher, for example, regarding work flexibility.

Women's work: expansion but not emancipation

One of the most significant yet contradictory consequences for gender relations was the growth of female employment within the welfare state. If the promotion of traditional family values had been the main agenda of Beveridge's vision of a welfare society, then the unintentional consequence was the expansion of female employment, taking women outside the home. The creation of a national health service, local authority departments responsible for health and welfare, childcare and housing, and educational expansion provided the context for the establishment of new forms of female employment. Many of the new jobs resembled the kinds of work that women had previously been expected to carry out either at home or on a voluntary basis. The new welfare state was premised on the setting up of a range of 'caring professions' – what Bernstein (1977) called 'agents of symbolic control'. Such agents would provide the human face of welfare but at the same time increase the surveillance of the population, particularly in private familial worlds. In the event, the growth of the welfare professions created the conditions for a new 'feminized' arm of the state.

This occurred also because, in the early years of the welfare state, there was a shortage of manpower to 'man' or serve in both manual and non-manual work. Thus women were increasingly recruited for a variety of jobs. New state agencies required more professionals, such as teachers for the extended educational system, ranging from pre-school to higher education; social workers were recruited to organize the care of disadvantaged children, the elderly and those with physical and mental disabilities; and nurses and other medical staff were needed to staff hospitals, community health care, school services, etc. Additionally, there were increased labour demands for support services, such as hospital cleaning and clerical work (Bradley, 1996; Crompton, 1997).

Significantly, the creation and development of the welfare state was relatively uneven because of the need for new forms of labour and the requirements for newly trained individuals. In some areas, expansion was slowed by the lack of trained personnel. Education therefore needed to respond to these requirements: for example, an expansion of teacher training took place in the 1950s and courses opened up at colleges and universities to train social workers. The training of nurses, however, was less of a problem in the early years of the National Health Service (NHS), as it was largely 'on the job'. In any event, education and training provision did not satisfy the need for 'manpower', and many untrained staff were recruited in the early years. Partly for these reasons the formalization of training requirements for nursing and its transfer to universities and colleges was deferred until much later.

Different strategies emerged to address labour shortfalls. In some parts of the country where labour supply had previously been sparse, the ban imposed on married women teachers introduced in the inter-war years had never taken effect, such as in London. In the late 1950s, with the growth of the birth-rate in the aftermath of the war, there was a severe shortage of trained schoolteachers, and a major campaign to recruit women, known as the 'married women returners' scheme, was inaugurated for both full-time and part-time teachers. The ban on married teachers was formally reversed, and married women, including those with relatively young children, were actively recruited where insufficient trained men or unmarried women were available to staff the expanding number of schools. Moreover, to this end, some LEAs began to set up nurseries or crèches based in schools to retain women teachers who might otherwise have been forced to resign.

Economic growth coupled with the establishment of a welfare state thus continued to disrupt the traditional separations of home, work and school. Married women, as Beveridge had pronounced only a decade or so earlier, were not to be fully occupied or preoccupied with their home duties but also to serve the children's needs in the country as a whole. Although the impact of women teachers on post-war generations of children has generally not been well documented (an exception to this is Kean, 1990), the new role for women in the modernization of the British post-war economy signifies the start of the processes of gender transformation that we have witnessed, lived through and are now trying to explain.

Even though women, particularly married women, both working and middle class, took up paid employment in the new expanding economy of the 1950s and 1960s, they were not able to puncture the highly segregated structure of the labour market. Male jobs remained largely male, and female jobs largely female (e.g., nursing, teaching). Nevertheless, women's employment outside the home threatened the 'natural order' of the family division of labour, and concern was expressed about the growing generation of disaffected working-class youth neglected by their work-orientated mothers (CCCS, 1981). At the same time stay-at-home mothers were encouraged to 'learn' the skills of full-time motherhood. Despite the fact that, at school, working-class girls were channelled into the plethora of domestic subjects, preparing them for the family and domesticity, young mothers were still seen as undereducated in their primary role in life. The Plowden Report (1967), following fast on the heels of the Coleman Report *On Equality of Educational Opportunity* in the United States (1966), recommended forms of compensatory education, including the greater involvement of mothers/parents in the home-based education of their children. In other words, there was an active campaign to ensure that home–school relations, particularly for disadvantaged families, were tightened.

Social workers and teachers, many of whom had children, were recruited to help with 'parent education'. Interestingly, what had been seen as an entirely 'natural' process of educating and raising children for middle-class families was now seen as something that could be taught explicitly to the working classes by 'untrained', volunteer, middle-class mothers. As we have seen, some middle-class women had themselves been involved in establishing shared childcare for pre-school children, such as the Pre-School Playgroups Association (PPA), when cutbacks in provision of nursery education were introduced.

During the late 1950s and 1960s women (including for the first time married women and mothers) left home for the public sphere, either on a formal or an informal basis, as nurses, teachers, volunteers in the PPA and nursery workers. The increase in the number of women in employment during this period had comparable effects to the rise of women workers in the nineteenth century. The 'knock-on' effects were similar in terms of reductions in family size, new markets for time-saving domestic appliances, and the increase in need for 'ready made goods' (Oakley, 1974). More significant, however, was the changing relationship between marriage, motherhood and a career, which was visible to many of those who lived through that period. Even Margaret Thatcher noted:

> The fifties marked the start of a major change in the role of women. Until then they tended to be well into middle age when the last child of an often large family fled the nest: work within the house, without the benefit of labour-saving devices, took much longer; and home was also more of a social place, visited throughout the day by a wide range of tradesmen. . . . Consequently fewer women had the opportunity or felt the need to go out to work. The

fifties marked the beginning of the end of this world, and by the eighties it had changed out of all recognition. Women were young when the children left home because families were smaller; domestic work was lightened owing to new home appliances; and home deliveries were replaced by a weekly visit to the mall or supermarket.

(1995: 83)

Working-class women who worked in the informal and/or casual labour market, however, were not in a position to devote themselves similarly to the home (Land, 1976). Thus, during this period, the complex interplay between the needs of various segments of the labour market, particularly those segments within the welfare state itself, and the need for effective family socialization of the new generation of children began to generate change of an unprecedented nature.

As the welfare state continued its inexorable growth, so did women's employment, both inside and outside the welfare state. Within it, as noted above, women were increasingly employed in what Etzioni (1969) called the semi-professions, as teachers (at all levels from nursery/primary through to higher education) and as nurses. They were also employed as doctors and as social workers and as administrative support staff. Others were employed as cleaners or caretakers and in other kinds of manual work. Outside the welfare state, women's employment also continued to grow – in the service industries, such as catering, food, retailing, etc., and in the law and media. In the 1960s and 1970s tensions between women's emancipation and their domestic responsibilities mounted as gender relations themselves became the target of attack, from both the political left and right.

The era of feminist politics

Women's economic advancement coincided with critiques of women's economic dependence in the family and growing dissatisfaction with the institution of marriage. This growing 'problem', ranging from higher divorce rates, separations, or 'refusals' to marry ('cohabitation') and/or economic independence, through to single status, was created either by force or by choice, as Riley (1983) put it. There were several different solutions. Some women decided not to have children; others chose to have children 'out of wedlock', either by cohabiting and/or by becoming 'single' parents; others were forced into lone parenthood through the desertion of men. Thus by the 1970s the patterns of family life and 'family-households' (Barrett & McIntosh, 1983) became more varied and less likely to privilege the traditional nuclear family, despite the fact that the 'traditional' family has continued to remain the majority form of household. Many children under the age of sixteen experienced a family divorce and found themselves living in one of a variety of 'family worlds' (CERI, 1982). Moreover, there was a questioning of the impact of these various changes on the growth and psychological development of children, not only on young children but also on teenagers and young adults.

Many of these trends were underpinned by the liberalization of social policies – for instance, changes in abortion and contraception and divorce law reforms in the late 1960s. Thus the social and economic transformations identified above were supported by welfare policy developments in the same way as earlier shifts in gender relations were generated by technological developments. The relationship between welfare and technological developments (e.g., advances in contraception and abortion as well as the more far-reaching developments in fertility control) and women's responses to them have been demonstrated by Rose (1994). By the late 1970s and early 1980s changes in official policy and the new opportunities to control biological reproduction contributed to the possibilities of change in women's family lives. Women to some extent were responsible for these scientific developments, both as producers and as consumers, although, as Rose points out, they were frequently excluded from the knowledge production involved and from any accolades for such 'scientific discoveries'.

Women also contributed to other social changes, including moves towards divorce law reform, although here too it was more as consumers than as key players in legal change. However, the trends that were identified as in need of some form of legitimation during the 1960s were largely a result of women's views of the constraining effects of marriage and parenthood and their activities and desires for change. Thus women, particularly middle-class women, began to identify with what Betty Friedan called 'the problem without a name' (1963), that is, the frustrations and limitation of marriage and motherhood in the context of wider socio-economic transformations and the increased availability of forms of employment.

During the 1970s and 1980s, partly as a response to the liberalization of divorce laws, contraception and abortion practices, and partly as a response to the changing labour-market conditions and to minor changes in childcare practices, the patterns of family formation and dissolution began to shift (e.g., Coote, Harman & Hewitt, 1990). The prime movers on this were women who began consciously to transform their private family lives. The patterns of change, as noted above, were varied and diverse. The influences and causes were also diverse, including, for example, women as mothers having an influence upon their daughters; women who had foregone higher education after school choosing to return as mature students; and women with dependent children taking up paid employment. Women also chose to leave their marriages, or not to have children, or to have children outside of conventional family structures. By 1995 over a third of all babies were born outside marriage, although their parents were likely to cohabit and/or jointly to sign the birth certificate/registration of the birth, etc. (Haskey, 1998).

Women's liberation: politicizing the personal

The post-war economic boom in welfare services, and in educational and employment opportunities, as we have seen, created a new context for many women, especially in terms of the balance between public and private life. The stirrings of feminist consciousness about their lives were articulated locally, nationally and internationally through writings and through groups of women getting together to organize themselves informally. In the USA, as we have already mentioned, Betty Friedan (1963) wrote evocatively of married middle-class women trapped in their homes. Simone de Beauvoir (1953) wrote about women as the 'other' in her important book *The Second Sex*. The work of such women was indicative of a widely felt unease, especially among educated and middle-class women, and particularly those who were married and confined to hearth and home.

These stirrings began to take shape and form themselves into what became known by the end of the 1960s in the United States as the Women's Liberation Movement. Begun in kitchens, in classrooms, in lecture theatres and in workplaces, this movement started campaigning for social change, particularly by making demands *for* and *by* women. The state, having assumed the power to redefine the boundaries between family, work and government, was in a position to push back the boundaries between the public and the private. Key to feminist demands was a recognition of the significance of private life, or, to use a key concept of the times, the 'personal is the political'. In 1969 the Women's Liberation Movement (WLM) in the UK formulated four demands – all of them targeted upon the state. They were: equal pay for equal work; equality of educational opportunity; abortion and contraception on demand; and twenty-four-hour nurseries (Coote & Campbell, 1982).

The third and fourth demands explicitly addressed the problem of the balance between what later became known as the 'public' and the 'private'. A slogan of the time for abortion and contraception – 'Not the church and not the state, women must decide their fate' – aptly summarizes the WLM position: that women had the right to abortion, contraception and family planning. Another memorable slogan, 'Smash the family', sought to draw attention to what was seen as the patriarchal nature of the nuclear family. When women decided their fate by having children, the WLM also demanded public support in the form of nurseries (and later schools). Three further demands were added early in the 1970s: legal and financial independence; the right to decide one's own sexuality; and no sexual harassment or violence.

Government responses to these 'demands' were somewhat lukewarm. For instance, in the late 1960s and early 1970s policies were formulated in the UK for equal pay and the reduction of discrimination in employment. Eventually these measures were translated into legislation – for example, the Equal Pay Act (1970), first implemented in 1975, and the Sex Discrimination Act of 1975. The Abortion Act (1967) resulted more from the demand from women for their rights than from the demands of either the state or the church. However, plans to extend abortion rights in the 1970s and 1980s were obstructed by the political right, which argued for a limit to such moves on ethical grounds. And there was no move to establish twenty-four-hour nurseries. A muted response came in 1973 from Margaret Thatcher, as secretary of state for education, in the form of an extension of nursery education (Circular 2/73), but the policy entailed a strong commitment to family support and involvement for three- and four-year-olds, if only on a part-time basis. However, such responses signalled also the shift away from all-consuming care within the privacy of the home and family towards a limited sharing or partnership between family and state. In other words, they provided further instances of the shifting boundary between public and private, and a further move towards destabilizing the Victorian family.

Reflections

By the 1970s, in the UK as in most advanced industrial/capitalist societies, the opportunities for employment for women had mushroomed in educational, welfare and other service industries. Indeed, in analysing economic developments towards what he called modernization, Rostow (1963) described this period as one which was characterized by a 'take-off into self-sustained growth'. This might also be an apt description of what happened to women's employment. Women gained a taste of economic independence where job opportunities became available, and also experienced the contradictions between their roles in the public world of work and the privacy of the family.

The incremental growth in women's employment was accompanied by changes in the family – changes to patterns of marriage, separation and divorce, and shifts in patterns of parenthood from the 'traditional' family to families experiencing cohabitation, separation, divorce and lone parenthood, and to reconstituted families and step-parenthood. Women were at the vanguard of moves for family change, with many already pursuing divorce and a release from what they saw as oppressive family relations.

Women's work and mothers' work was thus transformed in the first three decades after the Second World War through the rise of the welfare state and associated educational and economic policies, and through the response of women to these diverse changes. Paradoxically, the Bowlby heritage of family values, which had its roots in the Victorian era, remained a viable response, and it continued to retain a powerful influence on conservative thinking. The effect, therefore, of what has been called the 'social democratic consensus' of the post-war period in the UK (Mishra, 1984) was to create dissonance between policy, ideological rhetoric and the lived experiences of family life in late modern Britain. Most importantly, the lived experiences of family life of girls bore little resemblance to those of traditional families and their mothers' and grandmothers' role within them. Indeed, from the 1950s onwards, the majority of girls growing up in the new 'Elizabethan England' witnessed their mothers working and struggling with 'family' relationships in highly constrained circumstances – a reality which was to have considerable effect, as we shall see in Chapter 7, on their own aspirations.

5

Schooling, Teachers and Feminism

The struggle for women's educational equality, like that of the right to employment, in the post-war period, was not new. As we have already seen in Chapter 2, it had a long history dating back to Mary Wollstonecraft's intervention in the eighteenth century and to the campaigns of the nineteenth century which attempted to improve women's access to education – in particular to secondary and university education. The opening up of educational opportunities was enormously important for women because it challenged the 'prison' of Victorian domestic ideology. In the years preceding the Second World War, acknowledgement had come from government (for example, in the Hadow and Spens reports) that some girls aspired to a career or working outside the home, at least in the period before marriage and motherhood. This limited recognition facilitated access to a broader curriculum, albeit mainly for middle-class girls, but, more importantly, it legitimated more adventurous aspirations among a new generation of girls.

The particular version of 'educational feminism' (Stone, 1994, refers to 'education feminism' in the USA) in England and Wales, and in other parts of the UK, in the second half of the twentieth century was closely tied to the nature and role of the school system, especially its decentralized form. The educational system, although centrally controlled, was locally administered, providing teachers with an active role in the expansion of equality of opportunity. At the same time educational feminism in the UK was affected by the restructuring of the teaching profession in the light of fears of population decline and economic crisis. The coincidence of a movement to reform girls' aspirations with a reduction in teacher training places in the 1970s, for example, provided young women with a powerful disincentive for remaining within conventionally narrow feminine paths (Crompton, 1992).

Educational feminism was developed in the UK by teachers who were committed to finding what has been called a 'counter-hegemony' (Weiler,

1988) – an alternative version of femininity to the legacy and authoritarianism of Victorian family values. In contrast fewer incentives were offered to boys; indeed, educational feminism's main target was to change girls rather than to redefine contemporary masculinity or challenge stereotypical male public and private roles. If redefining femininity was the goal of feminism, the reconceptualization of masculinity was held to be the provenance of men.

What was remarkable about educational feminism, and indeed feminism in general, was its adaptability and capacity for survival through periods of crisis in education and shifts in educational ideologies. Initially educational feminism was integral to the era of social democracy, drawing inspiration from the concept of social citizenship promoted by welfare reformers (Marshall, 1950). The 'floor of entitlements' for all citizens, including health, housing and education, created new opportunities for women. In this context, educational feminism reflected many of the then current assumptions about the role education could play in 'compensating' for society (Bernstein, 1971). In the 1980s, a pivotal decade for feminist initiatives in education, it was assumed that schools (and particularly the teaching profession) could be used as agencies of social change in order to reduce if not eliminate inequalities between the sexes in education, and also ideally in the economy and in the family. The opportunities afforded by having a devolved curriculum, organizational structures and considerable teacher autonomy in the English/Welsh context could be exploited by those wishing to shape the content and structure of school teaching. This first wave of activity therefore used *voluntarism*, bottom-up approaches to change, encouraging teachers to become pioneers of anti-sexist and 'girl-friendly' educational reform. The aim was to persuade both classroom practitioners and educational policy-makers of the need for gender reform.

In the early 1980s this strategy proved remarkably resilient when faced with the Conservative educational upheavals, seemingly adaptable, for example, to the reforms of the school system and local government introduced by Margaret Thatcher's first government (1979–88). By the late 1980s educational feminism had grafted gender equality onto prevailing concerns about the need for accountability of the education service to politicians, to consumers and customers (parents, pupils/students) and to the new competitive performance-driven culture of schooling. In the second wave of educational feminism, from the end of the 1980s onwards, gender issues became part of the new *performance-oriented*, managerial discourses of the New Right, and latterly New Labour. Gender issues in education towards the end of the twentieth century, it seemed, had moved up the policy agenda instead of fading away.

The feminist challenge to the traditional, domestic roles and responsibilities of women developed slowly but insistently from the late eighteenth century, through the nineteenth- and early twentieth-century periods of high capitalism, through the social democratic era following the Second World War, to the New Right period of the late twentieth century. It is thus key to our understanding of the changed patterns of educational performance of girls in recent years. In this chapter we explore the first phase – the development of what we call feminist *voluntarism*, with its concerns for social justice and the liberal and critical educational feminisms which underpinned teachers' interventions in this period; we also discuss how voluntarism worked in practice. In Chapter 6 we look at the second phase of educational feminism – the development of feminist *managerialist* strategies in response to the marketization of schools in the late 1980s and 1990s.

Feminist voluntarism and the social democratic era

The demand for an equal education by modern feminists was affected both by the structure of the English/Welsh educational system and its forms of control. Post-war education legislation revealed the legacy of a deeply undemocratic educational system (Simon, 1994; Ainley, 1993) in which the principle of social-class differentiation, inherited from the Victorian age, was used to shape a new tripartite system of secondary schools (grammar, technical, secondary modern). Although the 1944 Act aimed to widen the life chances of children by giving free secondary education to all and by providing all children with access to education regardless of family or home socio-economic circumstances, the legislation assumed the existing structure of parental privilege and poverty (Ainley, 1993).

For working-class girls, the post-war expansion of education had relatively little impact because their educational outcomes remained similar to, even if in gender-segregated form, those of working-class boys. Access to different types of secondary schools was based upon children's performance on so-called measured intelligence tests at the age of eleven; yet proportionately fewer male and female working-class children succeeded in entering the grammar school and, later, university. The pattern in the post-war period established that middle-class boys were twenty-one times more likely to go to university than working-class girls (King, 1971). University education (only a quarter of students were drawn from working-class families) remained reserved for the elite (Committee on Higher Education, 1963). With few pretences to neutrality (such as that found in the United States, where competition was seen as the key to success), these patterns of educational provision in England and Wales, based on privilege as well as sex, made alliances possible between a range of activists (e.g., socialist, feminist, anti-racist) concerned to promote social justice in education more widely.

Because of constraints in the school building programme, most local authorities after the 1944 Act opted for a bipartite system of grammar and secondary schools (excluding provision of secondary technical or central schools). A number of bilateral schools were, however, built which later became known as comprehensives. Provision of comprehensive schooling increased slowly in the 1950s, quickening its pace with the election of a Labour government in 1964, which led to a commitment to removing class differences from education, and elsewhere. There was minimal discussion of the impact of comprehensivization on issues of gender, with the exception of Dale (1969, 1971, 1974). The expansion of comprehensive schools, however, was to have considerable significance for the development of educational feminism in the UK, not least because of the coeducational nature of many of these schools. By the 1970s most comprehensive schools were coeducational (often with male head-teachers), even though there had been no policy debate on the advantages of mixed as opposed to single-sex schools (Shaw, 1980; Deem, 1984). The concern expressed by mainly women teachers about the possible negative effects on girls' education of mixed-sex schooling in the 1920s and thereafter had been ignored. However, evidence collected by the HMI for the DES (1975) revealed that boys and girls were channelled into different subject areas and that, at secondary school, girls speedily lost any educational advantage gained at primary school. Debates about the respective merits of single-sex and mixed-sex secondary schooling were taken up by feminists, with calls for the reform of coeducational state schooling becoming a major area of focus of feminist activity in education in the UK.

Single-sex education was strongly associated with elite education, especially for state-maintained grammar schools, modelled largely on public/independent schools, although many voluntary church schools were also single sex. Until the 1980s most independent schools were single sex, excepting 'experimental' schools such as the exclusive Bedales, Dartington Hall and A. S. Neill's Summerhill. Similarly the majority of direct-grant grammar schools, which had been reviewed and reorganized in the 1940s by the Norwood Committee, developed along single-sex lines. Secondary technical schools created to provide for a 'middle way' between academic selection and non-selective education in coeducational secondary modern schools and provided by LEAs were also largely single sex. Thus, for those who attended grammar, direct-grant and independent schools, the education provided was largely single sex and university oriented, though from the 1970s onwards high-achieving girls were channelled towards teacher training colleges.

For the majority of girls and boys, however, large, coeducational secondary schools with an undifferentiated comprehensive pupil intake became the most common form of schooling. Feminist campaigners for the reform of coeducational schools therefore often found themselves engaging in debates about the class basis of the school system, since arguments for a return to single-sex education met with resistance from those whose primary aim was to eliminate selective schooling.

The selective system of secondary schooling established after the 1944 Act was revised in 1965, in a Labour government circular (10/65) which advocated the establishment of comprehensive schools. However, this divisive system remained largely intact (Ainley, 1993). A complex set of control mechanisms also ensured that neither central government nor the LEAs had exclusive responsibility for the school curriculum, testing or examinations (except for religious education and a regular school assembly, which were both compulsory). The school curriculum was largely the responsibility of educational professionals acting in accordance with generally agreed criteria, and ultimately shaped by the requirements of the examination bodies. Previous codes of what subjects should be taught remained in operation but did not have the force of law. Thus there was a large element of teacher and educational professional autonomy built into the post-war education settlement, involving a so-called partnership between the professionals and central and local government.

From the 1940s to the late 1960s there was relatively little change in official perception of equal opportunities, which centred mainly on social class. In 1964 Anthony Crosland, as Labour's secretary of state for education, signalled a shift from what he called the 'weak' to the 'strong' notion of equality of opportunity, from scrutiny of issues of *access* to those of *outcomes* of education. He argued that children should leave school with qualifications and achievements irrespective of their socio-economic origins and therefore enter employment on an equal footing. Crosland's notions were translated into policy measures by a Labour government in the second half of the 1960s. The political consensus over education between the two main political parties which had prevailed thus far began to break down, with disputes focusing upon Labour's commitment to comprehensive as opposed to Conservative support of selective education, and what was seen as Labour's ineffectual attempts to challenge the influence of the independent, 'public' school sector.

In contrast, educational goals in relation to gender (and race/ethnicity) remained weak. The discourse of progressivism that suffused primary education throughout the 1960s and 1970s proved inimical to concern about male and female educational inequalities. Progressivism, as we argued in Chapter 3, was premised on a notion of liberatory pedagogy where educational development and learning were seen as distinctive to the individual child within normative assumptions about age-related achievement (Walkerdine, 1981). A child's social background, sex and ethnicity were relegated to the personal and viewed as factors counting towards the shaping of an individual's learning and progress – thus little interest was expressed in countering what were perceived as 'natural' gender patterns.

Not surprisingly, the development of the second wave of the feminist movement in the late 1960s put considerable pressure (via concerned individuals, and teacher groups within and outside the unions) on the Labour government of the time to consider gender equality and its legislative and policy programme. Evidence was collected which pointed to high levels of sex discrimination in employment, social policy and education. The government responded promptly by passing the Equal Pay Act in 1970. However, its White Paper on equal opportunities was diluted by the incoming Conservatives. Once back in government in 1974, Labour passed the Sex Discrimination Act, as we have seen. There was some surprise and delight that education was included in the legislation – unlike other major areas of social policy, such as the NHS (Rendel, 1985). The Race Relations Act passed in 1976 focused on racial discrimination. The two regulatory bodies, the Equal Opportunities Commission (EOC) and the Commission for Racial Equality (CRE), were both designed by the legislation to be proactive regarding consultation on national policy issues, conducting formal investigations into possible discrimination, responding to complaints under the law, and promoting greater opportunities through educational activities. Both pieces of legislation signified major shifts in the understanding and interpretation of equal opportunities away from social class towards gender, race and ethnicity.

The passage of anti-discriminatory legislation in the UK has been claimed as a victory for equal opportunities campaigners, even if, until now, it has been sorely neglected by historians and analysts of contemporary educational policy (Rendel, 1985). This was the first time in English history that the concepts of *direct and indirect discrimination* were used, and also that responsibility for promoting social equality was not only at the discretion of providers. The courts and the law could be used to police discriminatory practice (albeit only if victims of discrimination or harassment could prove their case). The legislation left single-sex school provision intact, providing it was fair in terms of number of places available. Although textbook content was also excluded from the Act, the legislation provided for the first time the space for questions about single-sex provision and bias in curriculum and pedagogy to be discussed as a policy issue. Through various publications, the EOC encouraged schools and LEAs to review their provision in terms of gender equality and to develop strategies which aimed at promoting the full potential of both boys and girls.

Although the early EOC commissioners were criticized for leaving their 'feminist hats at home' (Meehan, 1982: 15), in the first ten years of its existence, mainly under Conservative administrations, teachers and the educational establishment were cajoled by the EOC into considering gender issues as important. This was at a time when schools and teachers saw themselves as largely responsible for the form and content of education, and autonomous from government. The strategy of reform (described by one of us as using the 'tea party principle') relied heavily upon gaining consent, rather than on coercion. It drew upon rational and legal arguments about the benefits of change, particularly in relation to women's economic advancement and their contribution to the economy. The main strategy for policy-makers, therefore, was to encourage changes by awareness raising and professional teacher development.

Increased professional awareness of teachers was also the prime target of feminist teachers and the growing number of feminist academics engaged in promoting gender change. The existence of the legislation was used to open up debates about inequalities in the schooling for girls – a theme which, despite its challenge to patriarchal relations, resonated with both the radical politics of the new social movements and the economic rationalism of the time. In the event, backed by the municipal socialism of a number of inner-city Labour-controlled LEAs, such political campaigning received official recognition and small-scale funding (e.g., through in-service budgets, the provision of specialist advisors, and the seeding of action research projects). Although in some notable instances pressure was put on head-teachers to deliver action plans on gender equality (and even compulsory attendance on in-service courses), for the most part, teacher-led change aimed at gender equality relied upon voluntary efforts.

From the late 1970s onwards, schools were challenged by feminist teachers too, about what was being done to implement the spirit of the Sex Discrimination Act. A common strategy was to provide evidence ('to prove') that inequalities existed in schooling – to put on record 'the hard facts of inequality' (Yates, 1985). Thus Cornbleet and Libovitch (1983) described the aims of one of the first working groups of gender established in a North London secondary school at the end of the 1970s as follows:

> The working party undertook to examine the effects of sexism in the classroom and throughout the school. This involved studying the sex-stereotyped option choices pupils were taking up, the provision made for pupils outside usual school time, the position of women teachers on the staff in relation to men teachers and the problem of unequal teacher time and attention being given to boys at the expense of the girls.
>
> *(Cornbleet & Libovitch, 1983: 145)*

Teachers and social justice

By the late 1970s and early 1980s, girls' education had been affected by the teaching profession in two major ways. The first way was the reduced access to teacher training on account of the closure of college courses. This had the effect of closing down opportunities for girls to enter teaching, which had been a popular career destination from the nineteenth century onwards, thus forcing them into alternative post-school choices (Crompton, 1992). The second way teachers influenced girls' education was the pressure they put on girls through feminist initiatives to perform well at school, to seek economic and personal autonomy in adult life and to broaden their career horizons. In Sweden for example, a similar rhetoric was of girls' 'breaking the mould'.

The presence of a large number of female teachers in the state system provided the foundation on which a new wave of feminist activity was built. Women teachers were a key audience for the messages of the women's movement and were critical to its success. They could be mobilized as 'insider reformers', especially since discriminatory practices affecting their employment could also be addressed. Although the marriage bar for teachers had been removed after the Second World War, women who temporarily left teaching during their child-bearing years returned to find their promotion opportunities limited and their skills learnt in child-rearing ignored. Few women were able to rise to the top of the profession (where men dominated and still continue to dominate headships, the inspectorate, university education departments and administrative/policy-making positions) and, moreover, women received scant support from the male-led teacher union movement, which was largely uninterested in the problems women faced as employees (Oram, 1987).

Although women had gained economically and socially from the expansion of the teaching profession since the late nineteenth century, the choice of teaching (alongside social work and nursing) continued, if only symbolically, to reflect the legacy of Victorian domestic ideologies. The channelling of academically successful girls into teaching was based upon naturalistic assumptions about female caring qualities, women's interest in children, and the usefulness of having employment which could dovetail, and not challenge, mothering roles and the need of women to be flexible in relation to their husband's employment opportunities. Any challenge to the Victorian domestic ideology as an educational goal would inevitably call into question the 'naturalness' and suitability of women's choice of profession.

As Crompton (1992) argues, such assumptions also led to the use of teacher training colleges up to the 1970s as 'the cheap solution' to meeting the requirements of higher education expansion recommended in the Robbins Report (Committee on Higher Education, 1963). Teacher training places cost £255, in comparison with £660 a year for undergraduates (Robbins Report, quoted in Crompton, 1992: 58) The demands of a rising number of newly qualified female school leavers was initially met by an expanded teacher training sector. In 1965, for example, 38,000 young men compared with 15,000 young women (approximately 30 per cent) were admitted as undergraduates to UK universities. The reverse was true for the colleges in 1965, 26,000 young women (approximately 70 per cent) could be found in the first year of teacher training, compared with 10,000 (approximately 30 per cent) young men.

However, as we have seen, by the 1970s cuts in teacher training hit women hard, but nevertheless provided a possible source of 'liberation' by compelling them to select other professional destinations. By 1980 the declining birth-rate, the falling pound, the economic crisis and a changed government led to the closure or merger of 100 teacher training colleges and the subsequent reduction in places from 43,700 in 1970 to 8700 in 1980. This was a time when girls' A-level results had risen faster than those of boys. As a result, a substantial proportion of academically successful girls joined the university system in order to take up professions and vocations other than teaching. This shift away from a pattern of work which had been premised on women's skills acquired in domestic gender roles (in the home and in the teaching profession) may have played a key part in increasing women's aspirations for change. The new paths and careers they chose were less 'domestically' oriented (Hutchinson, 1997).

The challenge to conventional sex roles was also sustained by teachers themselves in the early 1980s, despite the election of a Conservative government with seemingly little interest in promoting egalitarian issues. Feminist teachers continued to exploit the opportunities provided by the Sex Discrimination Act, focusing mainly on improving girls' schooling experiences and widening their career opportunities. The Equal Opportunities Commission published guidance booklets aimed at encouraging boys to take up home economics, but on the whole the thrust of reform was directed either at making schools more 'girl friendly' (Whyte, Deem, Kant & Cruickshank, 1985) or towards reducing the level of sexism found among boys (and teachers).

The next ten years were to see the increasing fragmentation of the teacher movement for change. Weiner (1994b) identified as many as *nine* different types of feminist educational discourse by the end of the decade. Such fragmentation reflected to some extent the tensions between those working with a model of *gender deficit* – the lack of achievement of girls in the educational system, where the causes of underachievement were assumed to be located in the psyche of the individual and in the school – and those teachers who recognized the significance of *social power* in shaping the experiences of certain groups of working-class, ethnic minority and/or black girls. Taking the latter perspective, school strategies were expected to assume a critical stance towards society more generally. The causes of school failure for both perspectives were assumed to lie in the unequal and discriminatory structure of society. Feminist activity in schools was thus affected by *liberal educational feminism* (the first type), with its politics of access and its concerns for curriculum reform. *Critical educational feminisms* (the second type) attempted to ally feminism to other more radical egalitarian movements by concentrating more upon localized 'consciousness'-raising activities, transforming school cultures and reshaping school subjects such as history or English to include women's experiences. Both strands of activity were concerned, in different ways, with harnessing education to the wider feminist aim of creating a more woman-friendly and equitable society.

Liberal educational feminism

Drawing on nineteenth-century movements to expand the political, social and educational rights of women (Banks, 1981), proponents of this position held a generally positive view of the role of education in a democratic society and of the importance of education in removing obstacles to girls' and women's progress. Equality of access to, and treatment in, education were fundamental goals, since it was believed that only through the provision of equal educational experiences for both sexes could a genuinely equal society be encouraged and developed. Liberal feminists' main aims were equal curricular access, experience and outcome for boys and girls (Byrne, 1978).

The failure (or underachievement) of girls and young women at school, in higher education and in the workplace in comparison with their male peers was understood at that time to be a result of different attainment patterns in certain subject areas (especially maths, science and technology), sex stereotyping in optional subject areas and in careers advice, bias in the construction and marking of examinations and tests, and sex differences in the role models (especially school staffing patterns). Such matters dovetailed well with the individualism underlying social democratic approaches to equality of opportunity and with concerns for the lack of skilled 'manpower', especially in the scientific and technological professions.

At the same time liberal educational feminists 'piggy-backed' on initiatives and schemes introduced by the Conservative government in the early 1980s which promoted new vocational education such as TVEI and Records of Achievement. These initiatives encouraged for the first time the removal of sex-divided barriers to educational and labour-market advancement in the interests both of the individual and the economy (Burchell & Millman, 1989). Premised on the perceived need to modify and raise the skill level of the British workforce, they utilized progressive languages (e.g., relevance and skills based) and pedagogies (e.g., student centred) to resocialize hitherto excluded, underskilled or underused students. Rather than signal the 'abandonment of equal opportunity as a central reference point for educational strategy', as asserted by Finn (1985: 113), such schemes introduced by the New Right suggested a new alliance between the 1980s liberal *laissez-faire* ideas about the need to promote labour-market flexibility and liberal/progressive ideas concerning freedom for girls and women to move up and across educational and occupational sectors and hierarchies. The process of 'degendering' the workforce as a means of freeing up labour and encouraging more enterprise and competition fitted in well with liberal education feminist desires to change gender relations in the public sphere.

Liberal educational feminism was thus able to forge alliances both with campaigners against sex discrimination in public life and with individualistic and free-market ideologies. Its main stance was pragmatic, and it was most effective when exploiting and working with mainstream educational concerns and in challenging formal, legalistic inequalities. Such alliances succeeded in challenging the assumptions that women's place was in the home, although at the same time they failed to address the constraints which the home placed upon women's full participation in an increasingly competitive society.

Critical educational feminisms

Other feminist perspectives (here we include radical, Marxist, socialist, lesbian, black feminisms, etc.) offer more trenchant ideas about the role of education, for example, in asserting the ethnocentric, male-centred nature of school knowledge and the white male domination of educational organizations and management within capitalist societies. Critical educational feminists thus spent more time on challenging the fundamental processes and experiences of education. They criticized, for example, the content of 'male' school subjects and the patriarchal processes of schooling which discriminated against female students and staff. Some focused on how forms of femininity encouraged at school are oppressive to girls and women in both the classroom and the staffroom (Jones & Mahony, 1989) and whether there might be a role for the single-sex school in the creation of an autonomous female learning culture (Deem, 1984). Other forms of critical educational feminism sought to understand, and therefore reduce, the impact of anti-school cultures on the eventual destinations of working-class and more affluent young men and women (Clarricoates, 1978; McRobbie, 1978; Wolpe, 1988).

The relationship between the family, schooling and the labour market, and particularly the under-appreciated and often invisible role of the mother and female teacher, were investigated by socialist feminists (David, 1980; Griffin, 1985; Walkerdine, 1990; Steedman, 1982). Simultaneously, black feminists drew attention to the effects of racism and sexism on black students' educational experiences generally and black girls' and young women's experiences specifically (Amos & Parmar, 1984; Brah & Minhas, 1985; Wright, 1987; Mirza, 1992).

The responses of critical educational feminists to how educational change could be achieved was more ambitious than that of their liberal feminist counterparts. They saw education and schooling as one of the terrains upon which struggles of class, gender and race are played out and as an arena in which wider patterns of social power and subordination are reproduced and sustained. Thus doubts were expressed about the extent and effectiveness of interventions in education by equal opportunities policy-making or by feminist activity, in the absence of wider social and economic change.

Voluntarism in practice

Such ideological differences were not as visible as might have been anticipated in the strategies chosen to generate change within schools. Liberal educational feminism placed greater emphasis on reform from the 'inside' in mounting a substantial number of small-scale initiatives in individual classrooms and schools aimed at persuading girls to opt for previously male-dominated subjects such as science, maths, technology and boys' crafts, and by challenging stereotypical assumptions in textbooks, in the curriculum and in pedagogies. On the other hand, critical educational feminisms suggested that young women would be more attracted to science and mathematics only if changes were made to the male orientation of curricula and to the science-related jobs available to them in the labour market. Thus demands were made that girls' and women's experience and achievements should have a larger presence in schooling.

There was also a willingness to address the more contentious gender issues in schooling, such as the extent of sex harassment in schools, the nature of sex education, school approaches to sexuality, how gay and lesbian students were treated and so on. Teachers were asked to think critically about how 'male'-identified organizational characteristics of hierarchy, competition and managerialism affected the women in the professions, who identified more with practices of valuing personal experience, co-operation and democracy (Measor & Sykes, 1992; Coppeck, Haydon & Richter 1995). Spender (1987), an influential Australian feminist then working in England, argued that, by emphasizing the role that the personal plays in learning,

> feminists have developed an educational paradigm which is sometimes diametrically opposed to the patriarchal one (where the person is seen as a source of contamination and the subjective, something to be avoided).
>
> *(Spender, 1987: 51)*

In reality, however, these different strands of educational feminism fused together as teachers sought to promote awareness of gender issues within a generally diversified and uninterested mainstream schooling system. Gender initiatives were designed to encourage critical reflection among both teachers and pupils, mainly in the form of *teacher-initiated* and *action-research* projects, most of which involved individuals and groups working together and/or with university-based or academic researchers.

The best-known work involving school-based and university-based feminists focused on the curriculum choices of girls, in particular, in mathematics, sciences and technology. The early 1980s *Girls and Technology Education Project* (GATE) investigated ways of improving the curriculum and assessment of craft, design and technology (CDT), and of developing 'good practice' in schools. The *Girls into Science and Technology Project* (GIST) (1980–84), on the other hand, worked directly with teachers to reduce sex-stereotyping on the part of both pupils and teachers, and to promote 'gender-fair' interaction in classrooms, so that girls would feel encouraged to study scientific subjects. Girls into Mathematics (GAMMA), a group of maths educators from the school and university sectors, met on a regular basis to discuss how girls could be persuaded to take up mathematics at sixteen- and eighteen-plus. Other developments included the Girls and Women into Science and Technology WISE year and roadshow, an HMI Report on Girls and Science (1980) and numerous smaller LEA and school events, training sessions, exhibitions and conferences. Such was the impact of many of these initiatives that in 1988 the high-status Royal Institute of Physics argued the case for girls to be better motivated to take up science, and that this needed to be recognized in the framing of any newly developed curricula.

In challenging the most consistently male-dominated subject areas, the emphasis was placed, for example, on addressing the different learning styles of girls and their lack of confidence in certain subjects ('learned-helplessness', as Komarovsky (1946) termed it); the masculine content and orientation of most textbooks, topics and tests; the methods of teaching laboratory-based subjects; and the importance of having female role models in areas where women were in a minority. In mathematics, for example, Walkerdine points to the fact that, despite girls' relatively good performance in the early years, every effort was made to diminish this achievement, for example, by attributing their success to the mediocre characteristics of rule-following and rote-learning. At secondary-school levels, boys were frequently entered for examinations despite poor results in their preliminary assessments or 'mocks', and girls excluded despite good performance (Walkerdine, 1988). Burton similarly highlighted the highly gendered definition of mathematical achievements, which privileged male success as 'gifted' and 'elegant', in contrast to female achievement, defined as 'routine' and 'rule'-following (Burton, 1986).

Other feminist initiatives concentrated on reducing the impact of sexism on girls. These involved extensive work with teachers in raising their awareness of the effects, for example, of detrimental sexist language, and male teachers' bonding mainly with boys through humour and shared male references (such as to football). It also included addressing the dominance of boys in terms of classroom discussions, control over playground space and sporting fixtures in schools, the reward system, etc. It remains problematic whether a connection can be established between participation in aspects of school life and girls' educational success. School policies on language, sexual harassment, mixed-sex sport, and the promotion of discussion of equal opportunities through personal and social education challenged, at the very least, the assumptions concerning gender differences and naturalistic inferences about girls as sex objects and carers.

The strategy adopted by many teachers and LEAs reflected the *Schools Council Sex Differentiation Project* (1981–2), which involved school-based, teacher-led research studies using, as far as possible, social science methods of research and data collection. Findings were fed back to school colleagues as a stimulus to discussions and eventual change. Sensitivity to 'audience' was a feature of this form of teacher activity:

> Classroom research, particularly in the areas of sex differentiation, is likely to raise some very sensitive questions and often teachers will find it hard to accept that their methods and interactions are sexist. In view of this, research findings will need to be presented in a full, thoughtful and objective manner so that teacher consciousness is raised as widely as possible.
>
> *(Millman, 1987: 31)*

It is difficult to ascertain how influential any of these small-scale initiatives were, though they undoubtedly helped maintain a feminist presence in education into the 1990s. Disappointment in the apparent slow pace of change voiced by Kelly, however, mirrored the frustrations of many feminists working in the 1980s.

> We [the GIST team] never anticipated that a small project . . . could produce massive changes in traditional beliefs and practices. However we do confess to a sense of disappointment in the teachers' reactions, and to a scepticism about the extent to which the innovations which were developed during the life of the project will survive its absence.
>
> *(Kelly, 1985: 138)*

In this voluntary phase, the pattern of reform in the UK was inevitably patchy. Initiatives and projects tended to be small-scale and short-lived, with consequent problems of underfinancing and resourcing. They generally involved teachers at the lower end of the school hierarchy, and were more common in the secondary rather than the primary sector because gender differences in subject choice and examination results provided more tangible evidence of gender inequality. Millman (1987) found the position of the teacher-activist in the hierarchy and within school culture to be all-important.

> Established and respected teachers had considerably more influence on school policy than those of supply or in their probationary year. . . . Moreover if the

school already had a tradition of teacher initiated debate on general curricular issues, the existing structures of staff and curriculum development were more likely to provide a forum within which research findings on gender could be presented to colleagues.

(Millman, 1987: 260)

Critical to the development of such projects was the sharing of information and strategies. In the UK context of a devolved curriculum the existence of professional organizations and networks was vital for generating and sustaining innovation. Contact and communication networks (prevalent in the women's movement) during the 1970s and early 1980s thus played a key role in spreading ideas across diverse social communities, schools and phases of education.

The range of networking across the teaching profession in the early 1980s involved subject groups such as Women in History, Women in Geography, Girls and Mathematics (GAMMA), Women in Computing, Women in Economics, etc. Another network was that of Women in Education groups, organized locally, in Hull, Oxford, Manchester, Cambridge, London, etc. Resource centres and newsletters were also prominent; for example, the London-based Women's Education Group had a resource centre and a journal, *GEN*. Feminist publishing ventures such as Virago, Pandora Press, and the Open University's Gender and Education series contributed to the generally buoyant ethos of the time, as did the creation of published materials, such as *Genderwatch* (Myers, 1987), and films, exhibitions, and in-service packs on different subjects produced by such groups as GAMMA.

A deliberately systematic approach to embed strategies to challenge gender inequality in mainstream educational structures was also adopted by local authorities such as Brent and the ILEA in London. In-service courses were designed around the concept of teacher-researcher with the aim of involving as wide a range of teachers as possible from the various sectors of education. These entailed a rejection of top-down management approach to change, preferring instead:

a bottom-up model [which] is harder to support and likely to produce divergence between institutions, but is the model philosophically most acceptable to the nature of the initiative . . . as it forces acknowledgement of the fact that much of the innovative work, both in defining the problems in providing an education for gender equality, and developing practice to bring it about, has been and is actually being done by teachers within their schools.

(Taylor, 1985: 126)

In a number of LEAs, equal opportunities advisors (and sometimes, local inspectors) were used to promote gender networks through courses, projects and materials; in schools, special responsibility posts for equal opportunities and the development of school policies reflected LEA policy at the school level. The survey of LEAs by the Women's National Commission (1984) found that the majority had briefed schools on the Sex Discrimination Act, and a large minority (about a third) had set up working parties, or encouraged schools to 'take countering action'. Interestingly, only 12 per cent had used or created special responsibility posts for gender.

In the UK in the 1980s teacher unions also played a key, if belated, role in supporting teachers' interests in gender equality. In 1978 a group of women in the National Union of Teachers (NUT) grouped together to respond to what they saw as the low priority given to women's rights issues in the union, the ghettoization of women in the lowest paid and poorest funded areas of education, and the general domination of the union and its policy-making by men (NUT, 1981). Such union activism highlighted male-dominated union hierarchies and the low status of women's issues on the union agenda.

The NUT set the pace for union activity on gender issues in the 1980s by sponsoring, together with the EOC, a survey, *Promotion and the Woman Teacher*. This resulted in a number of initiatives, for example, the creation of 'model' job descriptions, advice on maternity benefits, and formal policy on gender for the profession. The NUT also ran a series of training courses for women with the aim of promoting 'women's self-development, particularly in relation to their careers, their more active involvement in the Union and their role in establishing equal opportunities policies within their individual schools' (NUT, 1986: 4).

Other education unions in England and Wales, more reluctant to take up what were considered by some as issues which divided their membership, were slower to develop gender policy. Eventually, however, they established women's committees and/or regional panels (AUT, NATFHE), developed guidelines on equal opportunities policy (NATFHE) and published newsletters for their female members (AUT). Changes in teachers' conditions of service heralded by the 1988 legislation stimulated a flurry of documentation on equal opportunities in the late 1980s and early 1990s addressing appointment, appraisal and promotion procedures (e.g., NUT, 1990; NASUWT, 1990).

By the mid-1980s there was an optimistic belief among some that feminists' efforts to liberate schools would be recorded in the generations to follow (Acker, 1986). At the same time it was recognized that, given the short-term existence of the initiatives, the low status of teachers involved, and the marginality of gender to the main concerns of policy-makers, any impact would be necessarily muted (Weiner & Arnot, 1987a). Evidence of the continuing pattern of stereotypical subject choices of girls and boys pointed to the resilience of traditional school cultures and the need to use stronger intervention strategies to reduce the effects of gender differentiation. By the end of the 1980s, the introduction of a national curriculum ensured that schools were compelled to provide both sexes with a core curriculum covering the sciences and arts and also a range of craft and design subjects. As policy on gender was developed in the 1980s and 1990s, during the long period of Conservative government, attention shifted to whole-school approaches, with 'modern' management responsive to debates about educational achievement and the promotion of 'gender-fair' school cultures. For those involved in educational management, issues of *quality* and *equality* became fused in moves to ensure more standardization in the access and outcomes of schooling (Riley, 1994).

Reflections

Change within a devolved system of education is difficult to assess. As Orr (1985) argued, a strength of the English model of reform before the educational changes of the 1980s was that it encouraged a diversity of experiments. Its main weakness was its decentralized structure, which provided a major constraint on government action and on 'achieving any ambitious and co-ordinated intervention'. Equal opportunities in the 1970s and early 1980s lacked political clout and were often complied with only by policy-makers at the rhetorical level.

At school level, initiatives to promote greater sex equality were characterized more by their diversity than their uniformity. That is not to say that the momentum generated by such initiatives did not have an impact. Educational feminism deeply affected the climate and language of schooling around girls' education, in shaping teachers' understandings about suitable curriculum content, the need to guard against preconceptions about femininity and the role of women in society, and the requirement to act upon overt (if not covert) examples of discrimination against girls. The EOC study in 1996 found teachers and head-teachers who still spoke of their commitment to gender equality using a language which drew on feminism.

As we shall see in chapters 7 and 8, schoolgirls and schoolboys, living through a period when femininity was the subject of discussion and debate, could hardly fail to notice the challenge to (Victorian) gender values which schooling represented.

6

Markets, Competition and Performance

As we have seen, Margaret Thatcher came to power in 1979 committed to reversing the welfare state, reorientating education and reinstating Victorian family values in order to revitalize an economy which was in crisis. From the 1970s onwards there had been criticisms of the pervasiveness of the welfare state; and education was particularly targeted as not having helped to sustain economic growth. Crises throughout the 1970s – in the economy, in unemployment, and in international competitiveness – led to a breakdown in the political consensus about the purpose of education in a social democracy. The New Right, particularly, targeted both the welfare state and education for revision and reconstruction.

Analysts have differed in their understanding of what came to be known as Thatcherism (Hall & Jacques, 1985). Some saw it as a coherent political and economic strategy and others as an almost random clutch of economic and social approaches. Yet others identified distinct phases, beginning with economic retrenchment and followed by direct and explicit policies to privatize and deregulate the economy and social relations (Jessop, Bonnett, Bromley & Ling, 1988). Most agreed, however, that the main aims underlying New Right or neo-liberal/conservative administrations were to re-create individualism, consumerism and competition and to remove blocks, barriers and obstacles to the free play of market forces. Equality of opportunity was recast as the individualizing of opportunities, for economic and social enhancement – as, for example, articulated in the 1990s Citizen's Charter and the prioritization of user or consumer interest and/or involvement.

From the point of view of gender, the contradictions contained within the educational agenda of the Conservative administrations between 1979 and 1997 were highly significant. Three main trends were identified. On the one hand, there was an attempt to reverse the collectivist spirit, which Margaret

Thatcher perceived as dominating war-time Britain and which had shaped and 'distorted' British society in the process (Thatcher, 1995: 46). Part of that collectivist project, as we saw in Chapter 4, was the promotion of greater equality and a more profound commitment to the welfare and well-being of individuals and of communities. Two of the main outcomes of these social democratic goals were the challenge to sex discrimination in employment and education and the development of the women's liberation movement and promotion of gender equality in education. From Margaret Thatcher's perspective, such policy objectives needed to be abandoned, and education used as one means of promoting anti-collectivism.

Second, schools were to be concerned with the promotion of opportunities for families with values and backgrounds similar to those of the Thatcher family:

> It is my passionate belief that what above all was wrong with British Education is that since the war we have . . . strangled the middle way. Direct grant schools and grammar schools provided the means for people like me to get on equal terms with those who came from well-off backgrounds.
>
> *(Thatcher, 1993: 598)*

Margaret Thatcher articulated deep dissatisfaction with prevailing standards of education. She saw high standards of education (defined in terms of qualifications) as increasingly important if Britain was to compete in the global economy, and deregulation as the only means of reversing what she saw as the worst aspects of post-war collectivist education policy. Thus the raising of standards and the modernizing of the UK entrepreneurial culture constituted the main government agenda for education – an agenda described by some as neo-liberalism. In this context, boys and girls were to be encouraged to turn their hopes and aspirations towards the world of work (rather than family or community) and abandon their outmoded identities and aspirations. Instead, through schooling, they were to engage with the technologically oriented global culture and the new individualistic spirit of the age. In this context, schools would be encouraged to modernize, to produce a modern workforce that was not classed, sexed or racially classified. Thus the future educated worker would be mobile, flexible and qualified, well able to seize the opportunities made available to him or her.

The third strand of Thatcherism, and perhaps the least compatible with the other two, involved reinstating a version of Victorian family values in order to revitalize the social order. As we saw in Chapter 3, Margaret Thatcher herself had considerable respect for Victorians and revived the term 'Victorian virtues' to distinguish between the 'deserving poor and the undeserving poor' (Thatcher, 1993: 631). Both were to be helped but in different ways. Thatcher's mission was to eliminate the dependency culture which sustained the undeserving poor. Instead, she argued for the need to treat different families differently. Teenage single parents, one-parent families, absent fathers, and divorced couples were all seen as highly problematic and dys-functional. Also, because so much depended on how families operated, these groups became too important and central to the social order to remain outside the purview of the state. Schools would be used to educate a future generation in morality, respectful of authority, discipline and tradition. Education for parenthood, sex education, moral education were all cornerstones of this programme to 'remoralize' the nation.

These three areas of social welfare policy were all likely to have an impact on gender relations, that is, to impinge on men and women's work patterns and conditions, family life and education. The running down of manu-facturing industry, the restructuring of the economy, the instability of many middle-class occupations (particularly for skilled and technical workers; see Brown, 1995; Mac an Ghaill, 1994) and the reform of schooling would also have specific consequences. Educational feminism had done much to prepare girls for the demands of a technological world and the necessity of studying science and mathematics (although, paradoxically less so, for technology). However, boys were less well prepared for any attempt by government to broaden their curriculum (historically heavily focused upon the craft subjects, mathematics and science). No real attempt in the UK was made by the government or by feminists to encourage boys to engage more positively, for example, in the creative or performing arts or humanities.

The reforms under Margaret Thatcher and John Major from 1979 to 1997 were superimposed on a largely class-divided, sex-divided and racially divided education system and did little to reduce inequalities or consolidate the school as an effective preparation for work. At the same time, family patterns were changing, with higher divorce rates and increasing numbers of fathers disconnected from their children. As Campbell (1993) argued, dur-ing the 1980s Britain became a more dangerous place. Social commentators from the USA (Murray, 1994) were invited to Britain to discuss the rise of a new underclass and a new form of alienated youth – what Wilkinson and Mulgan (1995) called the 'under-wolves'. Rather than address such issues, however, schools were directed to emphasize the accumulation of academic qualifications.

In this chapter we explore the tensions between these agendas, making the case that such tensions created the means by which women were able to advance their position in the economy and girls to raise their performance in schools. In contrast, young men were faced with a contradictory set of agen-das, most of which failed to address the dilemmas they faced – for example, in work and family contexts. The transformation of gender relations was always likely to be uneven, especially in a school system undergoing radical overhaul. In the first section of this chapter we examine the significance for men and women of economic restructuring and the rolling back of the welfare state. Second we look at stances on the family and how the reconstruction of Victorian virtues through education was attempted, and third, we consider New Right educational reforms and feminist responses to what were perceived as new patriarchal and managerial educational discourses.

Economic restructuring and the welfare state

The first phase of economic change under Thatcherism saw a clear shift from the development of manufacturing (and from social services) to the development of the service industries, including financial services. Indeed, accompanying the growth in banking services and the re-emergence of the City of London as a global finance capital was a parallel decline in manufacturing industries and occupations, once central to the British economy. And one of Thatcher's early moves was to attack trade unions, and to restrict and curtail their powers.

Beynon (1992) describes how mass production and automation transformed manufacturing industry and conditions of work, breaking with long-established patterns of young people taking up jobs similar to those of their parents. The rise of the (non-unionized) service industries with 'flexible' working conditions and new forms of specialism related to new technologies is interpreted by some as indicative of the shift from Fordist to post-Fordist practices evident in post-industrial economies and societies (Kenway, Bigum & Fitzclarence, 1995). Significantly, high levels of unemployment and pressure to take any job obscured the fact that a transformation of work was taking place regarding hours and conditions of work, pay rates, company loyalty requirements, and increasing levels of 'workaholism'.

In this period the composition of the labour force in the UK also altered dramatically. For example, in 1946 construction, mining and manufacturing industries provided 45 per cent of employment, and service industries 36 per cent, of jobs. Employment in manufacturing had begun to decline relative to services from the 1950s onwards in absolute terms, and then, more speedily, from 1979 onwards. Thus in 1981 there were only 5.4 million working in manufacturing compared with 8.6 million in 1966. In 1989 the three great industrial sectors made up just 25 per cent of jobs in the country, while the service sector accounted for 15 million jobs – almost 70 per cent of total employment.

Rather than being reduced by such transformations, the segregation of male and female work was in fact aggravated. Women had been recruited to the new service-sector jobs, while workers who remained in industry were largely male. The industrial contributions made by coal, steel, shipyards, docks and shipping, and railways had been central to the national economy but strongly regionalized. Nationally, the presence of these groups of workers was distinctively masculine, as illustrated by the combative nature of trade union and employers' negotiations and bargaining. A specific heroic, working-class masculinity epitomized socialist and left-wing politics of the period.

During the 1970s and 1980s the rise of information technology allowed women workers to come in from the periphery. As Britain moved from industrialization to post-industrialization, class and gender relations in work and education for work changed. Complex economic, industrial and regional shifts in employment opportunities, particularly the growth of the public and the private service sectors, had a clear impact upon gender relations both within the family and in employment. Traditionally the preserve of women workers, opportunities for service-sector work expanded – even if on a casual, temporary, part-time and/or low-paid basis – whereas opportunities for male employment, especially for skilled or semi-skilled manual occupations, diminished. These kinds of shifts had a particular impact on already changing working-class families and households.

Margaret Thatcher's second phase of development also saw an attempt to redirect public social services into the private (or privatized) sector, which included the family. In other words, the push to privatization was both towards the implementation of business forms of organization of the private or commercial sector and towards allotting responsibility for social welfare and education to the private family. It was only in the third phase of Thatcherism that the full programme of privatization of public and welfare services, including health and education, was called into play.

The transformations of the welfare state started by Thatcher's first administration are now so familiar a part of the social landscape that it is difficult to remember what public provision of social welfare and education services was like in previous eras. Explicit regulation, rules and bureaucracy were created as a means of ensuring the right forms of deregulation. For instance, the role of local authorities' in the provision of education and social services was much reduced. In parallel, institutions and organizations (such as schools, polytechnics, universities and hospitals) were encouraged to mutate into independent 'businesses', run on commercial rather than service lines.

The marketization of British society, as well as the legislation necessary to deregulate, had an impact on the social organization of labour, such as housework, work, and family roles. The gap between the rich and the poor widened as Britain became what Hutton called a '30: 30: 40' society (Hutton, 1995: 14). As Crompton explains:

Only around 40% of the work force enjoy tenured full-time employment or secure self employment . . . another 30% are insecurely self-employed, involuntarily part-time, or casual workers; while the bottom 30%, the marginalised, are idle or working for poverty wages.

(Crompton, 1997: 131)

Concern was expressed about young people and, in particular, their involvement in rising rates of crime, anti-social behaviour, exclusions from school, and youth unemployment. Moral panics were frequent, for example, about the drift away from conventional family life, lone parents and 'parenting deficit' (Etzioni, 1993). One response was to campaign for a return to traditional family values, especially a re-emphasis on women's domestic responsibilities, and especially in light of young male behaviour.

Young men were increasingly characterized as disadvantaged, and intimations appeared in the media that masculinity was in crisis and that boys were being 'lost' (Evans, 1996). Those lower down the social scale were without jobs and those higher up were faced with increasing job insecurity and competition from women. Education was viewed as partly responsible for this, as the raised examination performance at GCSE of girls produced a reversal of previously male-dominated examination patterns and a closing of the gender gap (see Chapter 2).

However, it was also clear that the lack of job opportunities for young unskilled males offered little incentive for them to work harder at school. Traditional male working-class jobs requiring physical strength disappeared in large numbers. Whole communities were devastated as mines, steelworks, shipbuilding yards, docks and other heavy industries were closed altogether or subject to massive down-sizing and rationalization. It was apparent to many young men that, however hard they worked at school, the jobs just were not there.

In *Goliath: Britain's dangerous places* (1993) Campbell vividly documented the violent explosions in British cities in the late summer of 1991. Although the Conservatives had acted swiftly from the early 1980s onwards to remove the possibility of social protest or political action, a number of sites of protest remained – for example, Northern Ireland, the women's camp at Greenham Common, the miners' strike and the poll-tax protests. Additionally, towards the end of the 1980s, after a decade of Thatcherism, a large cohort of young men (and women) found themselves not only on the edges of politics but exiled from the worlds of both study and work. They were neither legitimate citizens nor consumers (Wilkinson, 1994). Mass unemployment among teenagers, the generation which constitutes the largest 'criminal' category, made specific provision for them problematic.

> Their student contemporaries may be poor, too, but they have an income and passport to the world of libraries, canteens, clubs, unions, seminars and conversations. Unemployed school leavers who are not enrolled in training schemes have no income and no access to the public domain.
>
> *(Campbell, 1993: 95)*

Campbell argued that schooling provided a terrain on which the changes induced by Thatcherism could be responded to. Boys and girls stayed on to pick up more qualifications and delay entry to the labour market, acting in largely similar ways. However, more boys preferred to try for early employment despite the relatively few options they had, while more girls tended to remain at school. According to Campbell (1993) the relationship between schooling and work was forged by these conditions:

> School was both their first and last point of contact with a society beyond their family and their neighbourhood, their first and last contact with a social culture of co-operation and compromise.
>
> *(Campbell, 1993: 95)*

Young people stayed 'on' at school but often were not 'in' school. For example, Campbell found that, by the last year of school, there could be anything up to 25 per cent of absenteeism among fifteen-year-olds, and in Newcastle's West End schools an average of twenty children a day, all white boys, were excluded for at least one day for violence.

> For a lad whose culture celebrated a man's authority and power, and lethal weapons as the solution to social problems, the discovery of his own illiteracy and incompetence could, of course, carry the dread that 'being inside society' meant 'being defeated' . . . power only meant brute force. 'They had no idea about how society works', says one of their lawyers.
>
> *(Campbell, 1993: 96)*

It has been argued that separate spheres for men and women has ultimately proved more of a handicap to men than women (Pahl, 1995). Pahl argues, for example, that modern masculinity is based on the model of the male as provider, mainly out in the public sphere and detached from the private sphere of emotions and caring. As a consequence, men are unable to cope with the interactive demands of the new 'people-related' jobs in customer-oriented service industries. Masculinity thus has become undermined as the role of provider disappears. Whether life was made excessively difficult for men, in particular, by Thatcherism, is a moot point. Men have retained their predominance in the world of paid work, and particular forms of masculinity are pre-eminent in the worlds of power, politics, commerce, the civil services, etc. (Connell, 1989), although there are also extensive class and ethnic differences between men. Thus care should be taken not to assume that all (or even most) men are more vulnerable than previously, although some groups of men have certainly suffered more under Thatcherism than others (see Chapter 8).

When young men and women tried to anticipate their futures after full-time education in the 1990s, they still received very different messages about male and female opportunities. Occupational opportunities and the youth labour market remain heavily structured by gender. In particular, given the extent of decline of traditional apprenticeships which conventionally eased the transition from school to work, young men now needed to think imaginatively and courageously about how to achieve their aspirations.

It is also clear that both men and women suffered from the greater poverty, joblessness and rising inequality generated by Thatcherism, and, thus, both needed to reposition themselves in the new economic order. Neither were the middle classes immune from Thatcherism, which was to destabilize the traditional security of male white-collar work. The link between a good education and qualifications and secure and well-paid employment could no longer be guaranteed (Brown, 1995) (see chapter 8).

Demonizing the family

Economic and social policy had an impact too on the family. Campbell argues that, especially for the black Afro-Caribbean family, women bore the brunt of family dislocations, with little support provided by the state for their attempts to hold together the fabric of social order. Particularly acute was the alienation of their sons and the interference of the police. Initial shifts towards privatization held the family rather than the state responsible for family members. Financial and social obligations were transferred back to families and households and away from the rather more universalist services of the social-democratic era. The state increasingly abdicated its responsibilities for the care, education and security of families, redefining this as a private rather than a public matter, and as an individual rather than a social or collective responsibility. One keenly felt outcome of this stance was that it dramatically widened social inequalities.

The expansion and growth in women's employment and professional activities described in Chapter 3 was not a phenomenon confined to the UK but one which occurred throughout the Western world, particularly in what were once referred to as the advanced industrial societies. By the 1980s such societies were characterized as late/high or post-modern societies (Giddens, 1991), in which the 'romanticization' of the traditional family (see Chapter 4) was now seen as constraining both to women and to children. The social democratic commitment to liberalizing family life was enhanced by support for measures around, for example, reforms in contraception and abortion, employment, childcare and divorce.

Despite Thatcher's efforts, the ideology of the traditional family no longer captured the hearts and minds of the majority of women or those forming families in the 1980s; in particular the institution of marriage for the purposes of legitimate parenthood was no longer the overall majority form but accounted only for about two-thirds of households at the time of the birth. Of these, many were reconstituted families and households (formed from the divorce of one or both of the partners). Of the remaining third, some cohabited but were not legally married, and others were in a variety of stable, non-married relationships. Unmarried teenage-mother households constituted a relatively small group within this diversity of family forms (Haskey, 1998).

By the middle of the 1990s, as we saw in Chapter 4, it had become clear that the Victorian patriarchal family – of husband and wife as biological/ natural parents and dependent children (under sixteen), with the man as the breadwinner and the woman as the non-working economically depend- ent wife – no longer typified households of late twentieth century Britain. Significant disruptions to this somewhat romanticized conventional family form were the realities of, for example:

- male unemployment
- female employment, though not necessarily full-time, and often involving non-standard hours and conditions
- lone-parent households, where men had left for other households or women had chosen to separate and live alone
- one parent not the biological/natural parent, usually the father, who may also be a parent of children in another household
- parents cohabiting but not (yet) married
- parents remarried, and the family therefore reconstituted
- single-parent family in which the mother had never married
- gay and lesbian partnerships and 'marriages', with or without offspring.

In contemporary Britain there could be found an almost infinite variety of family possibilities, involving a wide range of kin relationships, for example, siblings, step-siblings, step-parents, half-siblings, etc., rather than one pre- dominant family form (i.e., the nuclear family) and one deviant form (i.e., the single-mother family). The consequences for British culture were a range and diversity of family forms (some of which were affected by feminism) which departed substantially from the ideological prescriptions laid down fifty years previously by welfare reformers, and which, to some extent, had been idealized by Margaret Thatcher herself.

As we have argued in Chapter 3, Margaret Thatcher was ideologically committed to the Victorian family of 'pater familias' and home-maker mother and developed explicit policies to try to reinvigorate the traditional family as the cornerstone and building block of the community and 'society' as a whole. The liberalization of the family, however, brought with it changes specifically in the role of women that were seen by the Conservative government as deeply threatening to social stability. The key changes which were identified as problematic related to marriage and parenthood. For example, women were perceived as 'resisting' marriage both through divorce and/or separation, and were blamed for the 'new' forms of parenthood that were taking root, as we have seen above. Throughout the 1980s, therefore, a two-pronged ideological and political onslaught was mounted on these newer family forms, neither of which worked in the sense of restoring Victorian values. On the one hand, 'single-parent families' (often from minority ethnic groups) were demonized as the main cause of crime and juvenile delinquency, poverty and unemployment, and general social 'insecurity'. On the other hand, schools were to be used to re-establish traditional gender relations in the family.

The public spotlight was also turned on teenage mothers, and questions were raised about their ability to raise a 'proper family'. Even though lone-mother households were seen as responding to the call of the free marketeers or liberal economists, by 'choosing' their own family way, if not necessarily in circumstances of their own choosing, many were vilified. Much of the attack on such families in the UK was borrowed from the USA and ideologues of the New Right there such as Charles Murray (1994).

Murray argued, for instance, drawing from the American experience that Britain too would undergo a rapid rise in the growth of the 'underclass' such that, unless policy measures were taken to stem the tide, it would be the dominant form by the end of the twentieth century. Originally published in the *Sunday Times*, and reprinted in 1994, Murray's article compared and contrasted two boroughs through their census data, focusing in particular on rates of lone-mother families, juvenile crime and delinquency – and what he called 'working aged unemployment'. He identified two new forms, 'the New Rabble', based upon his analysis of Labour-controlled Middlesborough, and 'the New Victorians', based upon his analysis of Conservative-controlled Wokingham. Although his arguments were 'fundamentally flawed' (David, 1994), they were readily seized upon both by journalists and by politicians. Indeed, Margaret Thatcher devotes a whole chapter in her autobiography to these issues, arguing for welfare policies to stem the tide of 'welfare dependency'. Murray's diatribe was particularly addressed to gender relations. He argued that, with the passing of the Victorian family, boys and young men had lost appropriate father figures and models of fatherhood, and thus measures were needed to ensure its return, with the father as head of household. Murray presented the ammunition for the revival of Victorian family values which both attacked women as lone mothers and celebrated the necessity of women's economic and social dependence upon men.

The British conservative philosopher Roger Scruton took a slightly different tack. He argued that biological and natural instincts determined both the sexual division of labour within the family and the separation between the private and public spheres. The family, for Scruton (quoted in Williams, 1989: 119), was therefore a 'natural' form. Thus Scruton and others argued for the conventional family as occupying a privileged place in New Right ideology. On the one hand, the family was to be responsible for the 'defence of the individual against socialism and excessive state power'; on the other, it was to be the basis of private property and the location of the consumer responsible for the management of financial affairs. The family was also to be the 'centre of affections', 'the transmitter of traditions' and the ultimate authority. Such functions, according to Campbell (1987), transcended all allegiances of class and indeed of history itself.

Parenthood represented, for neo-conservatives such as Scruton, the political and moral values of hierarchy, authority and loyalty. Thus, 'the family had to be maximised in order to minimise the state'. By rehabilitating the family, the government aimed to break down the 'scrounger welfare state' and, through a 'moral crusade', to counter the effects of permissiveness that grew out of the 1960s (Campbell, 1987: 166).

Durham (1991) argues that the influence of the 'moral majority' was not as fully developed in the UK as in the USA, partly because government could not stem the tide of change – although it sought to do so, for example, by restricting sex education and making teaching about homosexuality illegal (Kelly, 1991). Moral campaigners could only be disappointed by the lack of progress on the restriction of abortion and divorce and the continuing rise in illegitimacy rates. The moralist position in UK politics in the 1980s thus remained weak despite the attraction of Margaret Thatcher and her ministers' to Victorian values and their attacks on 1960s permissive society.

In practice, the attacks on single parents and the attempts to develop a moralist position on the family had little effect on women's advancement. Early educational initiatives by the Conservative government promoting family life were less than successful. Curricular reforms (e.g., school courses on parenthood) which encouraged traditional parenting roles were hard to implement within a decentralized educational system and were an unlikely vehicle for a moral crusade, especially since such courses were not mandatory and occupied low status as non-examination subjects. Responsibility for sex education and parenthood education had been delegated to the new school governing bodies under the Education Act (1986), but children could be withdrawn from the classroom if their parents objected. The prohibition of teaching about gay and lesbian issues in schools, also in 1986, was symbolically and ideologically important but had little impact on practice, since few local authorities and schools had policies in place on teaching about sexuality.

Also the women's movement, even if fragmented, had clearly made an impact on public opinion. Segal argues that the Thatcher government was held back by the 'continual vigour and success of feminism in mobilising support for women's rights and equality' (1987: 214). Changes in women's employment, for example, had encouraged middle-class women to take up careers, and some of these were active members of the Conservative Party. As Campbell showed in her book on Conservative women, *Iron Ladies*, these women fought against any simple equation concerning women and motherhood and against excessive New Right moralizing, restructuring of sexual freedom and cuts in child benefits (Campbell, 1987). Women thus rejected strictures for their return *en masse* to the domestic sphere, continuing instead to carry on within their dual status of wife and worker (Wilson, 1987). The extent to which the New Right could promote traditional values, particularly surrounding women's domesticity, was therefore severely curtailed.

New Right notions of individualism and the unacceptability of excessive state control also militated against any new celebration of domestic/familial education for girls. And, of course, competitive individualism could be taken up by both men and women equally, as Margaret Thatcher herself argued, in 1952 and again in 1982.

> It is of course true that women of our generation are often still comparatively young by the time our children are grown up and therefore we have an opportunity further to develop our own talents. For many that experience can enhance their lives and enlarge their interests.
>
> *(Thatcher, quoted in Wilson, 1987: 295)*

Such modernizing tendencies in relation to women's roles, which were used to counter the 'blinkered ideologues' of the left,

> Fabians, Marxists, feminists and the like – whose time is past and who have got fatally out of step with the world we live in,
>
> *(Thatcher, quoted in Wilson, 1987: 205)*

could also be used in relation to economic agendas, as we shall see in the next section. The removal of previous social barriers to the educational advancement of women was likely to yield economic benefits to the individual and the economy, whether or not such advancement threatened the family form.

Feminism and New Right educational reforms

As we have seen, Margaret Thatcher held education largely to blame for Britain's economic problems, a position already adopted by James Callaghan, who, as Labour prime minister in the mid-1970s, instigated what was called the 'Great Debate' about whether education was giving value for money. As a consequence of both Callaghan's and Thatcher's interventions, the dual repertoire of social democracy (economic growth and equality of opportunity through redistribution and welfare provision) was abandoned in favour of a closer and more direct relationship between education and economic production (CCCS, 1981). New Right interpretations of this agenda were to transform the economy and public services as well as education. The processes of educational restructuring which were intended to move away from the collective and egalitarian principles of the welfare state (including education) were more difficult than originally envisaged and took until well into the late 1980s to complete.

In Chapter 5 we pointed out that the curricular reform which best exemplifies the ambivalence to gender of New Right policy-makers was the Technical and Vocational Educational Initiative (TVEI) in 1983. The new vocational thrust of Conservative government policy attempted to 'de-gender' the workforce through the promotion of equal opportunities and through grants targeted at innovatory practice in schools. Such de-gendering strategies also affected the conception of the national curriculum, although in an implicit rather than explicit form. In other words:

> liberal/progressive ideas concerning freedom for girls and women to move upwards in the educational and occupational hierarchies have become synonymous with 'liberal', 'laissez faire' ideas about labour market freedom.
>
> *(Weiner, 1989b: 121)*

Equal opportunities came to be seen by some free-marketers as crucial to ensuring that schooling delivered a flexibly skilled and undifferentiated (by sex in particular) workforce which could be suitably employed in whichever way capitalism developed.

Although New Right educational reforms were relatively slow, the ideological and value shifts were clearly in evidence from the end of the 1970s. Notions of equality of opportunity, whether on grounds of social class, gender or race, began to give way to notions of individualism, the ideals of competition and the reward for performance. One of the criticisms made by the Right of previous Labour policy was the extent to which education had become overbureaucratized in an attempt to ensure equal opportunities, and schools had thus become stifling in their 'sameness'.

When Kenneth Baker (then Secretary of State for Education and Science) announced in 1988 that 'the pursuit of egalitarianism is now over', he signalled a new era of 'standards, freedom and choice'. The new era would give the consumers a central part in decision-making. The legislation of 1988 dismantled the partnership between central and local government, with schools now controlled by their governing bodies and parents offered the possibility of deciding on whether their children's school should opt out of local authority control. Schools remaining within local authority control were to have greater financial autonomy through local management of schools (LMS). Of equal significance were the creation of a national curriculum, covering ten subjects to be taught to children between five and sixteen years old, national testing (SATs) and the publication of performance league tables of schools' results for sixteen- and eighteen-year-olds (later widened to include eleven-year-olds).

The Education Reform Act (ERA) 1988 became the cornerstone for educational policy for the next decade, emphasizing educational standards and quality, consumer freedom of choice and institutional autonomy. Subsequent legislation, particularly under John Major's administrations (1990–97) enhanced these elements, with the Citizen's Charter, Parents' Charter for Education, Education Act (1992) and Further and Higher Education Act (1992). New methods of quality control were introduced, through the creation of the Office for Standards in Education (OFSTED) administering a semi-privatized system of school inspections, as were attempts to increase choice for parents of pre-school children with the voucher scheme for nursery education.

The imposition of the National Curriculum, with its commitment to all pupils studying a common set of subjects, was clearly likely to influence girls' education (especially their take-up of traditional 'male' subjects such as science and technical crafts) and to encourage boys to study English and modern languages. As we discussed in Chapter 3, the pattern of subject choices which had been shaped by the domestic educational ideologies of the Victorian era was finally broken, ironically by Margaret Thatcher's Conservative government. The model of a core/common curriculum was something that feminists had argued for since the 1970s (Byrne, 1978). Nevertheless, feminist responses to the National Curriculum were relatively muted. They emphasized the failure, for example, to consult feminist teachers and academics with expertise in curriculum development. The National Curriculum was seen to have failed to address key gender concerns in the content of subjects, to set up adequate monitoring procedures to ensure that gender differences would not emerge within subjects, and to provide adequate training for teachers, governors and head-teachers on equality issues (see, for example, Miles & Middleton, 1990; Shah, 1990). Also noted was that, beneath the veneer of the overt curriculum, there was a 'hidden' curriculum which stressed competition and individualism above collectivist principles promoting social equality.

Change after change instigated by the Conservative government of the time led to feelings of 'shell shock' by teachers and others involved in education, and of exhaustion and helplessness as to how to respond. It was not clear what repercussions the new reforms would have, and what spaces were available for those critical of the new policies. How would the changes impact on girls' and boys' education, or on children from different social classes, or on children with disabilities, or in different parts of the country or from different ethnic groups? How would parental power be utilized and in whose interests? Many of these questions remain unanswered.

By the end of eighteen years of Conservative Party rule, the education landscape had shifted from one of a rhetorical commitment to social homogeneity to one of institutional variety and diversity, yet with an overriding centralism of policy steer, prescription of practice and inspection. At the same time Conservative educational reforms became associated with greater participation of pupils at all levels of education beyond compulsory schooling. Far more pupils entered and passed GCSE and A-levels than ever before. Conservative policies on the publication of examination results also made more visible the increasing educational achievements of girls. At the same time, evidence indicated that class and racial inequalities widened as a consequence of the Thatcher and Major administrations (Gillborn & Gipps, 1996; Gillborn, 1997; Furlong & Cartmel, 1997).

Why girls (particularly white girls) continued to raise their examination performance under these conditions is one of the questions addressed by this book. In Chapter 5 we suggested that the adaptability of British educational feminism to the shifting terrain of educational policy-making during the 1980s and 1990s played a key role in sustaining girls' achievement, despite the reservations of feminists about the reforms that we described above. To some extent the alleged neutrality of New Right reforms in relation to gender may have contributed to the development of what we term a third wave of feminist activity. Feminist campaigners (many of whom were not visible to the public – for example, the 'ordinary' classroom teacher) continued to inculcate in a new generation of girls a sense of what Whitty once called 'possibilitarianism' (Whitty, 1974). As in the case of family change and the rise of female employment, so in the case of commitment to gender equality: the Conservative reformers were unable to 'put the genie back in the bottle'.

Feminism, managerialism and performance

Feminist responses to New Right education policy were neither public nor organized, although feminist educational concerns were articulated in EOC submissions (e.g., EOC, 1989). The voices of women, in general, were not heard. Perhaps because of confusion over likely effects of the legislation, early commentators interpreted it more as a case of missed opportunities to tackle sex discrimination in education rather than as anti-feminist in intent. Such concerns were focused on the traditionally male orientation of the new curriculum, and it was argued that earlier feminist work in education had been overlooked – for example, there was a danger that the National Curriculum would push girls away from mathematics and science. Feminists, including ourselves, provided limited analyses rather than more theoretically sophisticated overviews of the restructuring of gender relations. Equal opportunities had been listed as a cross-curriculum theme by policy-makers in 1988 but then was viewed as too sensitive a subject to merit further development. There was no official commitment to monitoring sex bias in schools or in education more widely. In the event, the publication of examination results (rather than government statistics) culminated in the gender analysis of students' performance at the ages of sixteen and eighteen, which eventually heightened interest in gender once more.

The gender dimensions of the New Right reforms were neglected by other critical analysts of ERA and Thatcherism (Whitty, 1990; Ball, 1990). New Right attempts to deracialize education (i.e., by rejection of anti-racist strategies; see Troyna & Carrington, 1990; Gillborn, 1995) seemed to be better understood than its treatment of gender. In contrast the New Right in the USA was castigated by Dworkin (1983) as a social and political movement controlled almost totally by men and fundamentally anti-feminist in stance.

Feminism had been unprepared for the New Right counter-attack on social democracy and egalitarianism. The feminist movement seemed to be without any clear strategy to tackle emergent inequalities in the new era. It could be argued that the fragmentation of educational feminism described in the last chapter resulted in a failure to provide a unified response and had relied too heavily upon teachers' practice and autonomy. In the UK context it may have gone too far down the interventionist road without mobilizing popular, or parental, support. In that sense, teachers had not generated an effective counter-hegemony.

The structure and orientation of the English/Welsh educational system, which was different from that in other social democratic countries such as Sweden, with its stronger central state and a commitment to non-differentiated schooling, or the USA, with its meritocratic stance set in the context of looser federal ties and a decentralized framework of schools, produced a distinctive perspective on gender intervention in education. As we saw in Chapter 5 above, feminist teachers in the UK were able to mount a challenge because of the prevailing ethos of teacher autonomy and decentralization of power to LEAs. However, as educational policy became more centralized in the late 1980s and 1990s, and more overt forms of managerialism emerged, the balance shifted away from interventions that depended on teachers and LEAs and towards government agencies (such as the QCA and OFSTED) adopting more active roles. This shift from voluntarism to managerialism was a response to the new economic/educational structures described above.

The new centrally driven discourses of educational management and marketization which emerged in the UK from the late 1980s onwards sharply contrasted with the orientation of much of the feminist work already mentioned. As we have seen, the emphasis within gender initiatives until then had been on teacher or pupil participation and personal experience rather than on management and rational planning. Also, because of the *ad hoc* and 'alternative' character of many of the earlier feminist initiatives, generated by committed individuals and groups at the school and local level, the aims of educational feminism – that of raising gender as a legitimate area of consideration – were frequently seen as politically contentious, and the outcomes as unpredictable and non-finite.

As previous informal, often idiosyncratic, models of school organization were replaced by regimes of 'line management', clearly defined job descriptions, and boundaried responsibility, spheres of competence and expertise, educational feminism itself had to change. Indeed, the new managerialism was viewed by some as a new set of male power relations located within a performance-oriented culture (Ball, 1990; Maguire & Weiner, 1994).

The new organizational practices appeared to cut across feminist-identified styles of working, which had tended to be more 'open, democratic, friendly, and collaborative, and less confrontational and competitive' (Marshall, 1985). Also, with a focus on such practices as target-setting, service-delivery, efficiency and 'quality', the kind of managers which such managerial cultures required were less likely to be women or men sympathetic to feminist issues (Adler, Laney & Packer, 1993).

Thus, by the early 1990s, if it was to survive into the new managerial era, a repositioning of educational feminism was needed to accommodate newly constituted orthodoxies about school management and school effectiveness (see, for example, Handy & Aitken, 1986; Fullan & Hargreaves, 1992). Feminism, always 'a theory in the making' (hooks, 1984) showed itself adept at meeting the need to change. Significantly, feminists who had been appointed to inspector and advisor posts in LEAs and who received training in new managerial techniques led the way by putting pressure on feminist practitioners to 'manage' change more rationally and effectively, and, in some senses, to treat gender initiatives like any other attempt at change – equivalent, say, to the adoption of a new reading scheme or alterations in staffing policy (see, for example, ILEA 1986a, 1986b). The power of effective management had been asserted by Hazel Taylor, then an inspector in an outer London borough, as early as 1985:

> The implementation of equal opportunities initiatives cannot be divorced from an appreciation of the effectiveness of school's management; a desire to change that is not supported by effective management techniques to bring change about is no more satisfactory than no intention of changing, and can produce an extremely frustrating atmosphere for young teachers to work in.
>
> *(Taylor, 1985: 131)*

Criticisms of previous feminist work for weaknesses of planning and failure to distinguish between long-term and short-terms goals were addressed with the emergence of guidance on how gender policy-making might be broken down into smaller, more manageable parts and what appropriate performance indicators might look like (Myers, 1987; George, 1993).

To be 'seen' to be making a difference was also important within the discourse of management. This was particularly crucial in centrally funded schemes such as TVEI, where failure to 'deliver' changes in, say, option choices or stereotyped career patterns in the limited period offered by the schemes was likely to put in jeopardy government support for the equal opportunities elements of the schemes. The broader and more generalized aspirations of the earlier feminist initiatives, thus, were incompatible with the deliberate fast-pace and short-term nature of government funding requirements.

The kinds of gender initiatives which could flourish within what seemed a hostile period for feminist endeavour formed a topic of interest and investigation for our EOC project (see Chapter 2). As we noted earlier, we were surprised at the commitment to a more egalitarian society of many teachers and the resilience and adaptability of educational feminism itself. For example, we noted a changed language of gender and also a continuation of feminist work, though at the local level and engaging with prevailing government concerns. The ways in which gender issues were framed in the mid-1990s took a variety of forms, some of which were directly related to contemporary political and educational priorities. The emphasis of specific approaches might differ quite markedly, incorporating equal opportunities into various discourses such as value-addedness, raising standards, individual rights and responsibilities, and entitlement. We concluded the report with the following comment:

> ... the research revealed a mixed picture of beneficial procedures and policies arising from some of the reforms, pockets of thoughtful and knowledgeable practice from committed individuals and groups but overall no infrastructure for the delivery of equal opportunities on a wider and more systematic basis.
>
> Cultural, demographic and labour market changes have clearly influenced the way students and teachers think about the schooling of girls and boys such that few now consider girls' education to be less important. In fact high scoring female students are proving attractive to schools in the competitive climate of the 1990s, and it is poorly behaved and low achieving boys who appear to be the subjects of greatest concern.
>
> (Arnot, David & Weiner, 1996: 162)

Reflections

The struggle for gender equality using the educational system as the motor of change described in the last chapter made considerable inroads into a school system characterized by teacher autonomy and decentralization of curriculum decision-making. After 1988, with the introduction of market competition, standards and choice, educational feminism was compelled to address itself to a performance-oriented school system with a strong managerialist ethos. Paradoxically, even though a government was in power which criticized feminism as part of the excessiveness of the egalitarian era and as responsible for the collapse of family life, much was put into place that could only benefit girls' education. On the one hand, we have seen how the restructuring of the economy away from manufacturing industry towards the service sector, with its requirements for part-time, flexible and low-paid workers, offered opportunities for women to work, albeit in low-status and transitory occupations. More equal gender relations were seen by the promoters of the new vocationalism as important for labour-market freedom. Liberal feminism, with its concerns for open access and its commitment to de-gender the public sphere, in particular, was in a position to contribute to a new set of gender relationships. And, in fact, it was able to make the transition more effectively to the New Right's individualistic, consumer-oriented society, we suggest, than was critical feminism.

Critical educational feminism, with its agenda of attacking and eliminating patriarchal social relations, in contrast, became marginalized as schools were drawn into a closer relationship with the economy. In a context where the new agenda was one of increasing competition rather than promoting equality, the focus of feminist research, for example, on working-class girls' education was marginalized. It is only comparatively recently that evidence of the impact of New Right educational restructuring on working-class or ethnic minority girls and boys has emerged (Mahony & Zmroczek, 1997; Skeggs, 1994; Lucey & Walkerdine, 1996; Walkerdine, Melody & Lucey, 1996).

Margaret Thatcher's attack on social democracy and collectivism demanded a new response from those promoting gender equality. It showed that educational feminism in the UK was robust and adaptable and that flexibility would continue to be needed to address the inevitable backlash and hostility generated by girls' and women's educational advances and successes.

It is also important to recognize that women and men could not but be affected differently by the changes instituted by New Right policies. The contradictions were likely to be significant for young men and women trying to read the signs of the times. Although women might experience higher levels of unemployment than men, men lost their livelihoods as manufacturing plummeted. Young men witnessed the loss of status of their fathers when made redundant or unemployed. On the other hand, girls' experiences in the family, especially if headed by a single parent, were likely to add to their sense of change. One of the most neglected areas of discussion by critics of New Right policies has been their impact on the lived realities and work opportunities of succeeding generations of girls and boys growing up and being educated through these critical decades after the Second World War. This will form the discussion of the third and final part of this book.

Part III
New Generations of Girls and Boys

7

Schoolgirls and Social Change

In this chapter we review the evidence on girls' lives collected by social and feminist researchers from the 1970s to the 1990s. (In Chapter 8 we offer a similar review for boys.) We consider in what ways successive generations of girls have been affected by the contradictory messages of post-war social democratic policies and the recent promotion by the New Right of a more materialistic and competitive social ethos. A first impression is one of extensive change from that of forty years ago when Margaret Thatcher and Queen Elizabeth were young women. The image of those whom we might call 'Thatcher's daughters' is of young women who no longer seek economic dependency on a man or a husband and who wish to take their own place in the world of work. We explore here how shifts in social and economic life influenced the culture, values, identities and education of girls in different social classes and ethnic groups.

The socio-economic changes and political conflicts which we identified in Part 2 of this book can, with the benefit of hindsight, be interpreted as part of a far larger historical transformation of modern society. The underlying processes, such as increasing geographical mobility and the loosening of inter-generational family ties, have impacted on individuals' 'consciousness, identity, socialisation and emancipation' (Beck, 1992: 128). These processes of *individualization*, it has been argued, transform individuals' relationships with their class and ethnic status, family connections and traditional loyalties. They have to identify their own sources of meaning at the same time as handling 'the turbulence of the global, risk society' (Beck, Giddens & Lash, 1994: 7). Giddens (1991) argues that individuals need to cope with increasing diversification in employment by becoming more flexible, and by adopting a range of social identities and memberships of different groupings. Such diversification allows for greater reflexivity and a sense of possibility. A negative side is that individuals experience high levels of stress and anxiety about uncertain futures (Furlong & Cartmel, 1997).

Women, especially young women, have been symbolic of such social change. The new entrepreneurial culture has been represented as part of a process of 'feminization', especially since, it is argued, it has brought about the rise of the business woman. New magazines such as *Working Woman*, and new role models such as Anita Roddick, Madonna and Demi Moore (Sharpe, 1994), symbolize the growing status and earning power of women, not so much in the caring professions as in new positions in entrepreneurial capital. The emotional reaction to Princess Diana's untimely death in 1997 was represented as indicative of feminization (if not Americanization) of the British national character (Campbell, 1998; Burchill, 1998). The 'typical' modern woman in Britain has become the icon of the post-modern world.

Support for this view can be found in the study conducted by the left-leaning British think tank Demos on the values of a sample of some 2500 adults aged between eighteen and seventy-five (Wilkinson & Mulgan, 1995). The most significant finding of this controversial study is the evidence of a substantial generational shift in values between young adults aged eighteen to thirty-four and the older groups questioned. Younger women (eighteen to thirty-four years old) who have grown up in the aftermath of the Sex Discrimination Act (1975) are presented as 'setting the pace' of change, showing a desire for autonomy, self-fulfilment in work and family, and a valuing of risk, excitement and change. Supporting a realignment of work and female life and of male and female dependencies and androgyny (a blurring of gender boundaries), such young women appear to want the 'outer-directed' values of male working lives. They also seem to have 'a deepening attachment' to the values of individualism, as well as to be searching for complexity, more meaningful personal relationships, diverse sexualities and new work identities. They wish to articulate their own desires and expectations of others.

In this study teenage girls aged fifteen to seventeen, however, born and brought up under Thatcherism, have been found to be more contradictory. On the one hand, they are apparently even more likely than their older sisters to be attached to the values of risk, excitement, hedonism, sexuality and image-awareness. On the other hand, this optimism and sense of possibility appears as a form of romantic and sexual escapism, since teenage girls are unlikely to recognize the contradictions between the expectations of family life, the demands of being wives and workers and the stresses and strains of adult life such as divorce, partnership, poverty and unemployment.

At school, these shifts in expectations are revealed in the ways in which female pupils make their course choices, selecting new social science subjects (sociology, psychology, economics) and new business subjects (IT, business studies, technology) instead of high-status male subjects (Sharpe, 1994). Careers advice has aided this process, with girls showing far more awareness of the range of occupations now available in the business world and the service sector. Significantly more young women report wanting to set up their own small businesses (Sharpe, 1994; Wilkinson, 1994). Notes from the EOC study capture the new tone of confidence found among school-girls today:

> *C.* expects to study biochemistry, and then go into the private sector. Might have a husband and child.
> *A.* expects to study English. She was not sure what she might do after that, perhaps travel, writing, teaching. Does want to have children though is not sure whether she wants to get married.
> *S.* expects to study law and psychology and then to work for a 'big firm'. She would not be married nor have children in 10 years' time. She might have children in her 30s but first wants to own property.
> *L.* expects to study media studies, journalism and then go into the news-paper industry, journalism. She eventually wants to get married and have several children.
>
> *(Arnot, David & Weiner, 1996: 139)*

Such value changes, however, are unlikely on their own to account for the greater academic success of young women. They indicate a complex reshaping of the relationship between social class, gender and race. Once freed from social networks, from the certainties of collective and traditional identities, young people have to make their own way in the world and 'to put themselves at the centre of the plan', to take risks and to seize opportunities (Furlong & Cartmel, 1997). At the same time, these processes of individualization are mediated by the material conditions of their lives in what Roberts, Clark and Wallace (1994: 49) called 'structured individualization'. The continuities of class inequalities still remain (Chisholm & du Bois-Reymond, 1993; Furlong & Cartmel, 1997).

The ways in which change has worked its way into the lives of different groups of girls are explored here in relation to three distinctive patterns. The first of these, the rise of a female graduate elite, traces the raised educational achievement of predominantly upper-middle and middle-class girls, like Margaret Thatcher, attending girls' selective secondary schools in the independent and state sectors. Using accounts of what have been called 'typical girls' (Griffin, 1985), in the second section we consider how schoolgirls attending state secondary schools began to modify their values in relation to 'romance', marriage and dependency on men. The final section looks at recent evidence of new forms of autonomy and pragmatism among working-class and/or black girls and queries whether such responses have more to do with feminism or with the longer processes of individualization – or a combination perhaps of both.

The female graduate elite

One of the transformations in post-war British society was the growth of a 'female graduate elite'. The adaptability of selective girls' schools to new economic and social opportunities and the compromises reached with Victorian values on femininity in the twentieth century accounts to some extent for the consistently high levels of middle-class female academic performance up to the age of eighteen. The biggest increase in the intake of students who went to Oxford and Cambridge universities between the 1970s and the 1990s was found among girls from independent schools (McCrum, 1996). Such schools were affected not only by the increasing importance of qualifications as a means of gaining access to elite occupations, but also, we want to argue, by liberal feminist ideas, particularly in relation to equal opportunities in high-status, professional occupations.

To some extent their story is one of exploiting the meritocratic ethos of competitive elite education – a story that has remained largely invisible to social commentators and feminist and critical researchers (with notable exceptions: Lambart, 1975; Delamont, 1989; Roker, 1993), perhaps because of feminism's main concern with pursuing egalitarianism and eliminating the socially divisive effects of selective schools.

Delamont (1989) argues, somewhat controversially, that during the years of social democratic reform girls' grammar and public schools represented the 'only feminist sector' in the UK. Such schools educated the daughters of the upper and upper-middle classes, who 'have been the most influential group in rearing and marrying men who are the most successful products of the British educational system' (Delamont, 1989: 5). Educational equality for upper- and upper-middle class women meant their gaining access to the same quality of selective education as that achieved by the sons of the owners of capital and entrepreneurs, top managers in large bureaucracies and members of the elite professions (Heath, 1981). Not only did such schools provide girls with opportunities for higher education, but it was also mainly these schools which kept up the supply of female students taking science and mathematics from the 1950s to the 1980s, at a time when the system of co-educational state schools had failed to promote science for girls (Delamont, 1989).

Indeed, behind such 'successes' lies a long invisible war waged against conventional elite values so as to turn the daughters of the gentry into members of the elite professions in their own right. As we saw in Chapter 3, the Victorian legacy promoted a world which separated men and women into different spheres, with women located in the home and denied an autonomous existence. Educating elite women challenged the distinction that had been made between masculinity and femininity, since, as we have seen, the former was associated with public work, strength and superiority and the latter with the home, domesticity, virginity and sexual fidelity (Delamont, 1989).

The rise of the new middle classes and the opening up of professional training has been exploited by girls. Many more upper-middle class girls have used academic credentialism to find their way into the same social class category ('service class') as their professional fathers (Savage & Egerton, 1997). However, this strategy was not always encouraged. In the early post-war period there was an 'uneasy relationship' between femininity and academic success. In Judith Okely's private boarding school in the 1950s, marriage was still the ultimate vocation for a girl, and good marriages were essential. 'Our privileges were at the mercy of men' (Okely, 1978: 121). Marriage at that time offered the only chance to keep a 'financial hold' in the class system, dependent upon the exclusivity of accent and manners (1978: 121).

In comparison, some schools, such as that attended by Mary Evans (1991), offered new freedoms for girls to develop their academic ambitions and their desires for independent lives and careers alongside preparation for their future roles of wife and mother. Evans vividly describes the various compromises that were reached in her 1950s grammar school education. Successful girls were told that they could aspire to become the 'androgynous middle class person who is successful in a world that is apparently gender blind' (Evans, 1991: 23) and also to 'defer to and respect the authority of men'. The ideology of achievement presented girls with academic aspirations which involved imitating and encouraging masculine and masculinist habits of intellectual self-assertion and rational thinking (1991: 20).

> The world of the traditional grammar school provided an apparently perfectly coherent and congruent training ground for the managers – and their wives – of the new Elizabethan world.
>
> *(Evans, 1991: 40)*

Moreover, in the late 1970s many of the leading independent (public) schools for boys were moving towards coeducation, at the same time as male colleges in Oxford and Cambridge started admitting female students (McCrum, 1996). The incentives for such a transition, while being presented as progressive, could well have been pragmatic (Walford, 1986). Research suggests that young women found their second-class status reinforced in the strongly institutionalized masculine culture of boys' schools. Elite girls often provided the pool of art and humanities students at the age of eighteen, to make up the number and to complement the dominance of boys taking sciences (Walford, 1986). Nevertheless, in this way some young women were able to gain access to elite male educational institutions and to pursue academic success in mixed-sex settings. Elite girls' schools, in response, needed to ensure their place in the school market by pushing for exceptionally high levels of academic performance, especially in the sciences.

Since there have been few studies of such girls' schools in Britain, it is difficult to ascertain the extent to which feminist ideology affected pupils or teachers. Evans recalls how the twofold aim of trying 'to find a man' and of acquiring learning were exposed as unworkable. At the same time, sociologists in the UK and also in other countries such as Australia noted that the fusion of feminist ideas, changing patterns of women's employment and the new availability of contraceptives encouraged elite young women to escape the domestic sphere and to aim for equivalent high-status occupations to those of men (Connell, Ashenden, Kessler & Dowsett, 1982).

The threat of female advancement for the patriarchal order was contained, however, not least by business managers in commerce and industry, who steered women away from powerful positions in the control of finance, the economy and politics (Connell et al., 1982) and also by channelling upper-middle class girls into the caring 'semi-professions' of teaching, nursing, and social work. It was fortunate and driven individuals who won themselves places in other elite occupations (e.g., law and medicine). The breakthrough of women into such elite occupations, nevertheless, once achieved, had considerable impact (Hobsbawm, 1994: 317).

The tension between individualism (representing non-conformity to class values) and individual competition and achievement which exuded the class ethos (Evans, 1991) deeply affected the education of the post-war woman, who aspired, on the one hand, to high-level professional employment and, on the other hand, to achieve the modern manners and style of a lady. Kenway's more recent study of a highly selective ladies' school in Perth, Australia, showed how girls were encouraged to be a curious mixture of 'feminine but liberated': this meant they had to be 'clean cut', 'well groomed', 'frilly', beautiful', at the same time as being able 'to go out and get what they wanted'. Young women had the same levels of ambition for material success as young men of their social class but did not want to be seen as 'male' or masculine. Not surprisingly their relationship to feminism was cautious, and their awareness of the need to submit themselves to the 'male gaze' left them embarrassed rather than politicized (Kenway, 1990: 9).

Behind such meritocratic practices lay the active role which elite schools play in transforming cultural capital into economic capital (Bourdieu & Passeron, 1977). One of the key principles learnt by female pupils was the distinction between themselves and others. The schools themselves, through their entry procedures, organization and culture, were in the business of excluding 'others', such as the home and family, boys, the local community, urban culture, some ethnic groups and 'other' social classes (except those brought in through the scholarship route). A number of key markers (geographic, cultural, class) allowed pupils not just to differentiate themselves from other girls in other social classes, but also to define their own superiority.

In this context, although girls' individualism was and remained based upon a subversion of the patriarchal order, it was also associated with a series of damning comparisons with other girls, who are ascribed as non-ladylike, i.e., as 'lazy', 'dirty', 'having poor speech' or sexually promiscuous (Kenway, 1990; Okeley, 1978; Evans, 1991). Fine class distinctions based upon consumption patterns such as fashion and holidays were also used to differentiate cliques within elite schools. The girls in the ladies' school in Perth were seen as the 'boarding' or 'day' girls, the 'rejects' or 'the trendies' (Kenway, 1990: 141–6). Even in the late 1980s girls in independent schools were conscious of articulating a class identity and of using the concept of social class to inscribe their femininity. The language of class shaped the language of public schoolgirls (Frazer, 1988), and also their political understandings, which have been found to be right wing and highly individualistic (Furnham, 1982).

In the 1980s and 1990s, as we have seen, Conservative educational reforms, especially the production of school league tables and the celebration of individual achievement, encouraged greater competition between schools. As market competition affected both private and state schools, the need to sustain the reputation of schools became even more acute (Gewirtz, Ball & Bowe, 1995). Upper- and upper-middle class girls more recently have been driven, even more than in the past, by the ambitions of the school to retain its place within the hierarchy of educational establishments. At the same time the cultural, economic, social and emotional capital (Allatt, 1993) invested by families in the maintenance of their elite class position has begun to be used for daughters as well as sons. The new upper-middle classes clearly have had much to gain from their daughters' assumption of responsibility for the maintenance and development of their own class position.

Upper- and upper-middle class girls have thus become increasingly duty bound 'to succeed' along a predetermined, highly regulated set of academic and occupational choices. Upper-middle class girls in independent girls' schools may have more extensive careers education than their equivalents in the maintained sector, plan their careers earlier and specify the exact specialism within a profession than their equivalents in state schools (Roker, 1993). Domesticity as a goal may be viewed as a waste of the human and financial resources, but so too may be training for the lower status professions such as teaching and nursing. Such career planning from early secondary school onwards encouraged elite girls to head for the 'right' niche within a high-status profession, and offered protection from divergent or inappropriate choices. The greater 'degrees of freedom' from the constraints of gender and detachment from local labour markets that independent schoolgirls experienced has allowed them to be less influenced by gender stereotypes in choosing their higher education courses. Engineering, medicine, pure science, management have all been viewed as feasible and appropriate choices (Roker, 1993).

Yet, although seemingly liberated by wealth, a privileged education and high academic credentials, such girls can be trapped in 'an insular narcissistic ethic' (Kenway, 1990: 155) which paradoxically can also be associated with an underlying lack of self-worth and confidence. High levels of 'impression management' can hide the fear of failure and of letting the side down. One girl in Mann's (1996) study described feeling 'psychologically crowded' by high parental expectations of success. The upper-middle class girls Mann interviewed expressed this in a number of ways:

> 'Parents would not expect so much of men.'
> 'Give me more breathing space.'
> 'Not always expect me to get straight 'A's.'
> 'Stop comparing me with themselves or friends.'
> 'Stop putting so much pressure on me.'
>
> *(5.20)*

Middle-class women who were more able to develop their own careers expected their daughters to maintain both family domestic traditions and careers. As one young woman commented:

> All the women in my family have careers – thanks to Grandma. My mum says 'You're no good without that piece of paper' – the same message she got from her own mother. They have indirectly shown me what women can and should achieve.
>
> *(Mann, 1996: 5–19)*

However, these gains have not been without their problems, as Melody, Lucey and Walkderdine (1997) discovered in a recent study. They showed that middle-class girls cannot afford even to fantasize about the possibility of failure, or about achieving only 'ordinary' levels of attainment. Rather, these girls express acute fears in relation to the achievements of other clever members of the family (especially rival siblings) and of fears of letting others (not themselves) down.

In the 1970s, girls not wanting to alienate men by appearing too intelligent or successful were reported to have a 'fear of success' (Maccoby & Jacklin, 1974; Horner, 1972) which affected their approaches to education in the USA and Britain until well into the 1980s. By the late 1990s, however, evidence suggests that girls from elite schools aim for and achieve the highest educational levels both at school and university, whether or not this might alienate young men. University degrees have not only become more widely available and more essential for entry into new high-status occupations, but they have been perceived as useful in achieving 'good marriages' with men of similar social class. At the same time, consumerism and the development of youth cultures have emphasized alternative life styles to those traditionally promoted in the protected world of elite girls' schools.

Coeducation for the majority

The emergence of educational feminism in the 1970s was closely associated with a critique of coeducation (see Chapter 5). From the late 1960s the majority of female pupils in the state sector, unlike the girls in private and selective education, were educated in coeducational secondary schools, a process which developed without consideration of gender issues (Shaw, 1980). Delamont (1989) saw coeducation as both benefiting and betraying the cause of women's equality. Despite the expansion of education girls in mixed-sex schools had to confront daily not just a curriculum tipped towards domestic and 'female' arts-based subjects but also the presence of boys and the dominance of their masculinist culture. As we saw in Chapter 3, government policy from the 1940s viewed the futures of working-class girls differently from those of both their elite contemporaries and boys from the same background. Domesticity remained women's primary role, even though women increasingly worked in paid employment. Curricula offered in secondary modern schools, and later comprehensives, were focused around the provision of domestically oriented subjects or humanities, with a timetable and option choice system which prevented girls from broadening their education with 'male' science and technical crafts subjects (Deem, 1978). The patterns of subject choice were identified as strongly gendered in coeducational grammar and secondary modern schools (DES, 1975).

In the early 1980s the majority of pupils entering the humanities and domestic subjects at O-level (sixteen years) were girls, with only 1 per cent girls taking woodwork and metalwork O-levels, and only 3 and 4 per cent taking technical drawing and design and technology respectively in 1982. However, there was 100 per cent female take-up of needlework and 97 per cent take-up of cookery. This channelling of girls into so narrow a range of subjects was clearly one reason why the better performance of girls' in examinations at sixteen was not associated with success. Their education lacked the breadth and depth normally associated with 'good' schooling, and also precluded access to further and higher education. Feminist concerns about patterns of subject choice were expressed forcefully in the early 1980s, as described in Chapter 5.

However, at the time, girls seemed relatively untouched by the upsurge of feminism. For example, sexism was not part of the vocabulary of the London schoolgirls studied by Sharpe in the early 1970s, in that heterosexuality, marriage and motherhood were understood as inevitable facts of life (Sharpe, 1976). Similarly Griffin (1985) found few signs of feminism affecting her sample of urban seventeen- to twenty-one-year-olds; even girls who had stayed on to take A-levels expected to give up work on having children. Thus, it would seem that these girls had none of the economic privileges of upper-middle-class girls to 'hold off' marriage. Schoolgirls in coeducational secondary schools were reported to be sexist, using male 'sex talk' to label themselves and other girls as 'slags' or 'drags', 'virgins', 'one-man girls' and 'easy lays' (Lees, 1986; Shacklady Smith, 1978; Wilson, 1978). 'Success' was judged by schoolgirls according to the level of their sexual availability to boys and through negotiating their own sexual reputations. In Lees's view, the power imbalances and the dominance of boys on girls' lives played as great a part in shaping female academic careers and their adjustments to future life as that of social class inequality. The enduring nature of 'male in the head' patterns of sexuality and sexual behaviour has recently been well documented by Holland, Ramazanoglu, Sharpe & Thompson (1998).

Dependency on men appeared to be the main criterion in the early 1980s for white working-class girls in thinking about the labour market, the sexual market and the marriage market (Wallace, 1987). The high degree of sex segregation in the labour market, the pervasive sexual division of labour within the British family, and the lack of state-funded childcare had major repercussions on girls' long-term planning. It seemed an unavoidable and unalterable fact of life that child-rearing and childcare were to be women's responsibility. Without finance, the majority of girls would have little choice but to plan their way out of their predicament by ensuring marital and domestic support for their childrearing years.

The white young working-class women interviewed by McRobbie and Garber (1975) and McRobbie (1978) developed the alternative prospect of a romanticized future. Immersing themselves in the ideology of romance and glamour as an expression of female sexuality, they celebrated what they took to be their fate – marriage and motherhood – but in ways that repressed the domestic drudgery of the home and realistic appraisals of marriage. Marriage in this context was used both to confer status and as an opportunity to express individuality and sexuality.

Although there is no such thing as a 'typical girl' (Griffin, 1985), studies in the early 1980s offered an image of working class English girls 'inordinately preoccupied with romance' (Wallace, 1987), who cared little for educational success or secure long-term employment. This impression was reinforced by the statistics on higher education in England and Wales, which since the 1960s had shown working-class girls to be 'underachievers'. The Robbins Report (Committee on Higher Education, 1963) found that only 4 per cent of female graduates had fathers in skilled work and 5 per cent in semi-skilled and unskilled manual work. The Dearing Report (GB National Committee of Inquiry into Higher Education, 1997) confirmed this low level of participation, although other recent studies, suggest that there has been a considerable growth in black women students, particularly in new universities (Mirza, 1997; Morley & Walsh, 1996).

Revisiting school statistics, however, reveals that even in the 1970s more girls than boys achieved five or more O-levels or CSE grade 1 (Bristol Women's Studies Group, 1979) and fewer girls than boys left school with no qualifications (Arnot, 1986b). At the same time, paradoxically, schools encouraged girls to take up childcare and domestic science courses whilst discouraging them from exploring their sexuality by banning the wearing of make-up and jewellery. Resistance to such confused gender values united both pro- and anti-school groups of female pupils in challenging schools' containment of expressions of physical attractiveness (Meyen, 1980).

Like Willis's 'lads' (Willis, 1977), who celebrated an exaggerated model of masculine culture as a form of class cultural resistance to middle-class values, McRobbie's white working-class girls resisted schooling by developing a 're-markable if complex homogeneity' that celebrated a 'cult of femininity'. The repertoire of responses was typified by an 'ultimate if not wholesale endorse-ment of the traditional female role and of femininity, simply because to these girls these seemed to be perfectly "natural"' (McRobbie, 1978: 97). Later studies of female adolescents found that, even though some sixth-formers planned to study traditional male subjects at university (e.g., medicine, physics, economics), there was little evidence of a shift towards new forms of work, whether in traditionally male occupations or new female jobs in the service sector (Griffin, 1985). Even in the mid-1980s, when schools started to make a wider range of subjects available to all pupils, the majority of girls at sixteen remained unlikely to take up so-called boys' subjects. White working-class girls strongly identified with female work. Men's jobs were seen as hard, manual, with dirty, noisy work conditions and long hours and overtime; women employed in such occupations were likely to be seen as tokenistic, lonely, and harassed. A good job was more important for girls than qualifica-tions, and often girls stayed on after sixteen as they were not prepared to take what they saw as 'shit jobs' (Griffin, 1985: 98). Curricular reforms appeared not to disrupt this transition from school into work. Griffin concluded that, despite rising unemployment, femininity for most girls was still more linked to boyfriends, marriage and motherhood than the wage packet (1985: 99).

Black female autonomy and upward mobility

Brown's (1987) description of 'getting on and getting out' is fittingly applied to the instrumental approach of African-Caribbean and some Asian girls in the UK. Asian girls were noticeably the highest achieving among the working-class sample in a study conducted in 1985, doing well in comparison with their white counterparts (except among professional class families) (Drew & Gray, 1990). This was despite the stereotypical image of such girls, particularly

Muslim girls, as generally oppressed by their family, especially regarding 'arranged marriages' (Brah & Minhas, 1985). These data do not tell us about the differences between different groups from the Indian subcontinent, e.g., from Pakistan, Bangladesh and India. However, it is clear that the wish for better life chances and a delay in marriage led some Asian girls to use education and qualifications as a means of personal liberation.

Working-class African-Caribbean girls in the 1990s also appeared to perform better than their brothers (but not in the case of professional and intermediate classes) (Drew & Gray, 1990). Since the 1980s a number of research studies (Eggleston, Dunn, Anjali & Wright, 1986; Sillitoe & Meltzer, 1985) demonstrated that young black women obtained more qualifications than other groups, often in FE colleges rather than schools. However, as Mirza (1992) pointed out, black female students' academic success was not used to gain 'insights into the understanding of black educational issues and little attention was given to the fact that even when African-Caribbean girls chose non-traditional courses, their career routes were still highly stereotypical'. Their success was not used as a yardstick for the achievement either of white female pupils or of other ethnic minority/black students. Nor was attention paid to the fact that, in reality, after taking examinations at sixteen, many young black women faced major forms of sexual and racial discrimination and were, as Wallace (1987) put it, 'downwardly mobile'.

Different accounts of the culture of African-Caribbean families point to important triggers for their daughters' resistance to conventional gender values, in particular to becoming dependent on men. The group of African-Caribbean schoolgirls studied by Fuller (1980, 1983) in a multiracial comprehensive in Brent, London, claimed to be close to their mothers, but expressed resentment at the sexism of black men and the ways in which the sexual division of labour worked within the families. Thus girls were expected to do all the domestic work and at the same time boys ridiculed girls' efforts at school. African-Caribbean girls' response to such discriminatory practices, Fuller argued, was strategic – it involved the decision not to withdraw from school. They developed an instrumental approach to education, in order to gain more control over their personal lives as well as their employment prospects. If they were able to get a 'proper job', they would be able to look after themselves, help improve the quality of the black community, and also challenge racism in employment.

Similarly the Black Sisters, who were a group of Asian/African-Caribbean girls in a sixth-form college, developed educational strategies for institutional survival, a form of what could be called 'resistance within accommodation' (Mac an Ghaill, 1988). They rejected what they saw as racist curricula and stereotyping in school and teachers' assumptions that they would seek manual working-class jobs and traditional female work such as childcare and office studies, or, if they were Asian, have early arranged marriages on leaving school. Although the school saw them as 'diffident and devious', the young women used the school system to help them cope with the realities of what they saw as increasing competition for scarce jobs in the local economy. Qualifications, they believed, would provide them with a valued means of exchange and opportunity to escape conventional forms of black female work:

> Ye can't get anywhere without qualifications. We have to be better than the whites if we want to get away from the usual cleaning jobs an' shop work we're offered. I sometimes think that they built the hospitals, railways an' all that to keep us working (Joanne).

> *(Mac an Ghaill, 1988: 32)*

The Black Sisters' response, compared with that of their black male peers in the same college, perhaps resulted from their greater aspirations and relative invisibility to teachers. They reported being less likely than boys to be 'picked on'. The Black Sisters also seemed less likely to internalize an image of themselves as underachievers, less influenced by peer groups and to have greater freedom of choice in responses to school. Black women have to be strong, they argued, just to survive. Academic success meant that black girls could argue for greater equality with their brothers and could also establish independence from their homes and its unfair distribution of housework.

Gaining access, for example, to the caring professions such as nursing and social work was one means of securing occupational mobility for working-class black mothers and daughters (Bhavnani, 1994). Such jobs, it was believed, would also allow them to move up and out of their mothers' low-status factory or office work, and provide financial benefits and standing for black women and their families.

Mirza (1992) suggests that the freedom which African-Caribbean families offered girls over choice of education and jobs helped these young women to use the educational system as a means of social mobility away from their class and racialized positions. Their meritocratic orientations were similar to the sort of individual determination and perseverance found among white middle-class girls described in the section above. Their expressed desire for upward social mobility was to be achieved by the development of 'strategic careers' that challenged gender stratification in pragmatic and rational ways (Mirza, 1992).

The high proportion of African-Caribbean schoolgirls who opted for non-traditional courses such as plumbing, electronics and carpentry provides evidence of their greater gender freedom compared with white working-class girls. African-Caribbean girls appeared to have 'relative autonomy' to try out any route, to separate themselves from male dependence and to achieve economic independence. Femininity as a concept was not tied to dominant 'Eurocentric attitudes about gender oppositions' (Mirza, 1992: 159) nor was account taken of female marginality, economic dependence on men or female responsibility for childcare. 'Getting on' for such girls meant 'staying on', with many remaining in further and higher education and aspiring to high-status professions.

Similar perspectives on gender equality and upward social mobility have also been found among other girls where the conventional values of hetero-sexual femininity, marriage and motherhood might have been thought to be particularly strong. In 1996 Basit reported high aspirations among a sample of British Asian Muslim girls (fifteen- to sixteen-year-olds), who did not want to be 'just a housewife'. Thus, although many of their fathers were unemployed or in working-class occupations, they were supported in their wish to become lawyers, doctors, accountants and pharmacists, or to start their own business. Debnath's study of young Bangladeshi women in the East End of London also reported high aspirations for social mobility, even if it meant having to leave the community (Debnath, 1999). Similarly Haw (1998) found that the Muslim girls in state and private Muslim schools attempted to resolve the contradictions between being Muslim, academically able and highly aspiring. These studies suggest that girls in different Asian communities were encouraged to move away from manual patterns of female employment and to aim for careers and incomes in their own right in unam-biguously middle-class occupations (Bhavnani, 1991).

Unromantic realism and the working-class girl

On re-reading the accounts of working-class girls' lives from the 1970s to the 1990s, the 'moment of critique' of romance and traditional forms of femin-inity appears to have happened in the home rather than in the school. By the end of the 1970s Wallace (1987) found signs of what she termed 'unroman-tic realism' – an unromantic understanding of the relationship between men and women and women's likely fate. Girls, she observed, were beginning to distance themselves from centuries of emotional and financial dependency on men. They were observed challenging the outmoded Victorian values of other family members about women's place and work in the home.

Criticisms of the injustice of the sexual domestic division of labour were directly relevant to the experiences of girls, especially since, as study after study indicated, the main burden of domestic work fell on girls living at home – a burden which their middle-class sisters, especially those in board-ing school, were less likely to bear. Criticisms focused on their responsibil-ities to their families, which took most of their time and energy and imprisoned them in traditional gender roles. Domestic work, whether doing household chores, educating siblings or caring for the sick, was more than a set of tasks: it symbolized unequal and unjust male–female relations.

When asked, schoolgirls reiterated the statement 'I'm not a woman's libber but . . .' (Griffin, 1989). Despite negative connotations of being a feminist, not least because of feminists' perceived hostility to men and potential unattractiveness (Wilkinson, 1994; Wilkinson & Mulgan, 1995), the impact that feminism had on the role, status and equal opportunities in employment of women were 'resoundingly' admitted by the Ealing schoolgirls revisited by Sharpe in the 1990s.

Research on the differences between successive generations of predominantly working-class girls in their mid-teens in the UK, Canada and the United States captures this shift. The inevitability of domestic drudgery and women's subordination as wives and mothers appears no longer to be tolerated (McLaren, 1996). Although many young women still put employment second to domestic responsibility and were not prepared to contemplate non-parental childcare, not all young women in the Canadian study assumed they would be mothers; they expected to become mothers only if the conditions for childcare were right (McLaren, 1996: 293). The possible unwillingness of men to share parenting and the realities of interrupting their careers to bear and care for children had begun to shape young women's views (McLaren & Vanderbijl, 1998).

In a similar study conducted in the United States, it was found that working-class girls were not prepared to accept the 'double bind' of responsibility for work and family (Weis, 1990) but wished rather to set the conditions, the parameters, of 'future negotiations in the private sphere'; they wanted power to 'negotiate conditions of family life'. Individualistic solutions were to involve getting jobs outside the community, not marrying until they were settled in a career, and not allowing husbands to take control of their wives' personal lives.

In terms of sexual relations, young women increasingly appear to see marriage as only one option and cohabitation as an acceptable alternative. Marriage and husbands appear to have 'faded in priority' (Sharpe, 1994: 115). Some young women seem to be attracted to new models of family life, such as equal or co-parenting, contingency planning or role reversal (McLaren, 1996).

Sharpe showed that by the 1990s girls found it unthinkable to give up work automatically after marriage, or indeed after children. Mothers' occupations, particularly in what were perceived as limiting and 'boring' office work as secretaries, were not of interest, since girls wanted more interesting job content and a higher level of satisfaction. Nevertheless, as Sharpe commented: 'Twenty years later girls are less hampered by fears of maternal deprivation but guilt can still be provoked and nursery provision remains sadly lacking' (Sharpe, 1994: 220).

The reasons for these value shifts are complex and, as Weis (1990) argues for the USA, may be explained in several ways. They may be related first, on account of liberal cultural influences, to greater freedom from the conventions of sexual morality associated with marriage. At the same time young women no longer seem satisfied with being 'just' a housewife and mother. The devaluing of domestic work in society, the celebration of a vocational work ethic and the feminist challenge to domestic work as subordinating women, all may well have been influential. The development of a more realistic appraisal of male–female relations was also a reflection of girls' own perceptions of how women's lives had changed. In addition, their own mothers' experiences in trying to return to work after having children may have been significant influences. Sharpe found that:

> The ways girls see themselves and their lives have altered with the social and economic change of the intervening twenty years, reflecting changes in the structure and stability and a rise in the status of women – at least in women's eyes.
>
> *(Sharpe, 1994: 292)*

The majority of girls in Sharpe's second study rejected conventional views of gender differences and male dominance that had been accepted in the first study, having a greater sense of women's equal importance, their individuality and independence. More schoolgirls preferred being a girl than twenty years earlier. Racial differences in terms of valuing qualifications and staying on at school were less evident, as white working-class girls seemed to have more in common with 'West Indian' and Asian girls than previously.

Educational feminism may have touched girls' lives in ways that were not at all obvious from the outset. By ignoring the constraints on most women, teachers may well have played their part in encouraging girls, at least while at school, to think more imaginatively about their futures. Schools provided a relatively autonomous space, 'a safe haven', for girls away from the vicissitudes of family life and the labour market – a space in which young women could explore their gender identity, especially if it became the explicit topic of education. Young white women who had previously used conventional gender values as responses to their class and racialized positions within modern society may well have found such values challenged by teachers committed to providing equal opportunities in education. Such teachers had, for example, actively challenged what McRobbie called the 'class instinct' or 'the cult of femininity' of many white working-class girls.

Even though few girls self-identified with feminist issues or feminism as a political identity, the new entrepreneurial culture and the 'pull' of the economy under the New Right, and latterly New Labour, meant that such challenges to women's traditional roles could be sustained. Weis (1990) argues that the new working-class girl may well have been attracted to a concept of a 'new traditional woman', who sustains both modern and conservative values that are grounded in family life and expectations about stability as well as female employment. The shifts which we have identified, therefore, may have been associated not only with egalitarian movements of the 1970s and 1980s but also with the 'performance' ethic of schooling – or, as Mann (1996) discovered, the educational support of their mothers, who have themselves engaged with the project of social mobility and the challenge to conventional gender values.

Although there is evidence that girls are undergoing a sea-change in values, especially in relation to their own autonomy and dependency on men, it would be a mistake to generalize too far. Working-class girls have continued to be frustrated at school and to look forward to leaving as soon as possible. Just as many young women as young men make up the 10 per cent of young people who become what has been called the 'zero sum' generation – those who leave schools with no qualifications, have no home or job, and who cannot easily get back into society (Rees, Williamson & Istance, 1996). A significant number of girls subscribe to the conventional pattern of leaving school at sixteen, followed by local employment, steady boyfriend, marriage, settling down and having a family.

Any changing gender values have necessarily to address the sex-divided realities of the labour market. Providing equal opportunities in school of itself cannot change occupational choice patterns (Arnot, David & Weiner, 1996). The curious contradiction emerges of young women, no longer unaware of sex segregation and the lack of female bargaining power, still choosing to work as adults within rather than outside the 'realm of women's work' (Sharpe, 1994; Pilcher, Delamont, Powell, Rees & Read, 1989). The pressures on girls to resolve the family–work conflict by opting for security and by not resisting family conventions remain powerful. Consequently girls continue to choose traditionally feminine training routes and occupations, still wanting 'people jobs' and avoiding work contexts that might cause extra stress.

A range of circumstances has affected the extent to which working-class girls are able to upgrade their educational qualifications in line with those of their middle-class counterparts. Lack of training places for women has encouraged conservatism among working-class girls, who have tended to choose stereotypically feminine courses. Despite the higher levels of female performance in examinations, durable patterns of female higher education remain, the most obvious being the avoidance by female students of science, technology, IT and mathematics courses and the careers associated with these male subjects (as we argued in Chapter 2). The influence of gender (as well as class and race) on further education is also still prevalent (Bates, 1993), with female training courses, which draw upon the domestic and caring skills learnt in the home, being used as 'domestic apprenticeships' (Skeggs, 1988; 1997). Choosing such courses may be by default rather than by intent. The effect, as Buswell argues, is a training in the experience of dependency, low pay and 'realistic' expectations of their futures (Buswell, 1992: 94).

In Bates's study, some young working-class women squared their desire for autonomy and 'self-actualization' with traditional and low-status work by ascribing to the concept of 'choice'. They reconstructed low-skilled, often 'dirty' or difficult occupations as 'tough female work', claiming that they were 'no bleeding whining Minnies' (1993: 28). They celebrated the harsh physical conditions that they had already experienced in caring for sick family members, dealing with violence in the family or community and the hard domestic work they did at home. The lesson which girls learn today is that their sought-after academic qualifications may not easily convert into well-paid and skilled employment. Many take circuitous routes to higher education, or choose to go into further education, with early motherhood in some cases resolving these conflicts of identities (Lucey & Walkerdine, 1996).

Reflections

The particular cluster of meritocratic programmes, feminist influences, individualization and government support for Victorian family values (reworked in the context of an increasingly diverse set of family structures) was never likely to have simple effects. In this chapter we have indicated, using studies of girls themselves, how such forces for change can be understood. Key to girls' experiences of such influences while at school and living in different communities are the resources which they can draw upon. For middle-class girls, the transition to adulthood lies within known parameters. For the aspiring working-class girl, the future can feel less secure. In some cases high-achieving schoolgirls from working-class backgrounds are provided with strong support by their families, as in the case of the girls in Mann's (1998) study, where working-class mothers provided a critical force supporting their daughters 'up and out'. Similarly, in Lucey and Walkerdine's longitudinal study (1996), girls reported the significant encouragement from their fathers. Whatever variations, the reconstruction of family gender values has been found to be an essential ingredient in the development of 'distinctive orientations' among schoolgirls to formal education, to employment and to personal life goals (Chisholm & du Bois-Reymond, 1993).

There are groups of schoolgirls who articulate different values, using the language of individual achievement and gender equality, as they work within the school system to gain qualifications. However, a significant proportion still retain conventional gender values with respect to marriage. For the majority, it is still likely to be the case that the qualifications they achieve in such large numbers merely establish girls' intellectual credentials; they do not necessarily create a shift or transition out of their class destinations (Chisholm & du Bois-Reymond, 1993).

As Weis (1990) in the USA argues, these female values and new identities may represent the incorporation of women into the project of the New Right and a realignment of working-class women with *laissez-faire* conservatism, which expects individual women to solve their own economic and social subordination. On the other hand, such new values may represent a challenge to neo-conservatism – the beginnings of a 'moment of critique' – in which women are able to identify themselves as a sex class both in and for itself. They may acknowledge being female over and above the restrictions of their class identity (Eisenstein, 1984).

Young women in the UK in various settings tried to redefine traditional Eurocentric or Victorian values of femininity and to uncouple femininity from dependency on men. In the past, the norm of heterosexuality and the assumption that women were to bear the burden of domestic family care acted as a major break on women's aspirations, employment and married lives. Feminism, rather than neo-conservatism, encouraged young women to break with the past and to use the category of woman as a means of creating new sexual and gender identities.

For some girls, structural constraints, such as racism, family cultures and community values, have also acted as a catalyst to their efforts to improve their lives. For example, obtaining qualifications has been one of the few ways available to overcome the discrimination faced by black women as workers (Bryan, Dadzie & Scafe, 1985).

The balance between educating girls for the labour market, the marriage market and the sexual market which underlay previous gender values had already begun to shift by the time the Conservative government began its moral crusade of a return to traditional family values. The unfairness of doing so much more domestic work than their brothers was already a focus of anger for many girls, and indicative of their raised consciousness about gender relations. By the 1980s, the prospect of being a 'leisured' housewife no longer looked, for some, like a reasonable return on their parents' and school investment in their talents. The prospects for these girls, who faced a life of domesticity and job choices made on the basis of linking jobs to childcare responsibilities, seemed increasingly unattractive, especially when female earnings as part-time workers were so low. Political awareness, economic investment and personal security were already themes found in many girls' voices.

Discussion of male dominance in relationships rather than dependency on men formed the agenda of girls in the 1990s, even if not often articulated directly. Young women were increasingly reluctant to commit themselves to marriage, seeing it as but one option out of many forms of partnership. Different models for linking child-bearing with employment became a viable choice, as were alternative life styles and sexualities. In this context, educational qualifications would not only be an investment, they would be an essential part of self-protection and survival in an increasingly insecure world.

In the next chapter we consider whether similar processes were at work in shaping boys' identities. One critical element in the shaping of the agenda for girls has been that of boys. To what extent, we ask, have boys also found ways of challenging the conventional paths prepared for them?

8

Schoolboys and Social Change

Gender relations in the public sphere and within the family were transformed, as we have seen, in ways which have direct significance for societal definitions of masculinity, even though the transformation of masculinity in schools was not a priority for educational feminists. At the same time changes in production patterns, the decline in traditional male roles in manufacturing and construction, and the withdrawal of conventional modes of transition from school to work (e.g., traditional apprenticeships) also altered boys' understanding of masculinity. The processes of individualization had an impact on boys as well as on girls, but had different outcomes. In this chapter we consider the evidence from research on schoolboys. To what extent have boys had to rethink what it means to be male, to consider ways of using the educational system to gain access to new opportunities, or adapt to new work and family forms?

The evidence we presented in Chapter 2 of boys' patterns of academic achievement indicates at the very least that male school performance is highly complex. Boys are well represented among the highest and the lowest achievers. Many interesting questions have been raised by examination statistics, not least why boys have failed to raise their performance levels over the last decade at the same, or an equivalent, rate to girls. Why is it that boys have different patterns of educational outcomes to girls and why do proportionately fewer obtain academic qualifications at sixteen and eighteen? Yet at the same time we see the domination of professional occupations by men.

We show in this chapter how some of the changes in post-war society we identified led to educational success for some groups of boys, the possibility of adaptation for others and the marginalization of a substantial minority. Young men have been expected to adapt to an increasingly unstable set of circumstances in the work sphere, threatening the conventional basis both of masculinity and its associated ideal of the male as breadwinner. Such instability has been deepened, we suggest, not by the work of schools challenging and transforming masculinity, but rather by their failure to do so. While schools challenged girls to adapt to new circumstances, young men were not offered similar possibilities to adapt to social and economic change, even though the restructuring of the workplace and the family called for men with modern and more flexible approaches to their role in society. New sets of values, aspirations and skills were being asked of men as workers, husbands and fathers. The failure in the last two decades of government, society and schools to address the prevailing forms of, and ideas about, masculinity, particularly in relation to changing work identities and challenges to the patriarchal dominance of the male breadwinner, has had negative repercussions for boys.

In the first two sections of this chapter we explore the continuities with the past in terms of boys' romanticization of domesticity and their patterns of educational inequality. Later sections consider, in similar fashion to Chapter 7 on schoolgirls, how schoolboys from different social backgrounds understood social pressures and how they responded in terms of redefining masculinity. We review research on 'gentry' masculinity, middle-class masculinities and the 'new boys', and discuss how sexuality has been used as a form of social resistance to class and race inequalities. The final section looks at a central issue in the masculine experience of schooling, but one which has not in our view been sufficiently addressed in relation to inequalities of male and female performance – that of school violence.

The romanticization of domesticity

One indicator of how far young men have adapted to changes in gender relations in society is the extent to which they have taken up the principles of equal opportunities – that is, the notion that women have an equal right to work and to be respected as individuals in the family context. Wilkinson and Mulgan (1995) suggested that many more of the younger generation of men between the ages of eighteen and thirty-four, compared with older men, are in tune with the values of women in their age group. It is important however, they argue, not to overstate this convergence of interests between young men and women (Wilkinson & Mulgan, 1995: 36).

The greatest convergence between young men and women is among those who have completed some form of higher education and who seem to be attracted to similar progressive values in relation to gender and to employment, in particular. Alongside the majority of men who have 'superficially liberal values', there is evidence also of a backlash against feminism. Wilkinson and Mulgan identified a group of young men who asserted that the balance of equality legislation has tipped towards favouring women and discriminating against 'the white male'. Male unemployment was blamed in particular on women's increased labour-market involvement.

Data collected on the younger age group (fifteen- to seventeen-year-olds) suggested that, compared to young women of similar age, male adolescents are more pessimistic and introverted. They seem particularly dismissive of traditional forms of authority and are more attracted to excitement – perhaps even to crime – 'to bolster their fragile sense of masculinity'. Wilkinson and Mulgan suggest that their lack of a confident masculinity has made young men less ambitious, less willing to continue with their education and more likely to have lower self-esteem. (1995: 37). They draw attention to suicide rates for boys, which have doubled in the past decade, from 1 in 20,000 of fifteen- to twenty-four-year-olds in 1979 to 1 in 10,000 in 1989. Male pessimism, they suggest, is perhaps the result of the 'vicious spiral of male unemployment and low aspirations'.

The male as breadwinner

One of the key differences between young men and women today is not agreement with the principle of women's right to work, but rather support for Victorian models of the family, with men as breadwinners and women primarily responsible for child-rearing. Banks et al. (1992) found that most boys still attributed different roles to women, even though approximately half appeared to support equal opportunities and to have absorbed feminist arguments. These findings are echoed in many of the major studies of young people's attitudes in the UK. Furnham and Gunter (1989) found that, although boys endorsed equal opportunities for the workplace, even implying that women have as much to offer as men in the occupational sphere (70 per cent of boys aged ten to seventeen agreed with this), just under half (47 per cent) asserted that women should worry less about being equal with men and more about being good wives and mothers. Hence, 46 per cent of boys agreed with the statement that a woman's place is in the home looking after her family, in comparison with 74 per cent of girls, who indicated their opposition to this statement.

A similar gap between young male and female attitudes towards women's place in society was also evident in more recent findings from *Young People's Social Attitudes* (Roberts & Sachdev, 1996), a survey of 580 young people between twelve and nineteen years of age. Nearly 90 per cent of young women disagreed that it was a woman's job to look after the family and the home, while only 70 per cent of boys stated their opposition to this statement. At the core of this difference are assumptions about who should take responsibility for housework and childcare.

Despite the substantial increase in women's employment in post-war society, a number of studies have shown that the division of responsibility for housework in British families appears to have changed little (Furnham & Gunter, 1989; Oakley 1996; Wilkinson & Mulgan, 1995). Many men have not taken up new roles at home, and women are still held responsible overall for the housework. Women's move out of the home has not been matched by men sharing domestic responsibilities. Indeed, young men are reported to be less keen than young women to share shopping, to do the washing and ironing, or to acknowledge that women are able to carry out household repairs (Oakley, 1996). A significant minority of young men between eighteen and thirty-four, having been socialized to take up dominant male values, become 'social resisters and survivors' (Wilkinson & Mulgan, 1995). They still cling onto old identities attached to the male role of breadwinner and to the traditional division of labour which stresses male superiority.

In a set of interviews conducted in 1993 with a hundred girls and thirty boys in four comprehensive schools in London, Lees found that the 'unromantic realism' towards marriage of working-class girls described in the last chapter was not matched by boys from similar backgrounds. If anything boys wished to retain the role of male breadwinner, despite increasing evidence of male unemployment, rising female employment and girls' expectations of more equal partnerships. Girls discussed marriage as a domestic burden and boys as either 'letting you down' or 'not a good catch'. Most of the boys in the sample spoke of their desire to marry, and to find the equivalent of their mothers to cook and care for them. As Rajam, a Bangladeshi boy, declared: 'I don't want a girl who will leave you with the washing' (Lees, 1998). This model of a girlfriend resonates with the view expressed by one of Willis's lads in 1977:

> I've got the right bird. I've been goin' with her for eighteen months now. Her's as good as gold . . . She's fucking done well, she's clean. She loves doing fucking housework. Trousers I brought yesterday, I took 'em up last night, and her turned 'em up for me . . . She's as good as gold and I wanna get married as soon as I can.
>
> *(Willis, 1977: 44–5)*

Some African-Caribbean and white young men in Lees's recent study were more uncertain about taking this stance because of the instability of marriage and possibility of divorce, and because they were less concerned with keeping women subservient. The attachment to traditional family life symbolizes masculinity – linking male sexuality, male work identities and family responsibilities. The main reason given by men and boys for studying and working has been to support a family. The main reason given by men and boys for women having a conventional domestic role has been to support conventional versions of masculinity.

In Harland's (1997) study of young unemployed men in Belfast, the positive valuing of family life has been particularly important in times of stress. Achieving conventional manhood in the context of violence and the indignities of unemployment is critical to survival. One young man, commenting on the possibility of having a working wife, exclaimed: 'If my wife was looking after me, I'd feel crap' (Harland, 1997: 73).

> A man's gotta look after himself and his wife and he's to take care of them cause its his job to do that; if ya don't do that, then everyone thinks yer not a good man.
>
> *(Harland, 1997: 14)*

> It's up to the man of the house to provide; he's the one who has to do it – like my da says I've gotta get a job and bring in money to the house when I get married and all, cause he thinks it's dead important for a man to look after his family and I think that's right, so I do.
>
> *(ibid., 1997: 15)*

The restructuring of economic opportunities which were described in Part 2 above presents a serious challenge to the traditional male motivation to gain qualifications or jobs, and indeed to assume the male role in society. Economic and social change have together produced an identity crisis for men (Campbell, 1993), but so too has family change. Any understanding of a 'crisis in masculinity' must address such challenges to the role of male breadwinner and its implication for heterosexual masculinity.

While feminists and gay liberation groups have challenged dominant forms of masculinity, new alternative masculinities have also been explored by various men's groups and other agencies, who often adopt 'therapeutic' approaches (Kenway, 1995). However, research on youth cultures does not suggest that new concepts of fatherhood and family partnering are being addressed by more than a relatively small minority. On the whole, evidence of boys' greater reliance on parents (the 'perpetual adolescence' described by Wallace, 1987) and on women to maintain family life suggests the greater *dependency* of men rather than their independence.

Such attitudinal research suggests that young men have not become more attached to so-called feminine, caring values; rather they continue to eschew the feminine. Oakley found in her recent analysis of boys' and girls' social attitudes that:

> On many questions the young men's answers were significantly different from the young women's. It seems, then, that the social processes embedded in the cultural assignation to masculine or feminine gender still have a great deal of power to influence experiences, values, perceptions and ambitions.
>
> *(Oakley, 1996: 39)*

The promotion of gender differences therefore still appears to be a salient factor in shaping the aspirations of young men and their transitions to adulthood in ways that do not synchronize with those of young women.

Male patterns of educational inequality

The second factor which has influenced boys' educational experiences is that of social class inequality. Much has been written on the social and educational inequalities found among boys (e.g., Halsey, Heath & Ridge, 1980) and the possibility of boys (rather than girls) rising above their fathers' occupations, using educational credentials as the means of ensuring their advance. Class inequalities have been the major factor restricting the majority of boys from achieving access to male elite professions and managerial and political positions of power, as historically only a small elite of male school leavers (under 15 per cent until the late 1980s) went to university and acquired degrees.

Post-war society was well informed about the effects of male social class inequalities and their enduring character. From the Robbins Report (1963) to the more recent Dearing Report (1997), it has been clear that boys from professional middle-class families have a far greater chance of higher education, especially if they attend private (viz. independent and selective) schools. Other data, such as that collected by various LEAs, and the Youth Cohort Study (Drew & Gray, 1990) revealed the differences between male and female achievement in each social class and demonstrated that white boys in each social class were 'outperformed' by girls in GCSE examinations (a pattern not found among other ethnic groups). The higher achievement of girls from professional backgrounds compared to boys from the same background was even more noticeable in the statistics collected for Scotland by Furlong and Cartmel (1997). Clearly visible in figure 8.1 also is the relatively stable pattern over the last ten years of the low achievement level of working-class youth.

The relationship between gender, ethnicity and social class has been shown to be complicated. Data collected from Drew and Gray (1990) show Asian and African-Caribbean boys in professional and intermediate social classes achieving higher examination scores than girls from equivalent class and ethnic backgrounds (the reverse is true of white school leavers). The particular configuration of male and female working-class educational achievement is affected by local labour markets, as well as cultural and institutional practices and behaviours of individual schools (Mac an Ghaill, 1994). In some localities, those leaving school with the least qualifications are male and female working-class pupils; in other localities African-Caribbean boys or white working-class boys are the largest 'underachieving' group. As Gillborn and Gipps (1996) demonstrated, generalizations across localities are not productive, especially if they fail to take account of the particular class and ethnic distribution of population.

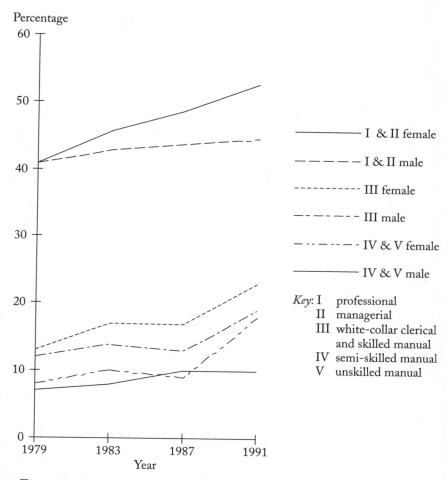

Figure 8.1 *Young people in highest attainment band, by class and gender*
Source: Furlong & Cartmel, 1997: 21, from the Scottish Young People's Surveys.

While some boys have redefined masculinity to respond to the pressures of individualization, competition and the new vocationalism, others have regressed into increased insecurity, anxiety and versions of 'hyper-masculinity' – or, to use common parlance, 'boys behaving badly'. We ask in the next sections of this chapter whether there are any 'new boys' to be found in schools today. We look at the responses of distinct groups of boys – the male elite, the middle-class and the white and black working-class 'lads' and 're-sisters' – to see how they have coped with the new school cultures, described in chapters 5 and 6, and the restructuring of male public worlds.

Gentry masculinity and the expert

In the nineteenth century there was much discussion about the relation-ship between 'gentlemen' and 'players', the former representing the landed aristocracy and 'blooded' elite and the latter, new money or the 'nouveau riche'. The compromise settlement was the muscular Christian masculinity of Matthew Arnold. By the twentieth century, however, as Connell describes, there was a 'displacement, splitting and remaking of gentry masculinity' (Connell, 1997: 611).

> Political revolution, industrialisation, and the growth of bureaucratic state apparatuses saw the displacement of gentry masculinity by more calculative, rational and regulated masculinities. The bureaucrat and the business men were produced as social types. The economic base of the landed gentry declined and with it the orientation of kinship and honor.
>
> *(ibid.)*

Gentry masculinity had been strongly tied to lineage and kin networks and to codes of family and personal honour. This hegemonic masculinity provided officers for the army and navy and recruits to government posts and the judiciary. However, in the twentieth century this changed:

> The enormous growth of school and university systems . . . the multiplying number of 'professional' occupations with claims to specialised expertise, the increasing political significance of technology and the growth of information industries are aspects of a large scale change in culture and production systems that has seen a further splitting of nineteenth century hegemonic masculinity.
>
> *(Connell, 1997: 612)*

Connell argues that a masculinity organized around *dominance* was incom-patible with masculinity organized around *expertise* or technical knowledge. Management elites therefore split off from the older professions, with power increasingly based in new and varied professional groupings. Tensions in creating upper-middle-class models of masculinity revealed themselves in terms of the type of character-building to be provided. The concept of man-hood described by a gentleman (involving personal endurance, unquestioned devotion to duty, education for leadership, ability to administer justice, a ser-vice ethic, etc.) did not necessarily prioritize intellectual pursuits. Rather it encouraged chauvinism, conservatism, and an unquestioning acceptance of hierarchy and privilege (Tolson, 1977: 35).

'Character-building' for gentry masculinity was organized institutionally through school practices involving hierarchy, competition, the removal of emotion, and institutionalized violence (Chandos, 1984). Schools became 'total' institutions where boys learnt the rules and rites of manhood to do with, for example, the treatment of women as subordinate, male sexuality, emotional life, and male camaraderie. The education provided was less about academic success and more about the building of a class culture for the protection of class interests:

> The 'English Gentleman' remains, morally if not politically, at the summit of civilisation. His manners, his sense of 'fairness', his devotion to 'duty' and 'service' together make up a socially legitimate character-type.
>
> *(Tolson, 1977: 39)*

Although the heyday of the classical public school education has passed, many elements of its gentlemanly ideal survive. Competitiveness, personal ambition, social responsibility and emotional restraint have continued as dominant masculine values of the high-status professions, although latterly selection has been more likely on the basis of competition and achievement than by ascribed right (1977: 39). Increasingly even this 'hierarchy of personal achievement' (1997: 87) has been threatened by competition from other sources of status (e.g., money), leading to a crisis in confidence over hegemonic notions of masculinity.

Post-war reconstruction of British society, according to Tolson, in part 'stripped away the idealistic cloak surrounding middle-class work', revealing for the first time 'its naked insecurity' (Tolson, 1997: 86). The association of masculinity with imperialism and the colonial era (Mangan, 1981, 1986) rendered it vulnerable as Britain's international economic power withered away, destroying the credibility of colonial concepts of duty and self-discipline. High levels of motivation and of work, rather than recourse to class-specific ideas about leadership or service, were required to achieve high social status.

This required a transformation of male elite education in line with the demands of a new form of meritocratic and technological society, as illustrated in Geoffrey Walford's (1986) case-studies of contemporary life in two public schools. The transformation of boys' public schools, like that of girls' independent schools discussed in the last chapter, indicated their ability to change with the times in order to retain class privilege. Change became a mechanism of class reproduction, propelling students towards new opportunities and new positions in society and levering them up new ladders of credentialism into the professions.

Walford's case-studies suggest the breaking down of the concept of the 'total' institution, with pupils now having access to modern media influences and parental values (1986: 63). Public schoolboys tended to come more from the local area and to see their parents during term time. The local recruitment of boys in one of the schools grew from 7 per cent to 33 per cent between

1962 and 1982. Such schools became 'greedy' institutions, expecting total commitment and expenditure of effort from staff as well as students in order to sustain the reputation of the school. Teachers were expected to be highly committed and school managers, to work hard to control the competition between their school and others. The mid-1970s were critical years for such schools, threatened by the impact of inflation, increased fees, the need for greater efficiency, and more pupils leaving after O-levels to do A-levels in more 'modern' state sixth-form colleges. Parents also became more demanding, holding higher expectations of teachers and pupils and requiring greater returns for their investment.

The schools studied by Walford managed to adapt by recruiting more pupils from overseas and by becoming coeducational. Girls were allowed in, particularly at A-level to support arts subjects. The proportion of girls taking science subjects remained far lower than boys, although a substantial number of girls took science. Such moves, however, highlighted the traditional values associated with gender relations rather than the transformation of such values. Nationally, only 2.6 per cent of girls from such elite independent coeducational schools took engineering or technology at university, compared with 17 per cent of boys. Although these schools were aware that there might be problems associated with the moves to coeducation, initially there was little evidence of the development of equality policies, anti-sexist training of teachers, preparation for teaching in mixed-sex classrooms or new staffing measures.

In parallel to the state sector, competition between pupils in these schools became increasingly individualized (Walford, 1986: 209); sporting prowess, for example, was encouraged at an individual rather than a team level, through tennis, squash, golf, judo, swimming, fencing, etc. At the same time, what was described as the 'anti-industrial/anti-practical attitude' of gentry masculinity (Wiener, 1982) began to break down. In Walford's case-study schools, the schoolmasters took the lead in promoting new curricula in mathematics, business education and science education, the last through the Association of Science Education. As subject specialists, public schoolmasters had contacts with universities, and sufficient autonomy and commitment to help with the development of their subjects. Thus A-level in business studies was pioneered at Marlborough and Sevenoaks, and an engineering science A-level was developed by other elite schools. Schoolmasters also played a part in the development of innovatory mathematics courses, such as the Secondary Maths Project (SMP) (Walford, 1986). Industrial initiatives and involvement in careers guidance also signalled the growth of new forms of instrumentalism in the independent school sector.

Pressure from upper-middle-class parents demanding value for money, and prioritizing career security, high levels of pay and long-term prospects for their sons, lent support to changes in independent schools (Heward, 1984). According to Walford:

As entry to more and more occupations and the universities has become more bureaucratically organised and competitive, fewer and fewer families could be indifferent to their son's educational qualifications. The schools that had once been the preserve of an élite with substantial independent means, who required a classical education to distance their sons from the possible contamination of having to earn one's living, found that these parents, too, were demanding a more solid and encashable return on their investment.

(Walford, 1986: 206)

This transfer of competitiveness from the sports field to the examination hall (Cross, 1983) took about fifty years. The 1930s slump, the Second World War, and the expansion of universities in the post-war period all had an impact. Also, by the 1980s, the male elite began to feel the effects of recession and de-industrialization. Their dominance in the senior civil service and the Church, though still marked, declined relatively between the 1930s and the 1970s. However, during the same period they maintained or increased their hold over appointments as ambassadors, judges and directors of clearing banks from 68 to 80 per cent. The dominance of public school alumni in politics was also sustained. Just under a half (42 per cent) of MPs in 1982 were educated in one of the elite (HMC) independent schools, while, of the twenty-two in Margaret Thatcher's cabinet of September 1984, seventeen were educated in elite independent schools: four from Eton, and three each from Winchester, Rugby, Stowe, Cheltenham, Clifton and Shrewsbury (Walford, 1986: 14).

Ease of access to Oxford and Cambridge has been a continuing feature of boys from public schools, although state-school educated students have increased their proportion of the intake. Nevertheless, boys from public schools remain highly represented in admissions figures (McCrum, 1996). The effectiveness of such educational routes and credentialism undoubtedly contributes to the maintenance of the male elite, although the rise of a female graduate elite has to some extent threatened that dominance.

Masculinities and the academically able boy

The story of middle-class boys' education is also a story of continuity and change. Although not sustained by the cultural and economic resources of their upper- and upper-middle-class counterparts, middle-class boys have been able to exploit the opportunities provided by the educational system in the post-war period and have used educational qualifications, especially within the sciences, to gain access to university education.

The extent to which middle-class boys in the 1970s were successful in gaining access to scientific and technological careers has been well documented.

Prepared through specialist educational routes for an 'expert' culture, middle-class boys who attended grammar and comprehensive schools were able to exploit the expansion of higher education and the variety of scientific and technological priorities of successive governments. Their ability to gain advantage in science and mathematics also stood them in good stead in the competition for skilled and scientific manpower (*sic*) between the 1960s to 1980s, and then from the 1980s onwards, in the restructuring of the economy towards specialist and international markets. The decline of manufacturing industry was of less importance to this group than the rise of information technology and the increased emphasis on consultancy and management services, finance capital, etc. To some extent such boys were able to take appropriate risks and adapt to new career structures using their credentials and developing a more individualistic orientation.

For middle-class boys, the new hegemonic values of masculinity involved a cluster of attributes as diverse as adventurousness, emotional neutrality, assertiveness, self-reliance, individuality, competitiveness, instrumental skills, discipline, reason, objectivity and rationality (see Kenway, 1995), attributes which were less problematic for them than for their more privileged peers. The grammar school, in particular, appeared to endorse such values for those who demonstrated appropriate social characteristics and excluded those who did not. In the competitive post-war climate, middle-class models of masculinity (in comparison with models of middle-class femininity) were compatible with academic success. For example, King (1971) found that 38 per cent of boys with fathers working in non-manual occupations achieved A-levels compared with only 28 per cent of girls from the same background, and a further 15 per cent of boys compared with 9 per cent of girls of the same social class entered full-time degree courses. Middle-class boys were clearly academically ahead of middle-class girls at that time. The separation of the sexes at the secondary stage also seemed to work in their favour; indeed, single-sex schools were viewed primarily as functional to their academic advancement. Arguments, however, were also put forward that boys should be educated with girls, not just to civilize them but to motivate them through gender competition (Dale, 1969, 1971, 1974).

Middle-class men maintained their elite professional positions, having 'the most extended of educational careers' (King, 1987). They had a status and a class interest in education compared with middle-class girls, who, as we have seen, were generally compelled to secure their class interest through marriage. According to Kelsall, Poole & Kuhn (1972), middle-class men constituted the highest percentage of university students. By the 1980s, however, evidence emerged that gender differences in academic achievement within the middle classes was narrowing, and that proportionately more middle-class girls were gaining places at university (Hutchinson & McPherson, 1976; Halsey, Heath & Ridge, 1980).

The academic success of middle-class boys at GCSE and A-level was affected by subject choice, especially their commitment to the sciences. As we saw in Chapter 2, in 1995 more boys than girls chose two or more A-levels with a science and maths basis: 56 per cent of male students compared with only 40 per cent of female. Similarly, 45 per cent of male students chose to study maths (compared with 22 per cent of female students), and 45 per cent of male students took physical science (compared with 20 per cent of female students) (Cheng, Payne & Witherspoon, 1995). Further, as the EOC study found, in the mid-1990s boys at A-level broadened their range of choices of science and technical subjects – physics, technology, economics and CDT were increasingly rather than decreasingly male-dominated subjects. Thus while academically able girls were specializing in courses which would lead them into the caring professions and the media/communications industries (e.g., publishing, journalism), boys' choices of three sciences at A-level could be exchanged for more highly paid and higher status careers and jobs.

However, economic recession made inter-generational succession less predictable for middle-class boys than in the past, with the result that some middle-class men since the 1970s have experienced downward social mobility. Indeed, Power, Edwards, Whitty & Wigfall (1998) suggest that recent publicly expressed anxiety about boys' educational performance (see Chapter 1) may well reflect the frustrations and ambitions of parents of middle-class origin for their sons.

The strategies of some middle-class boys to counter increasing academic pressure to do well at school were to develop alternative criteria of success. Responding to the uncertainty and utopianism of the 1960s and 1970s, some of the sons of the 'progressive middle classes' (teachers, social workers and creative artists) developed a critical detachment from 'bourgeois' middle-class values by seeking alternatives to respectability in employment and domesticity in the home (viz. a 'culture of gratification'). Although it is not clear whether this group was a 'sizeable minority' or whether it merely represented a middle-class fringe, it seemed to confirm male disenchantment with the consumer boom and also with conventional forms of work identity. Some young men challenged the forms of masculinity associated with middle-class employment, family life, and the unquestioning sense of duty associated with hegemonic masculinity.

As Tolson (1977) argued, the 'drop-outs' of the 1960s were not just a response to an affluent consumer-oriented society, but, paralleling the struggle for women's emancipation, a rejection of the traditional middle-class masculine role: 'The crisis of middle class masculinity is counterposed to the emancipation of middle class women' (1997: 115). Aggleton's (1987) ethnographic study of a group of young people illustrates these tensions. Drawn from the 'new middle class', the parents of these young people worked mainly as civil servants, FE/HE lecturers, teachers, architects or artists. In Aggleton's study, these young men saw themselves as midway between '[the] brutish manliness they associate with manual labour and the essential impotence they saw as characteristic of those whose involvement in mental labour was both committed and industrious' (1987: 73).

The consequences for such middle-class boys was that they rarely applied themselves academically in a sustained way for fear that they would be viewed as 'wimpish' or 'wet'. In perceiving themselves as positioned between the 'macho lad' and the 'sexless swot' (Aggleton, 1987: 72), they aimed for 'effortless achievement' (1987: 81) – a reverse of the protestant ethic! Thus, the educational values of the young people in Aggleton's study appeared 'markedly discontinuous' to those of their parents. They wanted to exert personal control, explore their individual creativity, and exercise personal autonomy. They tended to choose art or new school subjects such as psychology or media studies, and aimed for jobs in the creative industries or the media. Some, especially those whose academic grades were low, chose not to extend their education beyond schooling. Only three out of the twenty-seven young men in Aggleton's sample opted for higher education, and fifteen left college with no qualifications other than those they had gained before they enrolled. Most found employment, but the forms of work were generally less well paid and prestigious than that of their parents. Aggleton interprets this student response as a form of resistance to middle-class forms of control, but not to privileged class/power relations.

Mac an Ghaill's (1994) study of a multiracial comprehensive school describes the responses to schooling of a group of boys belonging to the 10 per cent from non-commercial middle-class backgrounds (parents in lecturing, teaching, public relations and work in the media and the arts). These pupils presented similarly ambivalent responses to the academic curriculum, and were one of the most problematic groups for teachers. These 'New Englanders', as they called themselves, displayed a publicly confident masculinity, defining themselves as 'arbiters of culture'. They refused to affirm teachers' authority, frequently seeing teachers as inferior to themselves. Their rebellion against schooling was more individualistic than collective. Here again the emphasis was on personal autonomy, which conventional middle-class cultures, it was felt, did not offer. Dismissive of both 'macho lads' and hard-working students (the 'sloggers'), these male pupils uncoupled the relationship between academic success and mental labour. While their orientation to work, according to Mac an Ghaill, was one of rejection, they also expressed self-confidence that they would eventually find employment when they chose to do so.

By the 1980s the crisis of confidence in professionalism described above was beginning to have an effect, particularly on middle-class boys confronted not only by competition from girls but by choices about whether to accept greater pressure to succeed academically or to 'drop out'. As Power et al.

(1998) comment, success for academically able pupils was 'by no means guaranteed':

> Although a close, unproblematic connection is sometimes presumed between middle class origin, middle class aspiration and middle class destination, there is considerable movement within, into and out of the middle class.
>
> *(Power et al., 1998: 136)*

Power et al.'s study of 342 academically able boys attending a range of independent and state schools (drawing on the original study of the Assisted Places Scheme) found that 92 per cent of the boys educated in the state sector achieved at least three A-level passes, 81 per cent obtained degrees and 14 per cent achieved masters degrees. For the independent sector, the figures were slightly higher: 93, 86 and 17 per cent respectively. Patterns of academic achievement were similar to those of a comparable group of girls, such that these boys could not be represented as 'underachieving'. Some academically able boys in the sample, however, were struggling, even among this relatively privileged group, and the extent to which they succeeded or failed in comparison with their peers depended, Power and her colleagues argued, on the development of their masculine subjectivity.

The unsuccessful (yet academically able) boys in the independent and state sectors did not constitute a 'group' in the same sense as other boys' groupings described below. What they had in common as individuals was their resistance to the dominant work ethos and its criteria of success. Their stories reveal similar negative effects of competition, where mediocrity is understood to be as damaging as outright failure (see Chapter 5).

In the three examples drawn from Power et al.'s study, each boy's failure to find an alternative subjectivity to academic work or sports (historically the alternative positive model of masculinity available in independent schools) led to what were regarded as weak academic outcomes and an uncertain future:

> Patrick attended an inner city comprehensive, was thought to be academically able but left at 16 with two GCSE passes. He had developed an alternative masculine identity in sport outside school, which was 'not integral to his academic identity' (Power et al., 1998: 144). He was not protected, for example, as in the case of selective schools, from such counter-academic distractions.
>
> Edward's parents paid for him to attend an independent school with a high academic record. Over time, his work declined, apparently because of academic pressure. He preferred to adopt the role of anti-hero – the intellectual who refuses to work hard (1988: 146). He passed only 2 A-levels and had to take another the following year at a FE college.
>
> Alex attended an elite public boarding school in which, however, he developed a 'relaxed' attitude to academic work. The alternative source of his masculine identity lay in his involvement in school sports – in particular, shooting and

karate. He gained two Ds and an E at A-level and took on posts as a security guard and in junior office jobs, while studying for an NVQ.

(1998: 149)

The boys in these schools who resisted and reacted to academic and social pressures in very academic environments showed high levels of anxiety. Peer-group solidarity plus a supportive, positive, academically based school identity, the authors argued, were clearly needed to bolster these pupils.

Research projects such as these remind us, as Connell (1989) found, that 'what privileged young men find at the end of the education conveyor belt is not necessarily to their taste' (1989: 297). Boys' motivation, like that of their sisters in equivalent schools, can come from the family rather than from the individual pupil. The prospect of studying 'dry' sciences at university was a particular form of the 'institutionalization of masculinity', and the extent to which there is flexibility in being male is another important factor in male academic performance.

New boys: getting on and getting out

The restructuring of education during recent decades and the processes of lowering and raising skill levels offer some opportunities for those brave enough to carve out a new masculinity. For working-class boys, the 'ordinary lads' who wish to 'get on' or 'get out' (Brown, 1987), this does not necessarily involve the adoption of middle-class versions of 'complicit' masculinity (Connell, 1987). Key aspects of social change for such boys has been the breaking down of the gendered division of labour and the opportunity to study more 'feminine' or modern subjects. In earlier chapters we referred to the rise of new vocationalism and the increased possibilities for girls to choose new modern occupations (business world, IT, consumer and service industries). An emphasis upon education for work and education as work also allowed the possibility of new forms of masculinity, along the lines of the 'expert' but without the connotations of elite upper-middle-class professionalism or of the traditional grammar school scientist. The version of masculinity which emerged was one of freedom, travel, opportunity and flexibility – offered potentially through the new vocationally oriented courses and other new avenues of study.

The boys most likely to respond to the modernizing entrepreneurial culture and its new vocationalism in schools were the 40 per cent of secondary school pupils to whom, for example, the TVEI initiative and the new vocational qualifications were aimed (see Chapter 6). An effect of the new vocationalist curriculum was to change existing school stratification processes, challenge curriculum organization, and focus pupils' and teachers' values on performance indicators, outcomes, and effectiveness (Mac an Ghaill, 1988). New definitions of school success were introduced, such as a positive orientation towards new subjects (e.g., business studies), new skills (e.g., information technology and computer literacy) and the choice of new jobs (hitherto unspecified).

This new performance culture in schools seemed to offer possibilities of upward social mobility to two groups of schoolboys in particular: the 'academic achievers' found a ladder of social mobility through valuing academic success/qualifications; and the 'new enterprisers', who wanted to make something of their lives, developed strategies to apply aspects of their traditional working-class identities to their school work (Mac an Ghaill, 1994).

What characterized the 'academic achievers' was their positive approach to the academic curriculum, even if not the school. The boys in Mac an Ghaill's study included a high proportion of Asian and white young men from skilled working-class backgrounds whose peer culture revealed shifting responses and criticisms of school discipline and of teachers' practices. Yet, tending to be in the top streams, they were provided with considerable support from the school when they chose to include in their studies drama and associated 'feminine' arts subjects. Significantly, these subject choices presented a challenge to the polarization of male and female school spheres and, for this reason, these boys attracted a higher level of bullying than might be expected, even occasionally from male teachers.

> Like in a school like this, a lot of the male teachers are very defensive, very macho and they've got a lot of power to put you down in front of everyone. So we just started talking together about taking on the sexual jokes and camping it up. And they just couldn't cope with it. It was great . . .
>
> *(Mac an Ghaill, 1994: 61)*

The success of 'academic achievers' was premised on the development of a masculine identity that was neither middle class nor working class. They used an ethic of hard work rather than that of 'effortless achievement', and put in long hours on their homework, assignments and revision. They nevertheless lacked the confidence of their more privileged middle-class peers. Their wish for professional careers also indicated their implicit acceptance of the mental–manual divide and their attempt to distance themselves from the macho lads.

Another route for social mobility for working-class boys created by the new vocationalism of the 1980s was opened up by the introduction of new technological subjects and skills. In this context, the 'new enterprisers' developed versions of masculinity based on rationality, instrumentalism, forward planning and careerism (Mac an Ghaill, 1988: 63). They signed up to mini-enterprise schemes, supported by newly entrepreneurial teachers, and they colonized the computer base often designed to encourage girls. They thus reaffirmed the teachers' authority, recognizing the need for professional support for their version of credentialism.

Both groups of working-class boys in Mac an Ghaill's study saw schooling as a means of gaining access to well-paid jobs in professional and modern, rather than 'old' or dying, industries and organizations. To some extent they wanted to extend themselves up and out of the limitations of working-class destinies, but in ways that did not alienate them from their class backgrounds. In this sense they were similar to black working-class girls, who took a pragmatic and instrumental approach in regard to their schooling (see Chapter 7).

Male sexuality as class resistance

Economic restructuring and the contraction of manufacturing industry in the UK during the three terms of Conservative government described in Part 2 above has had the greatest impact on those boys whose fathers worked in factory or other industrial jobs. The loss of jobs for their fathers was to reduce young men's expectations of finding 'real work' (Haywood & Mac an Ghaill, 1996). The collapse of the youth labour market, the replacement of factory work with new technologies and the expansion of the service industries all fundamentally affected the opportunities for these young men's employment after school. Traditional apprenticeships were no longer an option for many; neither was there necessarily any faith in the plethora of new training options and routes. According to Haywood and Mac an Ghaill (1996), de-industrialization created 'a crisis in working class forms of masculinity'.

Working-class boys were compelled to find ways of celebrating manhood without relying on work identity. Not surprisingly, how boys do this is potentially fraught with conflict – conflict with authority, conflict with girls, and conflict with other groups of boys. Manhood becomes the focus of resistance to what is seen as the meaningless of schooling. At the same time, when manhood is used to construct new 'rites to passage' into adulthood (Haywood & Mac an Ghaill, 1996), it runs counter to those tendencies within schools which might better prepare boys for modern society. Masculinity is premised often upon public collective allegiances to other boys, but such allegiances now run counter to the processes of individualization being encouraged by contemporary schooling. Bonding between boys can become a substitute, as we shall see, for class or ethnic collective identities, already undermined by late modernity, and simultaneously deflect any attempts by schools to help boys adjust to the demands of a society which values educational success and high levels of individuality and autonomy. Paradoxically, schools as social institutions both create the conditions for and reproduce working-class resistance; the celebration of masculine anti-learning culture and heterosexual masculinity (especially through the cult of the body) is a by-product of a school system that has not addressed the realities of working-class male lives.

The many studies of the school cultures of working-class boys point to how masculinity shapes school experiences and creates the form of their resistance to what is perceived by them as a hostile and unjust learning environment. The interaction between institutional school structures and practices and the 'making of masculinity' emerges as a major factor in explaining the educational disengagement of white and black working-class boys in the late 1970s. Willis's 1977 study of why working-class students were persuaded to take working-class jobs described how some white working-class boys coped with the stigma of being in the lowest sets of a secondary school by celebrating being working-class, white and male. At a time of relatively full employment, the 'lads' (in contrast with the more academic 'ear'oles') celebrated the tough physical manual labour of their fathers by adopting a 'macho' culture in which men were the main wage earners, future breadwinners and heads of the family. Rather than perceiving themselves as failures, the lads celebrated their early transition into employment as a secure means of achieving full manhood. Studies of working-class communities in Belfast and South Wales in the 1980s reported the continued presence of such working-class machismo among lads who aspired to become 'real men' (Jenkins, 1983; Brown, 1987).

Evidence from more recent studies suggests that the reforms of schooling from the late 1980s to the mid-1990s, at a time when traditional male working-class jobs were being lost in the 'heavy' manufacturing industries, exacerbated rather than reduced school resistance. By increasing emphasis on 'performance' and on competition both within and between schools, and by raising the stakes in terms of compliance to a school culture that was class oriented, schools were more rather than less likely to be viewed as hostile institutions. The sorting and selecting functions of schools were made more visible, with only weak support from any legitimating ideology. The re-introduction of streaming and the promotion of setting by school subjects for many such boys would confirm their failure to succeed in what were perceived as other people's educational designs. The rising rate of pupils excluded from school during the 1980s and 1990s was closely associated with such a competitive ethos.

It was likely that, in areas of high social deprivation, these organizational and regulative practices of schooling would be understood as new forms of social control rather than as mechanisms to improve young people's educational and work opportunities. The new school ethos, with its focus on high performance and competitiveness and its new regimes of monitoring and targeting, bore little relationship to the realities of economic dysfunction and community breakdown. As Haywood and Mac an Ghaill (1996) argue, in areas in which working-class youth are already marginalized, surveilled and excluded from the productive life of the society, the reconstruction of schooling according to market principles was most likely to force confrontations between young black and white working-class boys and their teachers. It was these confrontations that created and sustained counter-hegemonic masculinities among such youth that were both anti-academic and anti-school.

Parnell Comprehensive, where Mac an Ghaill (1988) conducted his research on masculinity, was the sort of school which restructured in line with the demands of the Conservative government's commitment to new entrepreneurialism, increased emphasis on academic performance and a perceived need for greater discipline. The male teachers themselves were divided on how best to respond to the new school ethos; while some ('the professionals') advocated authority, discipline and control through a paternalistic relationship with the boys, others ('the old collectivists') supported liberal pluralist ideals of meritocracy and anti-sexist and anti-racist policies and engaged with the boys in the school as if they were on the same side. Yet others ('the new entrepreneurs') favoured appraisal, effective management techniques, and new types of masculinity adapted by the 'academic achievers' and the 'new enterprisers', described above. While the messages from the teachers were mixed, so too were the contradictions between disciplinary practices which supported a polarization of the masculine and the feminine, and a curriculum which separated out different groups of boys according to academic and vocational hierarchies.

In such a school the continued presence of a group of disaffected 'macho lads' who celebrated a powerful version of heterosexual machismo appeared to be encouraged rather than discouraged by the new ethos. The responses of the 'macho lads' in this study were similar to those of unemployed working-class men in Australia studied by Connell (1987). Being denied access not just to the traditional male forms of power at school (e.g., access to higher qualifications and training) but also to secure jobs and higher wages, these men responded by becoming the 'cool guys', taking pride in courting trouble, challenging the authority of the school and claiming other sources of power, such as sporting prowess, physical aggression and sexual conquest. These forms of *gender power* became their new symbols of class identity and constituted a new content for their masculinity.

Although some working-class boys in Parnell School took on a new 'business-like masculinity', the 'macho lads' responded to academic failure and their poor employment prospects by celebrating the 3Fs – 'fighting football and fucking' (Mac an Ghaill, 1994). In short, they coped with the multiple uncertainties of their position by promoting a 'hyper-masculinity' – an exaggerated concept of heterosexual masculinity. Arguably it was the notion of 'behaving badly' that provided them with the prospect of regaining control of their lives.

Heterosexual masculinity has also become recognized as having played a key part in shaping the school experiences of black working-class pupils. The performance discourse of schooling, with its managerialist ethos, tended either to pathologize black working-class youth as 'having' problems, or to 'deracialize' the situation – to refuse to see race factors as central to their problems. Black pupils have frequently been portrayed as *the* problem, since they are understood to suffer from the 'decaying' urban contexts in which they live and are schooled. At the same time the Conservative government under Margaret Thatcher emphasized the importance of not differentiating pupils by ethnicity and treating all black pupils not as black but as British (Gilroy, 1986).

In reality, the schooling experiences of young black males were as varied and diverse as those of their white contemporaries. Some young black male pupils do well at schools academically, subscribing as much as possible to the white male and somewhat Eurocentric scholarly ideals. Indian schoolboys exemplify the complex relationship between ethnicity and class which allows them to 'get on' in the educational system; the patterns of vocational training, for example, identified by Felstead, Goodwin & Green (1995) suggest that Indian and Pakistani young men are more likely than young women from the same ethnic group to achieve vocational qualifications.

Significantly, both Mirza and Fuller found that, although African-Caribbean boys and girls tried to be pragmatic and use school as the means to an end, the latter were more successful than the former. 'Black girls have not got an exclusive hold on this coping strategy. What is different is that boys appear to find it less successful' (Mirza, 1992: 10). One of the suggested reasons for boys' lack of academic success is that the form of masculinity black schoolboys adopt, often in resistance – of aggressive heterosexuality – causes them problems in schools, particularly where teachers' morale is low. The teachers themselves generally have received little training in how to treat boys sensitively, and frequently fear being thought of as racist (Sewell, 1997). The education reforms, and especially the absence of funding for anti-racist work, appear to have undermined teachers' ability and willingness to address what they see as rebellious black youth.

Sewell found a range of responses to schooling among African-Caribbean male youth (similar to those identified by Mac an Ghaill, 1994; Connell, 1989; Brown, 1987). Sewell's boys were mainly 'conformists' (41 per cent) and 'innovators' (35 per cent), with only a minority in 'retreatism and rebellion' (18 per cent). As in other studies, black boys' school attendance was high compared with that of white boys. In order to succeed, Sewell argues, aspiring black youth needed to assume a form of 'racelessness', and lose their community and ethnic identity so as to avoid the wrath of their teachers.

The reaction to this 'racelessness' by the 'rebels' was the counter-promotion of a new black identity, which took the form of 'phallocentric masculinity' based on a powerful physical presence.

Sewell distinguishes between three types of teacher response to their male black pupils, two of which were negative. Teachers became 'irritated' (60 per cent) or 'antagonistic' (30 per cent), with only 10 per cent explicitly 'support-ive'. Perhaps not surprising, given such negative perspectives in this school, excluding black boys became the major strategy of classroom management (Sewell, 1997).

Gillborn and Gipps (1996) highlighted the fact that, in many urban com-munities in the UK, African-Caribbean boys left school with the lowest number of qualifications. They were also most likely to have been at the sharp end of disciplinary procedures such as suspensions and expulsions from school. For example, African-Caribbean pupils are reported to be up to six times more likely than white pupils to be excluded from school (Gillborn and Gipps, 1996; Ouseley, 1998). Figures from Lewisham for example show that 15 per cent of all exclusions were of black British (boys), although they formed only 8 per cent of the overall school population. Boys were more likely to be excluded if they were African, African-Caribbean, black British, or Turkish. At a conference on boys held by the authority, Lewisham's director of education reported that pupil motivation appeared to decrease from year 8 onwards (twelve to thirteen years), such that, by years 10 and 11, 40 per cent of pupils (mostly boys) were quoted as either 'disappointed' 'disaffected' or 'disappeared'.

Gillborn and Gipps (1996) mapped the local effects of changes as a result of the Conservative educational reforms and the introduction of competition between schools on the performance of ethnic minority pupils. They found that the number of permanent exclusions nationally had tripled over a three-year period (reaching more than 10,000 per annum in 1993–4), with the highest proportion being black boys (Parsons, 1995, para. 4.3). Wright, Weekes, McLaughlin & Webb's (1998) study of African-Caribbean pupils excluded from schools challenges the view that black masculinity is the prob-lem. The young black men in their study experienced an undervaluing of black masculinity and were never able to 'move beyond the equation of Black masculinity with conflict and confrontation' (Wright et al., 1998: 85).

African-Caribbean boys' subsequent failure to achieve educational quali-fications in GCSE is hardly surprising, since schools often mark them down as having learning and behaviour difficulties and as being in need of special-ist help (Daniels, Hey, Leonard & Smith, 1994; Cooper, Upton & Smith, 1991). Being overly represented among those identified as needing discipline or receiving 'help' often disadvantages black boys more than white working-class boys. In areas like Birmingham, Gillborn (1997) argues, while white pupils have improved their performance, the gap between white and black pupils has grown. The introduction of educational markets, the reintroduction of educational differentiation such as streaming and setting, and the failure to prevent high numbers of excluded pupils has it seems meant that the historical inequalities of race have been exacerbated over and above gender differences. Black and white working-class male pupils appeared to be at the receiving end of an educational philosophy which supported credentialism at whatever cost. New Labour has attempted both to sustain such a philosophy and to reduce its social consequences by, for example, taking a decision to 'name and shame' high 'excluding' authorities and schools. For male working-class youth, much will depend on whether this twin strategy is effective.

Routine violence in schools

The pressure to improve standards and to promote equal opportunities has marginalized concerns about the hidden curriculum and the culture of school. In the late 1970s and early 1980s interest had been shown in improving the quality of the school experience, particularly for girls. Attempts were made to reduce, for example, sexually or racially abusive language and harassment in the classroom, in playgrounds, in the interaction between teachers and taught, and in peer-group cultures. Such attempts highlighted the importance of tackling male aggression in the early years, but especially at adolescence. Research at that time indicated that boys constructed versions of heterosexual masculinity which are inherently unstable and thus need continued 'policing'. There were daily challenges, confrontations and re-ordering of insider and outsider groups which defined the membership of friendship groups and an individual's sexual identity. Boys also attempted to define heterosexual masculinity by putting girls down and even harassing them.

Most schools in the UK would probably also admit that homophobia is rife among boys and is a main focus of boys' bullying and harassment (Skelton, 1997). The attempt to distance themselves from femininity, and to confirm their own masculinity, leads boys to allege homosexuality in other boys. Such strategies serve a purpose of enabling boys to police the boundary between the masculine and feminine, to reassert the masculine heterosexual ideal, and to maintain their dominant position in the face of the academic challenges mounted by girls.

School inspectors have reported little evidence of bullying in British schools, with most schools claiming to have sound anti-bullying policies for dealing with incidents seriously (OFSTED, 1996). However, social researchers have found disturbingly high rates of bullying in primary schools, when children are at an age when their gender identities are still being formed. Whitney and Smith (1993) found that more than one in four primary pupils in Sheffield (compared with one in ten secondary pupils) reported being bullied at some time during a term. MacLeod and Morris's survey for Childline (1996), using open-ended questions, found that this rose to half of primary and 27 per cent of secondary children in London and the south-east of England who said they were bullied in school during the previous year. Bullying was reported as happening mostly in primary school playgrounds and in secondary school classrooms.

Although studies have shown that girls fear bullying more than boys, boys particularly in secondary schools are more likely to be victims and to experience physical violence (Pitts & Smith, 1995). Black pupils are also reported as more likely to be victims of bullying. The effects of bullying on pupils can take various forms, but the connection to male pupils' disengagement has been recognized. As Chaplain (1996) found, disengaged male pupils were more likely to be involved in bullying incidents, to feel that teachers were unaware of the amount of bullying they endured, and to feel under pressure from their immediate friends.

Another study, this time of twenty-five young male and female offenders between the ages of sixteen and twenty-one, found a correlation between bullying in school and dropping out of school and delinquency (Cullingford and Morrison, 1995). Cullingford and Morrison suggested that these boys retaliated aggressively because they were oversensitive to peer pressure: 'they feel caught up in and threatened by it' (1995: 555). Interviews with the offenders revealed fears of outright violence and more subtle forms of bullying, such as name calling, taunting, physical violence. As one interviewee said, bullying was 'just normal aspects of school life' (1995: 551). The authors argue that:

> from the point of view of young offenders bullying was part of the ethos of the schools. The problem is not a matter of clearly isolated incidents and individuals. It is pervasive in the social life of school, and therefore all children are affected by it in one form or other.
>
> *(1995: 547)*

The school processes involved in 'gendering boys' have been shown to involve routine violence being used as a resource in the strategies of both teachers and pupils. Beynon (1989) found that routine violence:

> was the means by which both parties projected themselves; provisionally typed each other; and settled the social charter of the Lower School at the start of the year as a 'school for men'.
>
> *(Beynon, 1989: 211)*

Reflections

This chapter has argued that boys' concepts of masculinity have been affected by the extensive restructuring of work in the UK in the 1980s. As heavy industry disappeared and new service and technological industries began to replace them, young men lost their previous security in the old labour market and found new jobs being taken by young women. Not surprisingly, these changes have differentially affected the level of motivation among different groups of boys, depending on their position in the social structure.

Research suggests that masculinity is shaped not just by society or local cultures but by individuals or groups, who take up positions in order to maintain their superiority in relation to other groups. Masculinity, historically, has been one of the key sources of power in society. The principal concern with heterosexual masculinities has been to present a counter to femininity. At the same time such masculinities have been shown to be complex, diverse and fragile. It is in this context that much of the violence that is a common feature of school life can be understood. Physical aggression can be used by some young males both as an achievement of, and as a challenge to, dominant forms of masculinity. The continuation of such models of heterosexual dominance, especially at a time when gender relations faced a challenge from women, has had major consequences for boys in school and at a critical time in their educational and personal development.

We argue, therefore, that behind the statistics of boys' achievements described in Chapter 2 lies the impact of social and educational change. The break with Victorian values and the family model of male breadwinner, coupled with the decline of male employment and conventional wage-earning roles, has had considerable yet also a differential impact on boys from different social groups. Social class, as Furlong and Cartmel (1997) note, remains a major determining influence on boys' educational outcomes. The male project of upward class mobility through education that dominated educational policy after the Second World War has been threatened and to some extent overturned by economic and political changes. For some boys, upward social mobility was rarely a viable option, especially if it meant having to abandon their collective class or ethnic male identity. Their response has been to call schoolwork girls' work. At the same time, as we have seen, some boys (e.g. the 'academic achievers') have succeeded in combining a working-class ethic (of hard work) with academic scholarship. For another middle-class group, schoolwork warrants 'effortless achievement' – that is, it is not to be taken too seriously. Alternative sources of male success are found in the new consumer worlds and industrial sectors. Significantly, elite boys seem not to have experienced a crisis comparable to that of their less privileged peers.

9
Closing the Gender Gap in Education?

Our main concern has been to account for the success of girls in closing the gender gaps which have traditionally shaped British schooling since its formation in the nineteenth century. By using examination statistics we have revealed one of the most extensive inversions of social inequality in contemporary times. A new gender gap in favour of girls appeared in the 1980s. Following that, the proportions of boys and girls who achieved the national benchmark of five higher grade (A*–C) GCSEs have remained constant. The relatively low literacy levels of boys in primary schools and the failure to modify boys' relatively lower performance in secondary schools over this period indicates the persistency of this new gender gap. It is unlikely to shift without attention to what has caused this inversion. It will require considered and considerable national effort on the part of government and schools if patterns of boys' achievement are to replicate those of girls.

We have argued that girls' academic achievement nationally cannot be accounted for by educational actions, whether small-scale changes in individual school subjects, new forms of assessment, including coursework, or examination modes and attention to classroom behaviour. There is no proven link between such educational programmes, policies and procedures and school effectiveness or improvement overall (Slee, Weiner & Tomlinson, 1998). The cluster of issues affecting school performance is complex and interactive. Moreover, it has been unstable over the last fifty years as successive governments have refashioned the shape and nature of the school curriculum. What is clear is that successive generations of girls have been challenged by economic and social change and by feminism.

Conservative commentators have expressed the view that feminism and the welfare state together have destabilized the family (Conway, 1998). They have argued that young women have been compelled to seek work outside the home to ensure a secure future for themselves and their children. 'Gender shock' (Eisenstein, 1991), or the sea-change in girls' attitudes to work, family life, childcare, choice of partners or equal opportunities in general, has been attributed to the impact of feminism both positively and negatively. But there remains deep hostility from conservative quarters to acknowledging feminism as a force for change in its own right. There is even more hostility to feminist efforts to improve conditions for girls and women as a group – what Faludi has called a 'backlash' (1992). In respect of education the effects of the backlash have been to convert girls' educational successes into a moral panic about boys' failure. Girls' achievements *per se* are not seen as representative of an educational revolution of modern times. They are rendered problematic, and teachers' work is thereby denigrated rather than praised. The threat of a future that is female is one which has captured the public imagination through media representations.

We have shown that the changes to the gender patterns in education in England and Wales in the 1960s and 1970s were not the result of national equality strategies. They derived from the space offered by a decentralized system of education and the associated notions of teacher professionalism and autonomy. In the 'secret garden of the curriculum' teachers were able to challenge traditional female roles and offer girls the chance to experiment and reflect upon their personal ambitions. The flexibility which British feminists have shown in riding the tide of change is also significant. In the 1980s and 1990s aspects of feminism became part of the language of schooling. When these ideas were related to the new performance and managerialist discourses of the New Right, they dovetailed with strategies for school improvement and pupil performance. The advantages of a female-dominated teaching profession were exploited by feminists who called for educational action for new generations of girls.

Paradoxically, in the future academically successful young women may turn away from teaching as a suitable female profession. They may well have new opportunities in the high-status graduate professions, such as finance and accounting, as inroads have been made into the higher reaches of education, where the gender gap has closed too. The continuation of the traditionally sex-segregated labour market overall, however, provides less incentive for girls than boys to aim for non-traditional qualifications. Girls' achievements in literacy and communication skills have put them in a strong position in the new technological and cultural industries. Some economic commentators have predicted that over 70 per cent of the new jobs that will be created in Britain over the next decade will be in areas traditionally dominated by women. The main areas of growth will be in managerial, professional and clerical occupations (Hughes, 1996).

The place of schooling in boys' lives, we argued, has also been transformed over the last two decades. It has been changed by the loss of traditional transitions from school to work and by the replacement of traditional skill-based, apprenticeships with modern ones. These have required boys to adapt their personal and occupational choices. Traditionally girls were 'protected' from the labour market, in ways which feminists challenged. Boys were not so protected; nor were they so challenged; nor were they prepared for the extent of national and global economic transformations. Adaptation educationally, personally and occupationally has proved more difficult for boys than for girls. Boys have remained more wedded to traditional notions of male and female roles in the family.

The historical legacies of social class and ethnicity we also argued still leave their mark, despite female educational successes and the closing of the gender gap. Old conditions still prevail, particularly in the constancy of traditional behaviour and in the continuing sex segregation of the labour market. This constancy has also cast a long shadow over young people's choices of training and careers. However, the new generations of young women have expressed a desire for equality over and above the conditions of the sex-segregated labour market. And new generations of young men have practised a rhetoric of equality without matching their words with deeds (Beck, 1992). 'In a risk society, the positions of men and women become increasingly unequal, *'more* conscious and *less* legitimated' (Beck, 1992: 104).

Beck, among other social theorists, has analysed global social changes. His depiction of the 'risk society' is similar to the account of social change that we have used to explain the closing of the gender gap in education. He too argues that epochal changes have occurred, but that they have had more influence on consciousness than on behaviour. The data on men and women speak a 'double language', is the way he expresses it. He too argues that the shift that has occurred over the last fifty to a hundred years has been dramatic and irreversible. 'It marks the very beginning of a liberation from the feudally ascribed roles for the sexes with all its associated antagonisms.' Early industrial society was dependent upon unequal positions of men and women in work and the private family. The crumbling of the bourgeois or Victorian patriarchal family and its traditional sexual division of labour has been crucial to what he calls 'the process of reflexive modernization' (1992: 104). It uncouples women from their status fate or the constraints of gender.

In this process, which Beck describes as 'I am I', new generations of young people have been divorced from the expected and traditional notions of men and women. They have had to begin to find new understandings of themselves. People have become more aware of the contrasting conditions under which they live. They have also become aware of the contradictory consequences and risks of their choices. The effects of these processes of individualization have produced some contradictions. Among young men at school, as we have seen, there has been a retention of strong traditional male identities. Yet these identities no longer provide the advantages of the past.

Feminist teachers and educators as we have seen encouraged reflexivity among young women at school and have helped girls to engage with the concept of woman and make it problematic. In the safe haven of the school young women have been able to consider themselves free from Victorian models of femininity and the patriarchal family. This has been helped by wider social changes such as technological developments applied to the home and housework, to families and family planning and to other forms of work. Successive generations of young women have witnessed and experienced changes in their own mothers' lives. They have variously seen the inter-generational effects of increases in women's employment, changes in marriage and divorce, developments in women's educational careers and experiences. The liberation of women from the cult of femininity and domesticity and the traditional family, it seems, cannot now be reversed.

Generations of girls have embraced the prospects of liberation in principle if not in practice, despite the attempts by the New Right in the 1980s and 1990s to revitalize Victorian values. Margaret Thatcher provided a very real role model of female possibilities: she was well ahead of her time in her personal life, becoming a 'working mother' at the 'dawn of the new Elizabethan era', to use her own words. Then she appealed to other women to 'wake up' and follow her lead. Yet three decades later, when she became leader of the Conservatives and prime minister, she hoped to reverse the broad social trends and, so to speak, 'put the genie back in the bottle'. It simply could not be done, since she was no longer unique. The shift in girls' aspirations resulted from the post-war welfare state which suggested that individuals could be uncoupled from their class fates. Girls have shifted as a result also of the increasingly individualistic culture which was promoted by the New Right restructuring of the educational system.

Political analyses of girls' educational achievements have, in our view, failed to engage with the complex processes of social change which have affected young women. The relationship between educational continuities and personal and social change provides a fascinating picture of how different social classes of girls engaged with the processes of individualization in high modernity. The continuities of class membership have been found most strongly in those girls attending private schools. Their education has been a way of retaining middle-class economic privilege while at the same time promoting the idea of individual success. For many other groups of girls the role of the school has changed dramatically. It has provided the institutional potential for personal liberation, even if the constraints and realities of economic insecurity have forced them into making traditional career choices. The lack of the transformation of the labour market has prevented such young women from leading autonomous lives through work. Many young women, as adults, have had to recognize the realities of reconnecting to conventional female forms of work after having had exciting engagements with the desire for economic independence and autonomy at school. Another inhibiting factor has been the lack of childcare at a time of increasing diversity of parenting.

Men's situations and boys' conditions have been very different from those of women. As we have shown the creation of the welfare state confirmed the position of men as head of the household and breadwinner (Land, 1976), and also legitimated their routine absence from regular parenting or fatherhood. The messages for men in the welfare reforms were far less contradictory than those for women, since the welfare reforms re-inscribed motherhood as essential to the stable family form at the same time as offering women new opportunities to enter paid employment in the service of the welfare state. At the heart of the male condition in contemporary society, by contrast, is the continuing coincidence between a traditional role identity and the need to make a living. Fatherhood, in other words, provides few obstacles to making a living or pursuing a career.

> All the factors which *dislodge* women from their traditional role are *missing* on the male side . . . In the context of male life, fatherhood *and* career, economic independence *and* familial life are not contradictions that have to be fought for and held together against the conditions in the family and society; instead their compatibility with the traditional male role is prescribed and protected. But this means that individualisation . . . *strengthens* masculine role behaviour.
>
> *(Beck, 1992: 112)*

Masculinity is a form of power in its own right and augments the power of those with bourgeois privilege, as Bourdieu and Passeron have argued (1977). The processes of accumulation of gender power, however, are complex and do not always presume educational advantage. Working-class boys, for example, gained their traditional dominance through physical prowess (sexual or sporting) rather than through cultural capital acquired within education. The processes of individualization have been experienced differently by boys and girls. The boundaries between masculinity and femininity have been at stake and the danger of adaptation lies in loss of masculinity. But different classes of boys have engaged with such processes of individualization in different ways. In the case of gentry masculinity, new generations of boys have adapted and reconstructed masculinity rather than abandoned it (in much the same way as the female graduate elite has successfully revised the concept of 'lady').

These processes of individualization have been uneven, given the education reforms of successive governments. They have not necessarily involved or encouraged an uncoupling from 'old identities'. The unintended consequences of educational reforms have been as significant as the intended aims. While social democratic reforms aimed to promote collectivism and a concern for the good of society, they retained the class legacies of the nineteenth century. The selection and sorting functions of education were built into the foundations of new forms of schooling in deeply undemocratic ways. At the same time the ethos of collectivism created an illusion of a common liberatory ideal.

The social and educational reforms of the Conservative governments of the 1980s and 1990s aimed rhetorically to mobilize popular support for what were essentially inegalitarian structures. They added new sets of distinctions between pupils and schools while at the same time they established a common curriculum, a standardized system of examinations and parental control over children's education. Their educational reforms promoted more competition between schools and pupils and encouraged stronger versions of individualism. Class and racial differences in educational opportunities were condoned and not reduced. Class distinctions and class identities were reinforced by the experience of schooling, especially for boys.

The educational policies of the post-war period have affected boys more negatively than girls. The emphasis on competition and performance and the heightened visibility of schools has called into play a new concept of the 'good pupil'. Pupils have been required to engage in the improvement of their academic performance for the sake of the school if not themselves. Educational success has been judged predominantly by the number of qualifications achieved at the age of sixteen, a yardstick which historically many boys have not met or have chosen not to get involved with. This shift in educational values has been successfully exploited by girls, resulting in raised educational performance. It has thus contributed to a decline of the relative advantage of boys over girls. This is what we have called the 'closing of the gender gap'. These trends have brought stress and anxiety to those boys who had understood masculinity as part of the equation between academic capital and class advantage. It also undermined the association of traditional working-class male success with leaving school early and going into work.

A minority of young men have learnt to generate new forms of masculinity that are able to engage with the requirements of the labour market. They have also negotiated feminism successfully and have worked on an ideal of masculinity which is not based on traditional forms of male employment or male power. Old masculinities, however, have been reworked as hyper-masculinities by other boys, who have placed even greater stress than in the past on dominant male heterosexuality and physical prowess. These versions of masculinity are incompatible with the new 'conservative' ethos of schooling. Schoolwork and academic scholarship have been portrayed by some boys as feminized and in conflict with emergent masculinities. The extent to which this has been to the detriment of male academic achievements has been dependent on the abilities of educationists to engage critically and constructively with such school-based masculinities. Male secondary schoolteachers in certain contexts have used masculinizing practices in ways detrimental to boys. One example is where teachers have exacerbated problematic relationships with black male pupils by confusing their masculine behaviour with a lack of intellectual abilities (Sewell, 1997).

The various studies of different class and educational settings have pointed to no one uniform shift in consciousness or aspiration. There has been a range of shifts for the new generations of boys and girls. What happened in the realm of selective and private education is not the same process as that found among those educated in state comprehensive schools. The national picture of female educational success masks the continuing significance of class inequalities in society. The high levels of academic achievement of those attending girls' selective and private schools is premised upon the continuation of class distinctions and the choice of such schools by upper-middle-class families. The anxieties found among high-achieving girls has recently become a topic of interest for education feminists (Walkerdine & Lucey, 1997; Mann, 1998).

Different models of femininity were offered to girls by their families and schooling. Different subcultures of female youth were not so clearly identifiable as in the case of boys. Indeed, recent feminist research shows girls' friendships as more significant forms of bonding than heterosexual relationships (Hey, 1997). Research studies have also highlighted the changing relations between girls of different ethnic groups, including those between black and white girls. This has suggested less difference and more continuity between white, Asian and African-Caribbean girls. The old model of the cult of femininity of white working-class girls' has been replaced by similar desires for upward social mobility, traditionally associated with African-Caribbean girls. The norm for schoolgirls, whether white, Asian or African-Caribbean, became, in the 1990s, that of 'getting on and getting out'.

The break with the principles of gender differentiation which were embedded in the development of mass schooling came about through a complexity of social forces. The tensions between the various value messages were augmented by complex social changes later inscribed in social democratic and New Right reforms of the education system. The contradiction between the promotion of individualism and the promotion of Victorian values has been critical to the processes of adaptation and individualization of young people. The school system has made various ambivalent responses to these processes of social change. The risk of dissolving the conventional family form for the maintenance of social order is great. Retaining a sense of continuity with the past is the function of school systems, since schooling contributes to the moral order as well as catering to the vicissitudes of the occupational structure. But in the UK, schooling appears to have broken with the traditions of the gender order. It is this decisive break with the social and educational past that lies behind the closing of the gender gap.

Authors' Note on Further Reading

The theme in each chapter is discussed more fully in the following articles and books in the References and Bibliography. Many of them involved earlier collaborations between ourselves.

Chapter 1

Arnot & Weiner (1987); David (1993); David, West & Ribbens (1994); David, Weiner & Arnot (1997); Weiner, Arnot & David (1997) (1998)

Chapter 2

Arnot (1986b); Arnot, David & Weiner (1996); Arnot, Gray, James & Rudduck (1998); Weiner, Arnot & David (1998)

Chapter 3

Arnot (1986b); Bristol Women's Studies Group (1979); David (1980) (1997); New & David (1985)

Chapter 4

David (1980) (1983a) (1983b); David & Land (1983); David, Edwards, Hughes & Ribbens (1993)

Chapter 5

Arnot (1983) (1984) (1985) (1986a) (1986b) (1997); Burton & Weiner (1990); Dillabough & Arnot (1999 in press); Weiner (1985a) (1985b) (1989b) (1993); Weiner & Arnot (1987a)

Chapter 6

Arnot (1989) (1991) (1992); (1993); Arnot & Blair (1993); David (1983a) (1983b) (1986a) (1986b) (1992) (1993) (1994); Millman & Weiner (1987); Weiner (1989b) (1993) (1994a) (1994b); Weiner, Arnot & David (1998)

Chapter 7

Arnot (1982) (1983)

Chapter 8

Arnot (1983) (1984); David (1993); David, Weiner & Arnot (1997); Weiner (1998)

References and Bibliography

Abbott, P. & Sapsford, R. (1987) *Women and Social Class*, London, Tavistock.

Abraham, J. (1995) *Divide and School: gender and class dynamics in comprehensive education*, London, Falmer Press.

Acker, S. (1986) What do feminists want from education?, in A. Hartnett & M. Naish (eds) *Education and Society Today*, Lewes, Falmer Press.

Adkins, L. & Leonard, D. (1997) 'The family work of young people: their education and post 16 Careers', London, ESRC [unpubd research report].

Adler, S., Laney, J. & Packer, M. (1993) *Managing Women: feminism and power in educational management*, Buckingham, Open University Press.

Aggleton, P. (1987) *Rebels Without a Cause: middle class youth and the transition from school to work*, Lewes, Falmer Press.

Ainley, P. (1993) *Class and Skill: divisions of knowledge and labour*, London, Cassell.

Allatt, P. (1993) 'Becoming privileged: the role of family processes', in I. Bates & G. Riseborough (eds) *Youth and Inequality*, Buckingham, Open University Press.

Amos, V. & Parmar, P. (1984) 'Challenging imperial feminism', *Feminist Review*, 17, 3–18.

Arnot, M. (1982) 'Male hegemony, social class and women's education', *Journal of Education*, 164/1, 64–89.

Arnot, M. (1983) 'A cloud over coeducation: an analysis of the forms of transmission of class and gender relations', in S. Walker & L. Barton (eds) *Gender, Class and Education*, Basingstoke, Falmer Press.

Arnot, M. (1984) 'How shall we educate our sons?', in R. Deem, *Co-Education Reconsidered*, Buckingham, Open University Press.

Arnot, M. (1985) *Race and Gender: equal opportunities policies in education*, Oxford, Pergamon.

Arnot, M. (1986a) *Race, Gender and Education Policy-Making*, module 4 E333, Milton Keynes, Open University Press.

Arnot, M. (1986b) 'State education policy and girls' educational experiences', in V. Beechey & E. Whitelegg (eds) *Women in Britain Today*, Milton Keynes, Open University Press.

Arnot, M. (1987) 'Political lip-service or radical reform? Central government responses to sex equality as a policy issue', in M. Arnot & G. Weiner (eds) *Gender and the Politics of Schooling*, London, Hutchinson.

Arnot, M. (1989) 'Consultation or legitimisation? Race and gender politics and the making of the national curriculum', *Critical Social Policy*, 20–38.

Arnot, M. (1991) 'Equality and democracy: a decade of struggle over education', *British Journal of Sociology of Education*, 12/4, 447–66.

Arnot, M. (1992) 'Feminism, education and the New Right', in M. Arnot & L. Barton (eds) *Voicing Concerns: sociological perspectives on contemporary education reforms*, Wallingford, Triangle Books.

Arnot, M. (1993) 'A crisis in patriarchy? British feminist education politics and state regulation of gender', in M. Arnot & K. Weiler (eds) *Feminism and Social Justice in Education: international perspectives*, London, Falmer Press.

Arnot, M. & Blair, M. (1993) 'Black and anti-racist perspectives on the National Curriculum and government education policy', in A. King & M. Reiss (eds) *The Multicultural Dimension of the National Curriculum*, Lewes, Falmer Press.

Arnot, M. & Weiner, G. (eds) (1987) *Gender and the Politics of Schooling*, London, Hutchinson.

Arnot, M., David, M. & Weiner, G. (1996) *Educational Reforms and Gender Equality in Schools*, Manchester, Equal Opportunities Commission, Research Discussion Series no. 17.

Arnot, M., Gray, J., James, M. & Rudduck, J. (1998) *A Review of Recent Research on Gender and Educational Performance*, OFSTED Research Series, London, The Stationery Office.

Askew, S. (1989) 'Aggressive behaviour in boys: to what extent is it institutionalised?' in D. Tattum and D. Lane (eds) *Bullying in Schools*, Stoke on Trent, Trentham Books.

Askew, S. & Ross, C. (1988) *Boys Don't Cry: boys and sexism in education*, Milton Keynes, Open University Press.

Baker Miller, J. (1978; 1986) *Towards a New Psychology of Women* (1st and 2nd edns), Harmondsworth, Penguin.

Ball, S. J. (1990) *Politics and Policy Making in Education: explorations in policy sociology*, London, Routledge.

Banks, M., Bates, I., Breakwell, G., Bynner, J., Emler, N., Jameson, L. & Roberts, K. (1992) *Career Identities*, Milton Keynes, Open University Press.

Banks, O. (1981) *Faces of Feminism: a study of feminism as a social movement*, Oxford, Martin Robertson.

Barber, M. (1994) *Gender Differences and GCSE Results*, Keele, Centre for Successful Schools, Keele University.

Barrett, M. & McIntosh, M. (1983) *The Anti-Social Family*, London, Verso.

Basit, T. N. (1996) 'I'd hate to be just a housewife: career aspirations of British Muslim girls', *British Journal of Guidance and Counselling*, 24/2, 227–42.

Bates, I. (1993) 'A job which is right for me? Social class, gender and individualisation', in I. Bates and G. Riseborough (eds) *Youth and Inequality*, Buckingham, Open University Press.

Bates, I. & Riseborough, G. (eds) (1993) *Youth and Inequality*, Buckingham, Open University Press.

de Beauvoir, S. (1953) *The Sexond Sex*, Harmondsworth, Penguin.

Beck, U. (1992) *Risk Society: towards a new modernity*, London, Sage.

Beck, U., Giddens, A. & Lash, S. (1994) *Reflexive Modernisation*, Cambridge, Polity Press.

Bernstein, B. (1971) 'On the classification and framing of educational knowledge', in M. Young (ed.) *Knowledge and Control: new directions for the sociology of education*, London, Collier-Macmillan.

Bernstein, B. (1977) *Class, Codes and Control*, Vol. 3, London, Routledge & Kegan Paul.

Beveridge, Sir W. (1942) *Social Insurance and Allied Services*, London, HMSO, Cmnd 6404.

Beynon, H. (1992) 'The end of the industrial worker?' in N. Abercrombie & A. Warde (eds) *Social Change in Contemporary Britain*, Cambridge, Polity Press.

Beynon, J. (1989) 'A school for men: an ethnographic case study of routine violence in schooling', in S. Walker & L. Barton (eds) *Politics and the Processes of Schooling*, Milton Keynes, Open University Press.

Bhavnani, R. (1991) *Black Women in the Labour Market: a research review*, Manchester, Equal Opportunities Commission.

Bird, E. (1998) 'High class cookery: gender status and domestic subjects, 1890–1930', *Gender and Education*, 10/2, 117–31.

Blackburn, R. M. & Jarman, J. (1993) 'Changing inequalities in access to British universities', *Oxford Review of Education*, 19/2, 197–215.

Board of Education (1923) *Report of the Consultative Committee on Differentiation of the Curriculum for Boys and Girls Respectively in Secondary Schools*, London, HMSO.

Bourdieu, P. (1977) 'The economics of linguistic exchange', *Social Science Information*, 16/6.

Bourdieu, P. & Passeron, J. C. (1977) *Reproduction in Education, Society and Culture*, London, Sage.

Bowlby, J. (1951) *Maternal Care and Mental Health*, Geneva, World Health Organization.

Bowlby, J. (1953) *Child Care and the Growth of Love*, London, Pelican Books.

Brabeck, M. (1996) 'The moral self, values and circles of belonging', in K. J. Wyche & F. J. Crosby (eds) *Women's Ethnicities*, Boulder, CO, Westview Press.

Bradley, H. (1996) *Fractured Identities: changing patterns of inequality*, Cambridge, Polity Press.

Brah, A. & Minhas, R. (1985) 'Structural racism or cultural difference: schooling for Asian girls', in G. Weiner (ed.) *Just a Bunch of Girls: feminist approaches to schooling*, Buckingham, Open University Press.

Branca, P. (1975) *Silent Sisterhood: middle-class women in the Victorian home*, London, Croom Helm.

Bristol Women's Studies Group (1979) *Half the Sky: an introduction to women's studies*, London, Virago.

Bron-Wojciechowska, A. (1995) 'Education and gender in Sweden: is there any equality?', *Women's Studies International Forum*, 18/1, 51–60.

Brown, P. (1987) *Schooling Ordinary Kids: inequality, unemployment and the new vocationalism*, London, Tavistock.

Brown, P. (1995) 'Cultural capital and social exclusion: some observations on recent trends in education, employment and the labour market', *Work, Employment and Society*, 9/1, 29–51.

Brown, P. & Lauder, H. (eds) (1997) *Education: economy, culture and society*, Oxford, Oxford University Press.

Bryan, B., Dadzie, S. & Scafe, S. (1985) *The Heart of the Race*, London, Virago.

Burchell, H. & Millman, V. (eds) (1989) *Changing Perspectives on Gender: new initiatives in secondary education*, Milton Keynes, Open University Press.

Burchill, J. (1998) *Diana*, London, Weidenfeld & Nicolson.

Burstyn, J. (1980) *Victorian Education and the Ideal of Womanhood*, London, Croom Helm.

Burton, L. (ed.) (1986) *Girls into Maths Can Go*, London, Holt, Rinehart & Winston.

Burton, L. & Weiner, G. (1990) 'Social justice and the National Curriculum', *Research Papers in Education*, 5/3, 203–28.

Buswell, C. (1992) 'Training girls to be low paid women', in C. Glendinning & J. Millar (eds) *Women and Poverty in Britain: the 1990s*, Hemel Hempstead, Harvester Wheatsheaf.

Byrne, E. (1978) *Women and Education*, London, Tavistock.

Campbell, B. (1987) *The Iron Ladies: why do women vote Tory?*, London, Virago.

Campbell, B. (1993) *Goliath: Britain's dangerous places*, London, Methuen.

Campbell, B. (1998) *Diana, Princess of Wales: how sexual politics shook the monarchy*, London, Women's Press.

Central Advisory Council for Education (England) (1959) *Fifteen to Eighteen: a report by Sir Geoffrey Crowther*, 2 vols, London, HMSO.

Central Advisory Council for Education (England) (1963) *Half our Future: a report by Sir John Newsom*, London, HMSO.

Central Advisory Council for Education (England) (1967) *Children and their Primary Schools: a report by Lady Plowden*, 2 vols, London, HMSO.

Centre for Contemporary Cultural Studies (CCCS) (1981) *Unpopular Education: schooling and social democracy in England since 1944*, London, Hutchinson.

Centre for Educational Research and Innovation (CERI) (1982) *Caring for Children*, Paris, OECD.

Chandos, J. (1984) *Boys Together: English public schools, 1800–1984*, Oxford, Oxford University Press.

Chaplain, R. (1996) 'Making a strategic withdrawal: disengagement and self-worth protection in male pupils', in J. Rudduck, R. Chaplain & G. Wallace (eds) *School Improvement: what can pupils tell us?*, London, David Fulton.

Cheng, Y., Payne, J. & Witherspoon, S. (1995) *Science and Mathematics in Full-time Education after 16*, Youth Cohort Report no. 36, London, Department for Education and Employment.

Chisholm, L. & du Bois-Reymond, M. (1993) 'Youth transitions, gender and social change', *Sociology*, 27/2, 259–79.

Chisholm, L. & Holland, J. (1987) 'Anti-sexist action research in schools: girls and occupational choice', in G. Weiner & M. Arnot (eds) *Gender Under Scrutiny: new inquiries in education*, London, Hutchinson.

Chodorow, N. (1978) *The Reproduction of Mothering: psychoanalysis and the sociology of gender*, Berkeley, CA, University of California Press.

Christian Smith, L. (1990) *Becoming a Woman through Romance*, London, Routledge.

Clarricoates, K. (1978) 'Dinosaurs in the classroom: a re-examination of some aspects of the "hidden curriculum" in primary schools', *Women's Studies International Quarterly*, 1, 353–64.

Clarricoates, K. (1980) 'The importance of being earnest . . . Emma, Tom, . . . Jane: the perception and categorisation of gender conformity and gender deviation in primary schools', in R. Deem (ed.) *Schooling for Women's Work*, London, Routledge & Kegan Paul.

Cohen, B. (1988) *Caring for Children*, London, European Commission.

Cohen, P. (1997) *Rethinking the Youth Question: education, labour and cultural studies*, London, Macmillan.

Coleman, J. (1966) *On Quality of Educational Opportunity*, Washington DC, US Government Office.

Committee on Higher Education (1963) *Higher Education*, London, HMSO [the Robbins Report].

Committee on Women in Science, Engineering and Technology (1994) *The Rising Tide: a report on women in science, engineering and technology*, London, HMSO.

Condor, S. (1989) 'Biting in the future: social change and the social identity of women', in S. Skevington & D. Barker (eds) *The Social Identity of Women*, London, Sage.

Connell, R. W. (1987) *Gender and Power: society, the person and sexual politics*, Cambridge, Polity Press.

Connell, R. W. (1989) 'Cool guys, swots and wimps: the inter-play of masculinity and education', *Oxford Review of Education*, 15/3, 291–303.

Connell, R. W. (1990) 'The state, gender and sexual politics', *Theory and Society*, 19, 507–44.

Connell, R. W. (1995) *Masculinities*, Cambridge, Polity Press.

Connell, R. W. (1997) 'The big picture: masculinities in recent world history', in A. H. Halsey, H. Lauder, P. Brown & A. S. Wells (eds) *Education, Culture, Economy and Something*, Oxford, Oxford University Press.

Connell, R. W., Ashenden, D. J., Kessler, S. & Dowsett, G. W. (1982) *Making the Difference: schools, families and social division*, Sydney, Allen & Unwin.

Conway, D. (ed.) (1998) *Free Market Feminism*, London, IEA Choice in Welfare 43, HMSO.

Cooper, P., Upton, G. & Smith, C. (1991) 'Ethnic minority and gender distribution among staff and pupils in facilities for pupils with emotional and behavioural difficulties in England and Wales', *British Journal of Sociology of Education*, 12/1, 74–94.

Coote, A. & Campbell, B. (1982) *Sweet Freedom: the struggle for women's liberation*, London, Picador.

Coote, A., Harman, H. & Hewitt, P. (1990) *The Family Way: a new approach to policy-making*, London, IPPR.

Coppeck, V., Haydon, D. & Richter, I. (1995) *The Illusions of Post-feminism: new women, old myths*, London, Taylor & Francis.

Cornbleet, A. & Libovitch, S. (1983) 'Anti-sexist initiatives in a mixed comprehensive school: a case study', in A. Wolpe & J. Donald (eds) *Is There Anyone Here from Education?*, London, Pluto Press.

Crompton, R. (1992) 'Where did all the bright girls go?', in N. Abercrombie & A. Warde (eds) *Social Change in Modern Britain*, Cambridge, Polity Press.

Crompton, R. (1993) *Class and Stratification*, Cambridge, Polity Press.

Crompton, R. (1997) *Women and Work in Modern Britain*, Oxford, Oxford University Press.

Cross, J. (1983) 'Prospects', *The Guardian*, 22 November.

Cullingford, C. (1993) 'Children's views on gender issues in school', *British Educational Research Journal*, 19/5, 555–63.

Cullingford, C. & Morrison, J. (1995) 'Bullying as a formative influence: the relationship between the experience of school and criminality', *British Educational Research Journal*, 21/5, 547–60.

Dale, J. & Foster, P. (1986) *Feminists and State Welfare*, London, Routledge & Kegan Paul.

Dale, R. R. (1969) *Mixed or Single Sex School?*, Vol. 1; (1971) *Mixed or Single Sex School? Some social aspects*, Vol. 2; (1974) *Mixed or Single Sex School? Attainment, attitudes and overview*, Vol. 3, London, Routledge.

Daniels, H., Hey, V., Leonard, D. & Smith, M. (1994) 'Gendered practice in special educational needs', in L. Dawtrey et al. (eds) *Equality and Inequality in Educational Policy*, Clevedon, Multilingual Matters.

David, M. E. (1980) *The State, the Family and Education*, London, Routledge & Kegan Paul.

David, M. E. (1983a) 'The New Right, sex, education and social policy: towards a new moral economy in Britain and the USA', in J. Lewis (ed.) *Women's Welfare: women's rights*, London, Croom Helm.

David, M. E. (1983b) 'Sex education and social policy: a new moral economy', in S. Walker & L. Barton (eds) *Gender, Class and Education*, Brighton, Falmer Press.

David, M. E. (1985) 'Motherhood and social policy: a matter of education?', *Critical Social Policy*, 12, 28–44.

David, M. E. (1986a) 'Moral and maternal: the family in the Right', in R. Levitas (ed.) *The Ideology of the New Right*, Cambridge, Polity Press.

David, M. E. (1986b) 'Teaching family matters', *British Journal of Sociology of Education*, 7/1, 35–57.

David, M. E. (1992) Parents and the state: how has social research informed education reforms?, in M. Arnot & L. Barton (eds) *Voicing Concerns: sociological perspectives on contemporary education reforms*, Wallingford, Triangle Books.

David, M. E. (1993) *Parents, Gender and Education Reform*, Cambridge, Polity Press.

David, M. E. (1994) 'Fundamentally flawed', in C. Murray, *Underclass: the crisis deepens*, London, IEA Health and Welfare Unit, pp. 53–8.

David, M. E. (1997) 'Family roles from the dawn to dusk of the New Elizabethan era', in G. Dench (ed.) *Rewriting the Sexual Contract*, London, Institute of Community Studies.

David, M. E. & Land, H. (1983) 'Sex and social policy', in H. Glennerster (ed.) *The Future of the Welfare State: remaking social policy*, London, Heinemann.

David, M. E., Edwards, R., Hughes, M. & Ribbens, J. (1993) *Mothers and Education Inside Out? Exploring family education policy and experience*, London, Macmillan.

David, M. E., Weiner, G. & Arnot, M. (1997) 'Strategic feminist research on gender equality and schooling in Britain in the 1990s', in C. Marshall, *Feminist*

Critical Policy Analysis: a perspective from primary to secondary schooling, London, Falmer Press.

David, M. E., West, A. & Ribbens, J. (1994) *Mother's Intuition? Choosing secondary schools*, London, Falmer Press.

Davies, B. (1993) *Frogs and Snails and Feminist Tales*, Sydney, Allen & Unwin.

Davies, L. (1984) *Pupil Power: gender and deviance in school*, Lewes, Falmer Press.

Dean, D. (1991) 'Education for moral improvement, domesticity and social cohesion: expectations and fears of the Labour government', *Oxford Review of Education*, 17/3, 269–85.

Debnath, E. (1999) 'Youth, gender and community change: a case study of young Bangladeshi in Tower Hamlets,' PhD diss., University of Cambridge.

Deem, R. (1978) *Women and Schooling*, London, Routledge & Kegan Paul.

Deem, R. (ed.) (1980) *Schooling for Women's Work*, London, Routledge.

Deem, R. (1981) 'State policy and ideology in the education of women', *British Journal of Sociology of Education*, 2/2, 131–43.

Deem, R. (ed.) (1984) *Co-education Reconsidered*, Milton Keynes, Open University Press.

Delamont, S. (1980) *Sex Roles and the School*, London, Methuen.

Delamont, S. (1989) *Knowledgeable Women*, London, Routledge.

Delamont, S. & Duffin, L. (eds) (1978) *The Nineteenth-century Woman: her cultural and physical world*, London, Croom Helm.

Dench, G. (1996) *The Place of Men in Changing Family Cultures*, London, Institute of Community Studies.

Department of Education and Science (DES) (1965) *The Re-organisation of Secondary Schools on Comprehensive Lines*, Circular 10/65.

Department of Education and Science (DES) (1972) *Education: a framework for expansion*, London, HMSO.

Department of Education and Science (DES) (1973) *Nursery Education*, Circular 2/73.

Department of Education and Science (DES) (1975) *Curricular Differences for Boys and Girls*, Education Survey 21, London, HMSO.

Department of Education and Science (DES) (1980) *Girls and Science*, London, HMSO.

Department of Education and Science (DES) (1983) *Education for All: report of the Committee of Inquiry into the Education of Children from Ethnic Minority Groups*, Cmnd 9453, London, HMSO [the Swann Report].

Dillabough, J. A. & Arnot, M. (1999 in press) 'Feminist perspectives in sociology of education: continuity in transformation in the field', in D. Levinson, A. Sadnovik & J. Cookson (eds) *Education and Sociology: an encyclopaedia*, New York, Garland.

Dinnerstein, D. (1976) *The Rocking of the Cradle and the Ruling of the World*, London, Souvenir Press.

Drew D. & Gray, J. (1990) 'The fifth year examination achievements of black young people in England and Wales', *Educational Research*, 32/3, 107–17.

Durham, M. (1991) *Sex and Politics: the family and morality in the Thatcher years*, London, Macmillan.

Dworkin, A. (1983) *Right Wing Women: the politics of domesticated females*, London, Women's Press.

Dyhouse, C. (1981) *Girls Growing up in Late Victorian and Edwardian England*, London, Routledge & Kegan Paul.

Eddowes, M. (1983) *Humble pi: the mathematics education of girls*, York, Longman.

Egerton, M. & Halsey, A. H. (1993) 'Trends by social class and gender in access to higher education in Britain', *Oxford Review of Education*, 19/2, 183–96.

Eggleston, J., Dunn, D., Anjali, M. & Wright, C. (1986) *Education for Some: the educational and vocational experiences of 15–18 year olds, members of minority ethnic groups*, Stoke on Trent, Trentham Books

Eisenstein, H. (1991) *Gender Shock: practising feminism on two continents*, Sydney, Allen & Unwin.

Eisenstein, Z. R. (1984) *Feminism and Sexual Equality*, New York, Monthly Review Press.

Elwood, J. (1995) 'Undermining gender stereotypes: examination and coursework performance in the UK at 16', *Assessment in Education*, 2/3, 283–303.

Equal Opportunities Commission (EOC) (1975) *Do you Provide Equal Educational Opportunities?*, Manchester, EOC.

Equal Opportunities Commission (EOC) (1989) *Gender Issues: the implications for schools of the Education Reform Act*, Manchester, EOC [EOC response to the legislation].

Etzioni, A. (1969) *The Semi-professions and their Organisation*, New York, Free Press.

Etzioni, A. (1993) *The Parenting Deficit*, London, Demos.

Evans, A. (1991) *A Good School: life at a girls' grammar school in the 1950s*, London, Women's Press.

Evans, M. (1996) 'Perils of ignoring our lost boys', *Times Educational Supplement*, 28 June, 20.

Faludi, S. (1992) *Backlash: the undeclared war against women*, London, Chatto & Windus.

Felstead, A., Goodwin, J. & Green, F. (1995) *Measuring up to the National Training Targets: women's attainment of vocational qualifications*, Research Report, Centre for Labour Market Studies, University of Leicester.

Finch, J. (1984) 'The deceit of self-help: pre-school playgroups and working class mothers', *Journal of Social Policy*, 13/1.

Finn, D. (1985) 'The Manpower Services Commission and the Youth Training Scheme: a permanent bridge to work', in R. Dale (ed.) *Education, Training and Employment*, Oxford, Pergamon.

Flude, M. & Hammer, M. (eds) (1990) *The Education Reform Act, 1988: its origins and implications*, Basingstoke, Falmer Press.

Foster, V. (1995) 'Barriers to equality in Australian girls' schooling for citizenship in the 1990s', *Lärarutbildning och Forskning i Umeå I*, 2, 3/4, 47–60.

Frazer, E. (1988) 'Teenage girls talking about class,' *Sociology*, 22/3, 343–58.

Frazer, E. (1989) 'Feminist talk and talking about feminism: teenage girls' discourses of gender', *Oxford Review of Education*, 15/3, 281–90.

Friedan, B. (1963) *The Feminine Mystique*, Harmondsworth, Penguin.

Frith, S. & McRobbie, A. (1978) 'Rock and sexuality', *Screen Education*, 29, winter, 3–20.

Fullan, M. & Hargreaves, A. (1992) *What's Worth Fighting for in your School? Working together for improvement*, Buckingham, Open University Press.

Fuller, M. (1980) 'Black girls in a London comprehensive school', in R. Deem (ed.) *Schooling for Women's Work*, London, Routledge & Kegan Paul.

Fuller, M. (1983) 'Qualified criticism and critical qualifications', in L. Barton & S. Walker (eds) *Race, Class and Education*, London, Croom Helm.

Furlong, A. (1986) 'Schools and the structure of female occupational aspirations', *British Journal of Sociology of Education*, 7/4, 367–77.

Furlong, A. & Cartmel, F. (1997) *Young People and Social Change: individualisation and risk in late modernity*, Buckingham, Open University Press.

Furnham, A. (1982) 'The perception of poverty amongst adolescents', *Journal of Adolescence*, 5, 135–47.

Furnham, A. & Gunter, B. (1989) *The Anatomy of Adolescence: young people's social attitudes in Britain*, London, Routledge.

Furnham, A. & Stacey, B. (1991) *Young People's Understanding of Society*, London, Routledge.

Gaskell, J. (1992) *Gender Matters from School to Work*, Milton Keynes, Open University Press.

George, R. (1993) *Equal Opportunities in Schools: principles, policy and practice*, Harlow, Longman.

Gewirtz, S., Ball, S. J. & Bowe, R. (1995) *Markets, Choice and Equity in Education*, Buckingham, Open University Press.

Giddens, A. (1991) *Modernity and Self-identity: self and society in the late modern age*, Cambridge, Polity Press.

Gillborn, D. (1995) *Racism and Antiracism in Real Schools: theory, policy, practice*, Buckingham, Open University Press.

Gillborn, D. (1997) 'Young, black and failed by school: the market, education reform and black students', *International Journal of Inclusive Education*, 1/1, 65–87.

Gillborn, D. & Gipps, C. (1996) *Recent Research on the Achievements of Ethnic Minority Pupils*, OFSTED Reviews of Research, London, HMSO.

Gilligan, C. (1982) *In a Different Voice: psychological theory and women's development*, Cambridge, MA, Harvard University Press.

Gilroy, P. (1986) *'There Ain't No Black in the Union Jack'*, London, Hutchinson.

Gipps, C. & Murphy, P. (1994) *A Fair Test? Assessment, achievement and equity*, Buckingham, Open University Press.

Great Britain National Committee of Inquiry into Higher Education (1997) *Higher Education in the Learning Society*, London, NCIHE [the Dearing Report].

Griffin, C. (1985) *Typical Girls? Young women from school to the job market*, London, Routledge & Kegan Paul.

Griffin, C. (1989) 'I'm not a woman's libber, but . . . feminism, consciousness and identity', in S. Skevington & D. Baker (eds) *The Social Identity of Women*, London, Sage.

Hall, S. & Jacques, M. (eds) (1985) *The Politics of Thatcherism*, London, Lawrence & Wishart.

Halsey, A. H. (1957) *Social Class and Educational Opportunity*, London, Heinemann.

Halsey, A. H., Heath, A. F. & Ridge, J. (1980) *Origins and Destinations: family, class and education in modern Britain*, Oxford, Clarendon Press.

Hamilton, D. (1987) 'What is a vocational curriculum?', paper presented at annual conference, British Educational Research Association, Manchester.

Handy, C. & Aitken, R. (1986) *Understanding Schools as Organisations*, Harmondsworth, Penguin.

Harding, J. (1982) 'CDT: what's missing?', *Studies in Design Education, Craft and Technology*, 15/1, winter.

Harding, J. (1983) *Switched Off: the science education of girls*, York, Longman.

Hargreaves, D. (1967) *Social Relations in a Secondary School*, London, Routledge & Kegan Paul.

Harland, J. (1986) 'The new inset: a transformative scene', *Journal of Educational Policy*, 2/3, 235–44.

Harland, J. (1987) 'The TVEI experience: issues of control, response and the professional role of teachers', in D. Gleeson (ed.) *TVEI and Secondary Education: a critical appraisal*, Milton Keynes, Open University Press.

Harland, K. (1997) *'Young Men Talking': voices from Belfast*, London, Working with Men Publications.

Hartmann, H. (1976) 'Capitalism, patriarchy and job segregation by sex', in M. Blaxall & B. Readgan (eds) *Women in the Workplace: the implications of occupational segregation*, Chicago, University of Chicago Press.

Haskey, J. (1998) 'Families: their historical context and recent trends in the factors influencing their formation and dissolution', in M. David (ed.) *The Fragmenting Family: does it matter?*, London, IEA Choice in Welfare 44.

Hatcher, R. (1989) 'Anti-racist education after the Act', *Multicultural Teaching*, 7/3, 24–7.

Haw, K. (1998) *Educating Muslim Girls: shifting discourses*, Buckingham, Open University Press.

Haywood, C. & Mac an Ghaill, M. (1996) 'What about the boys? Regendered local labour markets and the recomposition of working class masculinities', *British Journal of Education and Work*, 9/1, 19–30.

Heath, A. (1981) *Social Mobility*, London, Fontana.

Heron, E. (1985) *Truth, Dare or Promise: girls growing up in the fifties*, London, Virago.

Heward, C. M. (1984) 'Parents, sons and their careers: a case study of a public school, 1930–50', in G. Walford (ed.) *British Public Schools: policy and practice*, Lewes, Falmer Press.

Hey, V. (1997) *The Company She Keeps: an ethnography of girls' friendship*, Buckingham, Open University Press.

Hillman, J. & Pearce, N. (1998) *'Wasted Youth': dissaffection and non-participation amongst 14–19 year olds in education*, London, Institute for Public Policy Research.

Himmelfarb, G. (1995) *The Demoralisation of Society: from Victorian virtues to modern values*, London, Institute of Economic Affairs.

Hobsbawm, E. (1968) *Industry and Empire: from 1750 to the present day*, Harmondsworth, Penguin.

Hobsbawm, E. (1994) *The Age of Extremes*, London, Abacus.

Holland, J., Ramazanoglu, C. & Sharpe, S. (1993) *Wimp or Gladiator: contradictions in acquiring masculine sexuality*, WRAP Paper 9, London, Tufnell Press.

Holland, J., Ramazanoglu, C., Sharpe, S. & Thompson, R. (1998) *The Male in the Head: young people, heterosexuality and power*, London, Tufnell Press.

hooks, b. (1984) *Feminist Theory: from margin to centre*, Boston, South End Press.

Horner, M. S. (1972) 'Toward an understanding of achievement related conflicts in women', *Journal of Social Issues*, 8/2, 157–75.

Hughes, G. (1996) 'The implications of employment trends in Ireland, the Netherlands and the United Kingdom for the occupations today's students will enter', paper for the European Union Conference on Gender Equality for 2000 and Beyond.

Hutchinson, D. & McPherson, A. F. (1976) 'Competing inequalities: the sex and social class structure of the first year Scottish university population', *Sociology*, 10, 111–16.

Hutchinson, G. (1997) 'The decline of a subject: the case of home economics', PhD diss., South Bank University.

Hutton, W. (1995) *The State We're In*, London, Jonathan Cape.

Hymas, C. & Cohen, J. (1994) 'The trouble with boys', *Sunday Times*, 19 June.

Ingham, M. (1981) *Now we are Thirty: women of the breakthrough generation*, London, Eyre Methuen.

Inner London Education Authority (ILEA) (1986a) *Primary Matters*, London, ILEA.

Inner London Education Authority (ILEA) (1986b) *Secondary Issues: some approaches to equal opportunities in secondary schools*, London, ILEA.

Jackson, D. (1998) 'Breaking out of the binary trap: boys' underachievement, schooling and gender relations', in D. Epstein, J. Elwood, V. Hey & J. Haw (eds) *Failing Boys: issues in gender and achievement*, Buckingham, Open University Press.

Jenkins, R. (1983) *Working Class Youth Life Styles in Belfast*, London, Routledge & Kegan Paul.

Jessop, B. (1992) 'From social democracy to Thatcherism: twenty five years of British politics', in N. Abercrombie & A. Warde (eds) *Social Change in Contemporary Britain*, Cambridge, Polity Press.

Jessop, B., Bonnett, K., Bromley S. & Ling, T. (eds) (1988) *Thatcherism: a tale of two nations*, Cambridge, Polity Press.

Johnson, L. (1993) *The Modern Girl: girlhood and growing up*, Buckingham, Open University Press.

Jones, C. & Mahony, P. (eds) (1989) *Learning our Lines: sexuality and social control in education*, London, Women's Press.

Judd, J. (1994) 'The trouble with boys', *The Independent*, 18 October.

Kamm, J. (1965) *Hope Deferred: girls' education in English history*, London, Methuen.

Kean, H. (1990) *Challenging the State? The socialist and feminist educational experiment 1900–1930*, London, Falmer Press.

Kehily, M. J. & Nayak, A. (1997) 'Lads and laughter: humour and the production of heterosexual hierarchies', *Gender and Education*, 9/1, 69–88.

Kelly, A. (ed.) (1981) *The Missing Half: girls and science education*, Manchester, Manchester University Press.

Kelly, A. (1985) 'Changing schools and changing society: some reflections on the Girls into Science and Technology project', in M. Arnot (ed.) *Race and Gender: equal opportunities policies in education: a reader*, Oxford, Pergamon.

Kelly, L. (1991) 'Not in front of the children: responding to right-wing agendas on sexuality and education', in M. Arnot & L. Barton (eds) *Voicing Concerns: sociological perspectives on contemporary education reforms*, Wallingford, Triangle Books.

Kelsall, R., Poole, A. & Kuhn, A. (1972) *Graduates: the sociology of an elite*, London, Methuen.

Kenway, J. (1990) 'Privileged girls, private schools and the culture of success', in J. Kenway & S. Willis (eds) *Hearts and Minds: self esteem and the schooling of girls*, London, Falmer Press.

Kenway, J. (1995) 'Masculinities in schools: under siege, on the defensive and under reconstruction', *Discourse: studies in the cultural politics of education*, 16/1, 59–79.

Kenway, J. & Fitzclarence, L. (1997) 'Masculinity, violence and schooling: challenging "poisonous pedagogies"', *Gender and Education*, 9/1, 117–34.

Kenway, J., Bigum, C. & Fitzclarence, L. (1995) 'Introductory essay', in J. Kenway (ed.) *Marketing Education*, Geelong, Australia, Deakin University Press.

King, R. (1971) 'Unequal access in education: sex and social class', *Social and Economic Administration*, 5/3, 167–75.

King, R. (1987) 'Sex and social class inequalities in education: a re-examination', *British Journal of Sociology of Education*, 8/3, 287–303.

Komarovsky, M. (1946) 'Cultural contradictions and sex roles', *American Journal of Sociology*, 52/3, 184–9.

Kristeva, J. (1974) 'Women can never be defined', trans. in E. Marks & I. de Courtivron (eds) (1981) *New French Feminisms*, Brighton, Harvester.

Lacey, C. (1970) *Hightown Grammar*, Manchester, Manchester University Press.

Lambart, A. M. (1975) 'The Sisterhood', in M. Hammersley & P. Woods (eds) *The Processes of Schooling*, London, Routledge & Kegan Paul.

Land, H. (1976) 'Women: supporters and supported', in D. Barker & S. Allen (eds) *Sexual Divisions and Society: process and change*, London, Tavistock.

Larner, W. & Spoonley, P. (1995) 'Post-colonial politics in Aotearoa/New Zealand', in D. Stasiulus & N. Yuval-Davis (eds) *Unsettling Settler Societies: articulations of gender, race, ethnicity and class*, London, Sage.

Lawton, D. (1975) *Class, Culture and the Curriculum*, London, Routledge & Kegan Paul.

Lees, S. (1986) *Losing Out: sexuality and adolescent girls*, London, Hutchinson.

Lees, S. (1993) *Sugar and Spice: sexuality and adolescent girls*, Harmondsworth, Penguin.

Lees, S. (1998) 'Will boys be left on the shelf?', in G. Jagger & C. Wrigher (eds) *Changing Family Values: differences, diversity and the decline of the male order*, London, Routledge.

Levin, M. (1994) 'Children and feminism', in C. Quest (ed.) *Liberating Women . . . from Modern Feminism*, London, IEA Health and Welfare Unit.

Lloyd, B. & Duveen, G. (1992) *Gender Identities and Education: the impact of starting school*, London, Harvester Wheatsheaf.

Lucey, H. & Walkerdine, V. (1996) 'Transitions to womanhood: constructions of success and failure for middle and working class young women', paper presented at British Youth Research: the New Agenda conference, Glasgow University.

Luttrell, W. (1997) *School Smart and Motherwise*, London, Routledge.

Mac an Ghaill, M. (1988) *Young, Gifted and Black*, Buckingham, Open University Press.

Mac an Ghaill, M. (1994) *The Making of Men: masculinities, sexualities and schooling*, Buckingham, Open University Press.

Mac an Ghaill, M. (ed.) (1996) *Understanding Masculinities*, Milton Keynes, Open University Press.

Maccoby, E. E. & Jacklin, C. N. (1974) *The Psychology of Sex Differences*, Stanford, CA, Stanford University Press.

McCrum, N. G. (1996) 'Gender and social inequality in Oxford and Cambridge universities', *Oxford Review of Education*, 22/4, 369–96.

McLaren, A. T. (1996) 'Coercive invitations: how young women in school make sense of mothering and waged labour', *British Journal of Sociology of Education*, 17/3, 279–98.

McLaren, A. T. & Vanderbijl, A. (1998) 'Teenage girls making sense of mothering: what has (relational) equality got to do with it?', in S. Abbey & A. O'Reilly (eds) *Redefining Motherhood: changing identities and patterns*, Toronto, Second Story Press.

MacLeod, M. & Morris, S. (1996) *Why Me? Children talking to Childline about bullying*, London, Childline.

McRobbie, A. (1978) 'Working class girls and the culture of femininity', in Women's Studies Group, Centre for Contemporary Cultural Studies (ed.) *Women Take Issue: aspects of women's subordination*, London, Hutchinson.

McRobbie, A. & Garber, J. (1975) 'Girls and subcultures: an exploration', in S. Hall & T. Jefferson (eds) *Resistance through Rituals: youth subcultures in post war Britain*, London, Hutchinson.

Maguire, M. & Weiner, G. (1994) 'The place of women in teacher education: discourses of power', *Educational Review*, 46/2, 121–39.

Mahony, P. (1989) 'Sexual violence in mixed schools', in C. Jones & P. Mahony (eds) *Learning our Lines: sexuality and social control in education*, London, Women's Press.

Mahony, P. & Zmroczek, C. (eds) (1997) *Class Matters: 'working class' women's perspectives on social class*, London, Taylor & Francis.

Mangan, J. A. (1981) *Athleticism in the Victorian and Edwardian Public School: the emergence and consolidation of an educational ideology*, Cambridge, Cambridge University Press.

Mangan, J. A. (1986) *The Games Ethic and Imperialism: aspects of the diffusion of an ideal*, Harmondsworth, Penguin.

Mann, C. (1996) 'Finding a favourable front: the contribution of the family to working class girls' achievement', PhD diss., University of Cambridge.

Mann, C. (1998) 'The impact of working class mothers on the educational success of their adolescent daughters at a time of social change', *British Journal of Sociology of Education*, 19/2, 211–26.

Marshall, C. (1985) 'From culturally defined to self-defined: career stages of women administrators', *Journal of Educational Thought*, 19/2, 134–47.

Marshall, T. H. (1950) *Citizenship and Social Class and Other Essays*, Cambridge, Cambridge University Press.

Measor, L. & Sykes, P. (1992) *Gender and Schooling*, London, Cassell.

Meehan, E. (1982) 'Implementing equal opportunities policies: some British-American comparisons', *Politics: Journal of the PSA*, 2/1, 14–20.

Meyen, R. J. (1980) 'School girls' peer groups', in P. Woods (ed.) *Pupil Strategies*, London, Croom Helm.

Miles, S. & Middleton, C. (1990) 'Girls' education in the balance: the ERA and inequality', in M. Flude & M. Hammer (eds) *The Education Reform Act, 1988: its origins and implications*, Basingstoke, Falmer Press.

Millman, V. (1987) 'Teacher as researcher: a new tradition for research on gender', in G. Weiner & M. Arnot (eds) *Gender Under Scrutiny: new inquiries in education*, London, Hutchinson.

Millman, V. & Weiner, G. (1985) *Sex Differentiation in Schooling: is there really a problem?*, York, Longman.

Millman, V. & Weiner, G. (1987) 'Engendering equal opportunities: the case of TVEI', in D. Gleeson (ed.) *TVEI and Secondary Education: a critical appraisal*, Milton Keynes, Open University Press.

Minhas, R. (1986) 'Race, gender and class: making the connections', in ILEA (ed.) *Secondary Issues: some approaches to equal opportunities in secondary schools*, London, ILEA.

Ministry of Health and Social Affairs (1995) *Shared Power Responsibility*, national report by the government of Sweden for the Fourth World Conference in Beijing 1995, Stockholm, Ministry of Health and Social Affairs.

Mirza, H. (1992) *Young, Female and Black*, London, Routledge.

Mirza, H. S. (1997) 'Black women in education: a collective movement', in H. S. Mirza (ed.) *Black British Feminism: a reader*, London, Routledge.

Mishra, R. (1984) *The Welfare State in Crisis: social thought and social change*, Brighton, Harvester Wheatsheaf.

Mitchell, J. (1971) *Women's Estate*, Harmondsworth, Penguin.

Mitchell, J. (1974) *Psychoanalysis and Feminism*, London, Allen Lane.

Modood, T. & Shiner, M. (1994) *Ethnic Minorities and Higher Education*, London, PSI/UCAS.

Moore, R. (1996) 'Back to the future: the problem of change and the possibilities of advance in the sociology of education', *British Journal of Sociology of Education*, 17/2, 145–61.

Morley, P. & Walsh, V. (1996) *Breaking Boundaries: women in higher education*, London, Taylor & Francis.

Moss, P. & Penn, H. (1997) *Transforming Nursery Education*, London, Paul Chapman.

Murray, C. (1994) *Underclass: the crisis deepens*, London, IEA Health and Welfare Unit.

Myers, K. (1987) *Genderwatch*, London, SCDC; rev. and repr., 1992, Cambridge, Cambridge University Press.

National Association of Schoolmasters & Union of Women Teachers (NASUWT) (1990) *ERA and Equal Opportunities for the Teacher: a practical guide*, Birmingham, NASUWT.

National Union of Teachers (1981) *Promotion and the Woman Teacher*, London, EPC/NUT.

National Union of Teachers (1986) *Briefing*, 2, London, NUT.

National Union of Teachers (1990) *Fair and Equal: guidelines on equal opportunities in the appointment and promotion of teachers*, London, NUT.

Nava, M. (1992) *Changing Cultures: feminism, youth and consumerism*, London, Sage.

New, C. & David, M. E. (1985) *For the Children's Sake: making child care more than women's business*, Harmondsworth, Penguin.

Oakley, A. (1974) *Housewife*, Harmondsworth, Penguin.

Oakley, A. (1996) 'Gender matters: man the hunter', in H. Roberts & D. Sachdev (eds) *Young People's Social Attitudes: having their say*, Basildon, Barnardo's.

OFSTED (1996) *Exclusions from Secondary Schools*, London, Office for Standards in Education.

OFSTED/EOC (1996) *The Gender Divide: performance differences between boys and girls at school*, London, HMSO.

Okely, J. (1978) 'Privileged, schooled and finished: boarding education for girls', in S. Ardener (ed.) *Defining Females: the nature of women in society*, London, Croom Helm.

Open University/Inner London Education Authority (1986) *Girls into Mathematics*, Cambridge, Cambridge University Press.

Oram, A. (1987) 'Sex antagonism in the teaching profession: equal pay and the marriage bar 1910–39', in M. Arnot & G. Weiner (eds) *Gender and the Politics of Schooling*, London, Hutchinson.

Orbach, S. (1979) *Fat is a Feminist Issue*, London, Hamlyn.

Ord, F. & Quigley, J. (1985) 'Anti-sexism as good educational practice: what can feminists realistically achieve?, in G. Weiner (ed.) *Just a Bunch of Girls: feminist approaches to schooling*, Buckingham, Open University Press.

Orr, P. (1985) 'Sex bias in schools: national perspectives', in J. Whyte, R. Deem, L. Kant & M. Cruickshank (eds) *Girl Friendly Schooling*, London, Methuen.

Ouseley, H. (1998) Presidential Address, North of England Education Conference, 5–7 January.

Owen, U. (ed.) (1983) *Fathers: reflections by daughters*, London, Virago.

Pahl, R. (1995) *After Success*, Cambridge, Polity Press.

Parsons, C. (1995) *Final Report to the Department of Education: national survey of LEAs' policies and procedures for the identification of, and provision for, children who are out of school by reason of exclusion or otherwise*, London, DfEE.

Parsons, T. (1952) *The Social System*, London, Tavistock.

Pascall, G. (1986) *Social Policy: a feminist analysis*, London, Tavistock.

Pateman, C. (1988) *The Sexual Contract*, Cambridge, Polity Press.

Penn, H. (1990) *Under Fives: the view from Strathclyde*, Edinburgh Scottish Academic Press.

Pilcher, J. (1997) *Age and Generation in Modern Britain*, Oxford, Oxford University Press.

Pilcher, J. & Wagg, S. (eds) (1996) *Thatcher's Children: politics, childhood and society in the 1980s and 1990s*, London, Falmer Press.

Pilcher, J., Delamont, S., Powell, G., Rees, T. & Read, M. (1989) 'Evaluating a women's careers convention: methods, results and implications', *Research Papers in education*, 4/1, 57–76.

Pitts, J. & Smith, P. (1995) *Preventing School Bullying*, Police Research Group, Crime Detection and Prevention Series, Paper 63.

Pollert, A. (1984) *Girls, Wives, Factory Lives*, London, Macmillan.

Power, S., Edwards, A., Whitty, G. & Wigfall, V. (1998) 'Schoolboys and schoolwork: gender identification and academic achievement', *Journal of Inclusive Education*, 2/2, 135–53.

Powney, J. (1996) *Gender and Attainment: a review*, Edinburgh, SCRE.

Powney, J. & Weiner, G. (1991) *Outside of the Norm: equity and management in educational institutions*, London, South Bank University.

Pratt, J., Bloomfield, J. & Seale, C. (1984) *Option Choice: a question of equal opportunity: a study sponsored by the Equal Opportunities Commission*, Windsor, NFER/ Nelson.

Purvis, J. (1981) 'The double burden of class and gender in the schooling of working-class girls in nineteenth-century England, 1800–1870', in L. Barton and S. Walker (eds) *Schools, Teachers and Teaching*, Lewes, Falmer Press.

Purvis, J. (1989) *Hard Lessons: the lives and education of working-class women in nineteenth-century England*, Cambridge, Polity Press.

Purvis, J. (1991) *A History of Women's Education in England*, Buckingham, Open University Press.

Pye, D., Haywood, C. & Mac an Ghaill, M. (1996) 'The training state, de-industrialisation and the production of white working class trainee identities', *International Studies in Sociology of Education*, 6/2, 133–46.

Radloff, L. S. (1975) 'Sex differences in depression: the effect of occupation and marital status', *Sex Roles*, 1, 249–66.

Raffe, D. (1993/4) *Participation of 16–18 year olds in Education and Training*, briefing for the National Commission of Education, London, Heinemann.

Reay, D. (1990) 'Working with boys' *Gender and Education*, 23, 269–82.

Rees, G., Williamson, H. & Istance, D. (1996) '"Status Zero": a study of jobless school-leavers in South Wales', *Research Papers in Education*, 11/2, 219–35.

Rees, T. (1992) *Women and the Labour Market*, London, Routledge.

Rendel, M. (1985) 'The winning of the Sex Discrimination Act', in M. Arnot (ed.) *Race and Gender: equal opportunities policies in education*, Oxford, Pergamon Press/ Open University Press.

Riley, D. (1983) *War in the Nursery*, London, Virago.

Riley, K. (1994) *Quality and Equality: promoting opportunities in schools*, London, Cassell.

Riseborough, G. B. H. (1993) 'The Gobbo Barmy Harmy: one day in the life of the YTS boys', in I. Bates & G. Riseborough (eds) *Youth and Inequality*, Buckingham, Open University Press.

Roberts, K., Clark, S. C. & Wallace, C. (1994) 'Flexibility and individualisation: a comparison of transitions into employment in England and Germany', *Sociology*, 28/1, 31–54.

Roberts, H. & Sachdev, D. (1996) *Young People's Social Attitudes: having their say, the views of 12–19 year olds*, Ilford, Barnardo's.

Roker, D. (1993) 'Gaining the edge: girls at a private school', in I. Bates & G. B. H. Riseborough (eds) *Youth and Inequality*, Buckingham, Open University Press.

Rose, H. (1994) *Love, Power and Knowledge: towards a feminist transformation of the sciences*, Cambridge, Polity Press.

Rossi, A. (1973) *The Feminist Papers*, New York, University of Columbia Press.

Rostow, W. W. (1963) *The Economics of Take-off into Sustained Growth*, London, Macmillan.

Rowbotham, S. (1989) *The Past is Before Us: feminism in action since the 1960s*, London, Pandora.

Rutter, M. (1972) *Maternal Deprivation Re-assessed*, Harmondsworth, Penguin.

Salisbury, J. (1996) *Educational Reforms and Gender Equality in Welsh Schools*, Cardiff, EOC.

Salisbury, J. & Jackson, D. (1996) *Challenging Macho Values: practical ways of working with adolescent boys*, London, Falmer Press.

Savage, M. & Egerton, M. (1997) 'Social mobility, individual mobility and the inheritance of class inequality', *Sociology*, 31/4, 645–72.

Sayers, J. (1986) *Sexual Contradictions: psychology, psychoanalysis and feminism*, London, Tavistock.

Scruton, R. (1986) *Sexual Desire*, London, Weidenfeld & Nicholson.

Segal, L. (1983) 'The heat in the kitchen', in S. Hall & M. Jacques (eds) *The Politics of Thatcherism*, London, Lawrence & Wishart.

Segal, L. (1987) *Is the Future Female? Troubled thoughts on contemporary feminism*, London, Virago.

Segal, L. (1994) *Slow Motion: changing masculinities, changing men*, London, Virago.

Sewell, T. (1997) *Black Masculinities and Schooling*, Stoke on Trent, Trentham Books.

Shacklady Smith, L. S. (1978) 'Sexual assumptions and female delinquency: an empirical interpretation', in C. Smart & B. Smart (eds) *Women, Sexuality and Social Council*, London, Routledge & Kegan Paul.

Shah, S. (1990) 'Equal opportunity issues in the context of the National Curriculum: a black perspective', *Gender and Education*, 2/3, 309–18.

Sharpe, S. (1976; 1994) *Just Like a Girl: how girls learn to be women* (1st and 2nd edns), Harmondsworth, Penguin.

Shaw, J. (1980) 'Education and the individual: schooling for girls, or mixed schooling: a mixed blessing?', in R. Deem (ed.) *Schooling for Women's Work*, London, Routledge.

Shaw, J. (1995) *Education, Gender and Anxiety*, London, Tavistock.

Sillitoe, K. & Meltzer, H. (1985) *The West Indian School Leaver*, Vol. 1: *Starting Work*, London, OPCS, Social Survey Division, HMSO.

Simon, B. (1988) *Bending the Rules: the Baker 'reform' of education*, London, Lawrence & Wishart.

Simon, B. (1994) 'Education and citizenship in England', in *State and Educational Change*, London, Lawrence & Wishart.

Skeggs, B. (1988) 'Gender reproduction and further education: domestic apprentice-ships', *British Journal of Sociology of Education*, 9/2, 131–49.

Skeggs, B. (1991) 'Postmodernism: what is all the fuss about?', *British Journal of Sociology of Education*, 12/2, 255–79.

Skeggs, B. (1994) 'The limits of neutrality: feminist research and the ERA', in B. Troyna & D. Halpin (eds) *Researching Educational Policy: ethical and methodo-logical issues*, Lewes, Falmer Press.

Skeggs, B. (1997) *Formations of Class and Gender*, London, Sage.

Skelton, C. (1997) 'Primary boys and hegemonic masculinities', *British Journal of Sociology of Education*, 18/3, 349–70.

Skelton, C. (1998) 'Feminism and research into masculinities and schooling', *Gender and Education*, 10/2, 217–27.

Slee, R., Weiner, G. & Tomlinson, S. (eds) (1998) *School Effectiveness for Whom?*, London, Falmer Press.

Spender, D. (1982) *Invisible Women: the schooling scandal*, London, Writers & Readers Co-operative.

Spender, D. (1987) 'Education: the patriarchal paradigm and the response to feminism', in M. Arnot & G. Weiner (eds) *Gender and the Politics of Schooling*, London, Hutchinson.

Spender, D. & Sarah, E. (eds) (1980) *Learning to Lose*, London, Women's Press.

Stanworth, M. (1981) *Gender and Schooling: a study of sexual divisions in the classroom*, London, Women's Research and Resources Centre Publications Collective.

Stanworth, M. (1983) *Gender and Schooling*, London, Hutchinson.

Steedman, C. (1982) *The Tidy House: little girls' writing*, London, Virago.

Steedman, J. (1985) *Examination Results in Mixed and Single Sex Schools: findings from the National Child Development Study*, Manchester, Equal Opportunities Commission.

Stone, L. (ed.) (1994) *The Education Feminism Reader*, London, Routledge.

Stones, R. (1983) *'Pour out the Cocoa, Janet': sexism in children's books*, York, Longman.

Swindells, J. (1985) *Victorian Writing and Working Women: the other side of silence*, Cambridge, Polity Press.

Taylor, H. (1985) 'A local authority initiative on equal opportunities', in M. Arnot (ed.) *Race and Gender: equal opportunities policies in education: a reader*, Oxford, Pergamon.

Teese, R., Davies, M., Charlton, M. & Polesel, J. (1995) *Who Wins at School? Boys and girls in Australian secondary education*, Dept. of Education Policy and Management, University of Melbourne.

Thatcher, C. (1996) *Below the Parapet: the biography of Denis Thatcher*, London, Harper Collins.

Thatcher, M. (1993) *The Downing Street Years*, London, Harper Collins.

Thatcher, M. (1995) *The Path to Power*, London, Harper Collins.

Thom, D. (1992) 'Wishes, hopes, fears and dreams: child guidance in the interwar period', in R. Cooter (ed.) *In the Name of the Child*, London, Routledge.

Tigar Mclaren, M. (1996) 'Coercive invitations: how young women in school make sense of mothering and waged labour', *British Journal of Sociology of Education*, 17/3, 279–98.

Tolson, A. (1977) *The Limits of Masculinity*, London, Tavistock.

Tomlinson, S. (1983) 'Black women in higher education: case studies of university women in Britain', in L. Barton & S. Walker (eds) *Race, Class and Education*, London, Croom Helm.

Tomlinson, S. & Smith, M. (1988) *The School Effect*, London, PSI.

Troyna, B. & Carrington, B. (1990) *Education, Racism and Reform*, London, Croom Helm.

Troyna, B. & Vincent, C. (1995) 'The discourses of social justice in education', *Discourse*, 16/2, 149–66.

Turner, E., Riddell, S. & Brown, S. (1995) *Gender Equality in Scottish Schools: the impact of recent educational reforms*, Glasgow, EOC.

Unattributed (1996) 'Boys revert to nature when future looks bleak', *Times Educational Supplement*, 12 January.

Unattributed (1996) 'Worried about an excess of women', *Times Educational Supplement*, 16 February.

Valente, M. O., Bárrios, A., Gasper, A. & Teodoro, V. D. (eds) (1996) *Teacher Training and Values Education*, Lisbon, ATEE.

Vicinus, M. (ed.) (1972) *Suffer and be Still: women in the Victorian age*, 1980 edn, London, Methuen.

Walford, G. (1986) *Life in Public Schools*, London, Methuen.

Walford, G. & Miller, H. (1991) *City Technology College*, Milton Keynes, Open University Press.

Walker, J. C. (1988) 'The way men act: dominant and subordinate male cultures in an inner city school', *British Journal of Sociology of Education*, 9/1, 3–18.

Walkerdine, V. (1981) 'Sex, power and pedagogy', *Screen Education*, 38, spring, 14–25.

Walkerdine, V. (1983) 'It's only natural: rethinking child-centred pedagogy', in A. M. Wolpe & J. Donald (eds) *Is there Anyone Here from Education?*, London, Pluto Press..

Walkerdine, V. (1988) *The Mastery of Reason: cognitive development and the production of rationality*, London, Routledge.

Walkerdine, V. (1989) *Counting Girls Out*, London, Virago.

Walkerdine, V. (1990) *Schoolgirl Fictions*, London, Verso.

Walkerdine, V., Lucey, H. & Melody, J. (1998) 'Class attainment and sexuality in late 20th century Britain', in P. Mahony & C. Zmroczek (eds) *Women and Social Class*, London, Taylor & Francis.

Walkerdine, V., Melody, J. & Lucey, H. (1996) Project 4: 21 *Transition to Womanhood*, London, ESRC.

Wallace, C. (1987) 'From girls and boys to women and men: the social reproduction of gender', in M. Arnot & G. Weiner (eds) *Gender and the Politics of Schooling*, London, Hutchinson.

WedG (1983) *Women's Education Group Newsletter*, October, London.

Weiler, K. (1988) *Women Teaching for Change*, New York, Bergin & Harvey.

Weiner, G. (1985a) 'The Schools Council and gender: a case-study of policy making and curriculum innovation', in M. Arnot (ed.) *Race and Gender: equal opportunities policies in education: a reader*, Oxford, Pergamon.

Weiner, G. (ed.) (1985b) *Just a Bunch of Girls*, Milton Keynes, Open University Press.

Weiner, G. (1989a) 'Professional self-knowledge versus social justice: a critical analysis of the teacher-researcher movement', *British Educational Research Journal*, 15/1, 41–51.

Weiner, G. (1989b) 'Feminism, equal opportunities and vocationalism: the changing context', in H. Burchell & V. Millman (eds) *Changing Perspectives on Gender: new initiatives in secondary education*, Milton Keynes, Open University Press.

Weiner, G. (1993) 'Shell-shock or sisterhood: English school history and feminist practice', in M. Arnot & K. Weiler (eds) *Feminism and Social Justice in Education: international perspectives*, London, Falmer Press.

Weiner, G. (1994a) 'Equality and quality: approaches to changes in the management of issues of gender', in E. Burridge and P. Ribbens (eds) *Improving Education: promoting quality in schools*, London, Cassell.

Weiner, G. (1994b) *Feminisms in Education: an introduction*, Buckingham, Open University Press.

Weiner, G. (1998) 'New era or old times: class, gender and education', *International Journal of Inclusive Education*, 3/1, 189–208.

Weiner, G. & Arnot, M. (1987a) 'Teachers and gender politics', in M. Arnot & G. Weiner (eds) *Gender and the Politics of Schooling*, London, Hutchinson.

Weiner, G. & Arnot, M. (eds) (1987b) *Gender Under Scrutiny: new inquiries in education*, London, Hutchinson.

Weiner, G., Arnot, M. & David, M. (1997) 'Is the future female? Female success, male disadvantage and changing gender relations in education', in A. H. Halsey, H. Lauder, P. Brown & A. Stuart-Wells (eds) *Education: culture, economy and society*, Oxford, Oxford University Press.

Weiner, G., Arnot, M. & David, M. (1998) 'Who benefits from schooling? Equality issues in Britain', in A. Mackinnon, I. Elgqvist-Saltzman & A. Prentice (eds) *Education into the 21st Century: dangerous terrain for women?*, London, Falmer Press.

Weis, L. (1990) *Working Class without Work: high school students in a de-industrialising economy*, New York, Routledge.

Whitney, I. & Smith, P. K. (1993) 'A survey of the nature and extent of bullying in junior and secondary schools', *Educational Research*, 35/1, 3–25.

Whitty, G. (1974) 'Sociology and the problem of radical educational change', in M. Flude & J. Ahier (eds) *Educability, Schools and Ideology*, London, Croom Helm.

Whitty, G. (1990) 'Central control or market forces?', in J. Flude & M. Hammer (eds) *The Education Reform Act, 1988: its origins and implications*, Basingstoke, Falmer Press.

Whyte, J. (1983) *Beyond the Wendy House: sex role stereotyping in primary schools*, York, Longman.

Whyte, J., Deem, R., Kant, L. & Cruickshank, M. (1985) *Girl Friendly Schooling*, London, Methuen.

Widdowson, F. (1980) *Going Up into the Next Class: women and elementary teacher training, 1840–1914*, London, Hutchinson.

Wiener, M. J. (1982) *English Culture and the Decline of the Industrial Spirit*, Cambridge, Cambridge University Press.

Wilkinson, H. (1994) *No Turning Back: generations and the genderquake*, London, Demos.

Wilkinson, H. & Mulgan, G. (1995) *Freedom's Children: work, relationships and politics for 18–34 year olds in Britain today*, London, Demos.

Williams, F. (1989) *Social Policy: a critical introduction: issues of race, gender, and class*, Cambridge, Polity Press.

Willis, P. (1977) *Learning to Labour: how working class kids get working class jobs*, Farnborough, Saxon House.

Willmot, P. (1966) *Adolescent Boys in East London*, London, Pelican Books.

Wilson, D. (1978) 'Social codes and conduct: a study of teenage girls', in C. Smart & B. Smart (eds) *Women, Sexuality and Social Change*, London, Routledge & Kegan Paul.

Wilson, E. (1977) *Women and the Welfare State*, London, Tavistock.

Wilson, E. (1980) *Only Halfway to Paradise: women in postwar Britain, 1945–1968*, London, Tavistock.

Wilson, E. (1987) 'Thatcherism and Women: after seven years', in R. Milliband, L. Panitch & J. Saville (eds) *Socialist Register*, London, Merlin Press.

Wollstonecraft, M. (1792) *Vindication of the Rights of Woman* (repr. 1985) Harmondsworth, Penguin.

Wolpe, A. M. (1976) 'The official ideology of education for girls', in M. Flude & J. Ahier (eds) *Educability, Schools and Ideology*, London, Croom Helm.

Wolpe, A. M. (1988) *Within School Walls: the role of discipline, sexuality and the curriculum*, London, Routledge.

Women in Education (1982) *Newsletter*, 24, Manchester.

Women in Higher Education Network (WHEN) (1991) *Access and After: conference report*, Nottingham, WHEN.

Women in the NUT (1981) *Newsletter*, London, NUT.

Women's National Commission (1984) *Report on Secondary Education*, London, Cabinet Office.

Wright, C. (1987) 'The relations between teachers and Afro-Caribbean pupils: observing multiracial classrooms', in G. Weiner & M. Arnot (eds) *Gender Under Scrutiny: new inquiries in education*, London, Hutchinson.

Wright, C., Weekes, D., McLaughlin, A. & Webb, D. (1998) 'Masculinised discourses within education and the construction of black male identities among African Caribbean Youth', *British Journal of Sociology of Education*, 19/1, 75–87.

Yates, L. (1985) 'Is girl-friendly schooling really what girls need?', in J. Whyte, R. Deem, L. Kant & M. Cruickshank (eds) *Girl Friendly Schooling*, London, Methuen.

Yates, L. & Leder, G. C. (1996) *Student Pathways: a review and overview of national databases on gender equity*, Canberra, ACT Dept. of Education & Training & Children's Youth and Family Bureau.

Young, M. (1963) *The Rise of the Meritocracy*, Harmondsworth, Penguin.

Index

Note: page numbers in *italics* denote figures or tables where these are separated from the textual reference.